THE CATHOLIC UNIVERSITY OF AMERICA
CANON LAW STUDIES
No. 199

SUSTENANCE OF RELIGIOUS HOUSES OF REGULARS

A DISSERTATION

SUBMITTED TO THE FACULTY OF THE SCHOOL OF CANON LAW OF THE CATHOLIC UNIVERSITY OF AMERICA IN PARTIAL FULFILLMENT OF THE REQUIREMENTS FOR THE DEGREE OF DOCTOR OF CANON LAW

BY

ROMUALD EUGENE KOWALSKI, O.F.M., A.B., J.C.L.

THE CATHOLIC UNIVERSITY OF AMERICA PRESS
WASHINGTON, D. C.
1944

Nihil Obstat:
FERDINANDUS PAWLOWSKI, O.F.M., L.G.,
Censor Deputatus.

Imprimi Potest:
ISIDORUS CWIKLINSKI, O.F.M.,
Minister Provincialis.

Nihil Obstat:

HIERONYMUS D. HANNAN, A.M., LL.B., S.T.D., J.C.D.,
Censor Deputatus.
Washingtonii, D.C., die 18 maii 1944

Imprimatur:
✠ MICHAEL J. CURLEY, D.D.,
Archiepiscopus Baltimoriensis-Washingtoniensis.
Baltimorae, Md., die 19 maii 1944

MURRAY & HEISTER—WASHINGTON, D. C.
PRINTED IN THE UNITED STATES OF AMERICA

9

To
My Father
and
Mother

TABLE OF CONTENTS

PART TWO

SOURCES OF SUSTENANCE

PART THREE

ADMINISTRATION OF TEMPORAL GOODS BY REGULARS

FOREWORD

In order to attain greater perfection and promote God's Kingdom on earth, various religious groups voluntarily renounce temporal possessions by the vow of poverty. The degree and manner in which this vow is observed differs from group to group depending on the particular rules, constitutions and legislation of each organization. Nonetheless, no matter how strict an observance of this vow may be enjoined by any particular rule or constitutions, in no case does this renunciation of private possessions eliminate the right to a proper sustenance. This right is a natural one, common to all. Its satisfaction is as necessary in the case of religious as of other persons, if they are expected to fulfill the obligation of their state and attain the end for which religious institutes have been established.

Precisely for this reason the Church has always granted to religious the rights either of possessing temporal goods in common or of enjoying the simple use or usufruct of temporalities without actual ownership. The Canon Law of the Church, emphasizing the natural right of sustenance, grants to all religious the right to employ means necessary to the adequate satisfaction of this right. Nevertheless, this concession does not grant all religious the right to use indiscriminately all and every means available for the acquisition of temporal possessions. The various different concepts of poverty, based on individual rules and constitutions, demand a certain restriction in the use of the means and methods of acquiring goods. Only in this manner can a certain modicum of conformity between the theory and practice of each group be safeguarded. This equilibrium between theory and practice will depend to a great extent upon the particular laws, as expressed in the rule of life and constitutions of each religious institute.

The present work is a study of the means and methods whereby the natural right of sustenance can be realized by houses of the regular religious. Its purpose, however, is not to offer an exhaustive study of canonical or particular legislation relative to the sustenance of all religious. Neither does it attempt to interpret this problem in the light of particular laws of any one institute of regular religious. It simply intends to show the past and present canonical legislation in the matter of the use of what can be considered ordinary methods of sustenance of houses of regulars.

The study is divided into three parts. The first deals with the natural law of sustenance in connection with the establishment and founding of houses of regular religious. In the second part the ordinary sources of sustenance, such as are derived from common possessions, almsgathering, etc., are considered. The third part presents the general norms of Canon Law relative to the administration of temporal goods by regular religious. In the course of this study the author has availed himself of the excellent studies of Drs. Flanagan [1] and McManus.[2]

The writer wishes to take this opportunity to express his sincere appreciation to all those who have aided him in the preparation of this study. Particular gratitude is due to the faculty of the School of Canon Law of the Catholic University of America for their considerate and generous assistance at all times.

[1] *The Canonical Erection of Religious Houses,* The Catholic University of America Canon Law Studies, n. 179 (Washington, D. C.: The Catholic University of America Press, 1943).

[2] *The Administration of Temporal Goods in Religious Institutes,* The Catholic University of America Canon Law Studies, n. 109 (Washington, D. C.: The Catholic University of America, 1937).

PART ONE

THE ESTABLISHMENT OF HOUSES OF REGULARS

CHAPTER I

Authorization for the Erection of a Religious House of Regulars

ARTICLE 1. PRE-CODE LEGISLATION

A. Council of Chalcedon (451) to the Council of Trent (1545–1563)

With the progress of religious life in the first centuries of the Christian era, one finds large numbers of men and women influenced by the great spiritual leaders of the day [1] banding together and dedicating themselves to the service of God and the cause of the Church. With the growth of membership in the various religious groups, there arose the question of their proper

[1] In the East, St. Paul (234–342), St. Anthony (251–356), St. Pachomius (292–346), St. Basil the Great (329–379). In the West, St. Benedict (480–543), St. Augustine (354–430). Cf. Schäfer, *Compendium de Religiosis ad Normam Codicis Iuris Canonici* (Münster i.W.: Ex Officina Libraria Aschendorff, 1927), nn. 10, 11. (Hereafter this work will be referred to as Schäfer, *De Religiosis.*) Steiger, "De Propagatione et Diffusione Vitae Religiosae,"—*Periodica de Re Canonica et Morali Utili praesertim Religiosis et Missionariis,* XIII (1924), (44)-(48); (73)-(75). (Hereafter this periodical will be cited as *Periodica.*) Turner, *The Vow of Poverty,* The Catholic University of America Canon Law Studies, n. 54 (Washington, D. C.: The Catholic University of America, 1929), pp. 5–18; Wernz, *Ius Decretalium ad usum Praelectionum in Scholis Textus Canonici sive Iuris Decretalium* (2. ed., 6 vols., Romae, 1906–1913), III, nn. 602, 603. (Hereafter this work is cited as *Ius Decretalium.*) Cf. also, Pourrat, *Christian Spirituality from the Time of our Lord till the Dawn of the Middle Ages,* transl. by Mittchell and Jacques (3 vols., London: Burns, Oates and Washbourne Ltd., 1922–1927), I, pp. 80–88, 136–168, 241–252.

habitation and sustenance. Thus, as early as the fourth century, following the cessation of the persecutions, numbers of religious, professing diverse rules, are found migrating to the cities and towns and vying among themselves for the good will of the people and their own livelihood. Coming into new localities they established homes wherever they pleased, very often without any authorization from any ecclesiastical authority.

In turn, this soon gave rise to serious clashes between the bishops and rectors of churches on the one hand and the religious on the other. The cause of all this was obviously the lack of any clear and definite legislation on the matter. The erection of religious houses in this early period was solely dependent upon some tacit approval of the local bishop. Lacking the authority of an express law, such a procedure could in no way be well regulated.[2]

To remedy these and similar abuses and to put an end to the promiscuous infiltration of religious into cities and towns, the General Council of Chalcedon (451) in its fourth canon, prohibited the building and foundation of monasteries or chapels without the knowledge and consent of the bishops of the city concerned.[3] The necessity of obtaining the local bishop's consent was further emphasized by the enactments of subsequent Provincial Councils, notably that of Agde in 506,[4] I of Orleans in 511,[5] Epâon in 518,[6] Lerida in 523,[7] Barcelona in 540,[8] and XVII of Toledo in 694.[9]

---

[2] Wernz, *Ius Decretalium,* III, n. 616. Cf. also, Schmalzgrueber, *Ius Ecclesiasticum Universum* (5 vols. in 12, Romae, 1843–1845), lib. III, tit. 36, n. 28.

[3] C. 10, C. XVIII, q. 2; Mansi, *Sacrorum Conciliorum Nova et Amplissima Collectio* (53 vols., vols. 1–31, Florentiae, Venetiis, Parisiis, 1759–1798; vols., 31b–53, Parisiis, Leipzig, Arnhem, 1901–1927), VII, 394. (Hereafter this work is cited as Mansi.) Cf. Schroeder, *Disciplinary Decrees of the General Councils* (St. Louis, Mo.: Herder Book Co., 1937), p. 92. (Hereafter this work is cited as *Disciplinary Decrees.*)

[4] C. 12, 13, C. XVIII, q. 2; can. 27, 58—Mansi, VIII, 329, 334.

[5] C. 14, C. XVIII, q. 2; can. 22—Mansi, VIII, 355.

[6] Can. 10—Mansi, VIII, 560.

[7] Can. 3—Mansi, VIII, 613.

[8] Can. 10—Mansi, IX, 109.

[9] Sententia 11—Mansi, XII, 105.

This legislation of the Council of Chalcedon was in effect throughout the ensuing centuries and constituted common law until the time of Pope Boniface VIII.[10] With the rise of exempt religious orders, particularly the Mendicants, in the thirteenth century, it was necessary to issue new provisions because the rights of the bishops to approve foundation of new houses had been questioned by these religious on the plea of universal exemption from the jurisdiction of the local bishops. In 1296 Pope Boniface VIII, in view of the diverse scandals and frequent appeals to the Apostolic See, notwithstanding contrary privileges, notably those of Pope Gregory X (1271–1276), prohibited the Friars Preachers, Minor and other Mendicants [11] from building, buying, changing or alienating homes or places without the special permission of the Holy See, which permission must also mention this prohibition.[12] This law was subsequently confirmed by Pope Clement V at the General Council of Vienne (1311–1312) and an additional sanctioning decree was issued whereby violators of the constitution of Pope Boniface VIII would *ipso facto* incur the sentence of excommunication.[13]

These enactments of Boniface VIII and Clement V remained

---

[10] Hostiensis, *Summa Aurea* (Lugduni, 1568), lib. III, *de statu monachorum et canonicorum regularium*, n. 4.

[11] Glossa ad v. *mendicantes* explains as mendicants those "quibus victus tribuit incerta mendicitas et qui redditus aut possessiones ex regula vel constitutionibus habere non possunt."

[12] ". . . hoc perpetuo prohibemus edicto, ne deinceps aliquis vel aliqui de praedictis [*Praedicatores, Minores et religiosi alii mendicantes*] . . . in aliqua civitate, casto, villa seu loco quocunque ad habitandum domos, vel loca quaecumque de novo recipere, seu hactenus recepta mutare, vel ea venditioni, permutationi aut cuiusvis alienationis titulo quocunque in alios transferre praesumant absque Sedis Apostolicae licentia speciali, plenam et expressam faciente de prohibitione huius modi mentionem; si secus egerint irritum decernentes."—C. un. *de excessibus praelatorum et subditorum*, V, 6, in VI°; *Bullarium Franciscanum* (7 vols., Romae, 1759–1904), IV, 424, n. 105. (Hereafter this work is referred to as *BF.*) Potthast, *Regesta Pontificum Romanorum inde ab anno Post Christum natum 1198 ad annum 1304* (2 vols., Berolini, 1874–1875), n. 24446. (Hereafter this work is referred to as Potthast.)

[13] C. 3 *de poenis*, V, 8, in Clem; Schroeder (*Disciplinary Decrees*, p. 440) states that without doubt this decree is a postconciliar addition.

in force as common law of the Church until the time of the Council of Trent. Neither, by virtue of these enactments, were the exempt religious freed from the old obligation to obtain the permission of the local bishops. In other words, the exempt religious had to obtain a double permission: a special one from the Holy See and another permission from the local bishop in whose territory they desired to build, buy, or receive a new house.

B. Council of Trent (1545–1563) to the Code

The General Council of Trent (1545–1563), in considering the reform of regulars, decreed, by a prohibitive law affecting all religious orders, that henceforth monasteries could not be erected licitly unless first the permission of the bishop in whose diocese they were to be established would be obtained.[14] This new law requiring only the permission of the bishop caused a difference of opinion as to whether it superseded the former decrees of Pope Boniface VIII and Pope Clement V requiring the mendicants to obtain a special permission from the Holy See.[15]

Prosper Fagnanus (1598–1678)[16] held that the legislation of the Council of Trent changed the old law. He asserted that there was no difficulty as to the eremitic and non-mendicant orders because the decree of Pope Boniface VIII speaks only of mendicant orders. In fact the difficulty arose only with the Capuchins and the Friars Minor *de observantia,* for the prohibition of the former decrees, particularly that of Boniface VIII, referred only to those mendicants "*quibus victus tribuit incerta mendicitas*"

---

[14] ". . . nec de caetero similia loca sine episcopi in cuius dioecesi erigenda sunt, licentia prius obtenta."—Sess. XXV, *de regularibus,* c. 3.

[15] C. un. *de excessibus praelatorum et subditorum,* V, 6, in VIo; c. 3 *de poenis,* V, 8, in Clem.

[16] *Commentaria in Quinque Libros Decretalium* (Venetiis, 1696), lib. III, tit. *de institutionibus,* c. 1, n. 62. (Hereafter this work is referred to as *Commentaria.*) Cf. also Rodericus, *Quaestiones Regulares et Canonicae* (3 vols., Antuerpiae, 1528), I, q. 23, art. 7. (Hereafter this work is cited *Quaestiones*) ; Bouix, *Tractatus de Jure Regularium* (2 vols., Parisiis, 1857), I, pp. 244–251; Schmalzgrueber, *Ius Ecclesiasticum Universum* III, tit. 36, n. 29; Wernz, *Ius Decretalium,* III, n. 616; *Acta Sanctae Sedis* (41 vols., Romae, 1865–1908), I (1865–66), 714–728. (Hereafter this work is referred to as *ASS.*)

and who did not possess anything, even in common. Furthermore, since the Council of Trent permitted common possession of immovable property to all regulars of whatsoever order with the exception of the two mentioned above,[17] the decree of Pope Boniface VIII could not be applied to them. The Friars Minor and the Capuchins had been included in the decree of Pope Boniface VIII and were excepted by the Council of Trent in its permission to the possession of goods by all other regulars.

The constitution of Pope Innocent X, "*Instaurandae,*" published on October 15, 1652 for Italy and the adjacent islands, did not clarify the issue. The Pope decreed that henceforth no religious order, whether mendicant or non-mendicant, no congregation or society, could build a monastery or home without permission of the Holy See to be obtained in writing and mentioning this prohibition.[18] The cause for the lack of clarity in this constitution on the erection of religious houses is found in the very words of the Pontiff, for he stated in the document that he intended to provide separately for the religious outside of Italy.[19]

Fagnanus (1598–1678), who was secretary of the Sacred Congregation *super statu Regularium* at that time, states that this decree was only local in character and did not apply outside of Italy and the adjacent islands. Therefore the permission of only the local ordinary sufficed for the foundation of a monastery or home for the religious outside of the mentioned territories.[20] Identical was the teaching of Pignatelli (1600–1675),[21] Reiffenstuel (1641–1703),[22] and Bouix (1808–1870).[23]

---

[17] Sess. XXV, *de regularibus,* c. 3.

[18] *Codicis Iuris Canonici Fontes cura Emi Petri Card. Gaspari editi* (9 vols., Romae [postea Civitate Vaticana]: Typis Polyglottis Vaticanis, 1923–1939) (Vols. VII–IX ed. cura et studio Emi Iustiniani Card. Serédi), n. 233. (Hereafter this work is referred to as *Fontes.*)

[19] Par. 5.: "Intendimus autem in praemissis etiam ultra Italiam insulas adiacentes, prout expedire volumus, providere."—*Fontes,* n. 233.

[20] *Commentaria,* lib. III, tit. *de institutionibus,* c. 1, n. 71.

[21] *Consultationes Canonicae* (11 vols., Coloniae Allobrogorum, 1700), tom. X, consult. 91, n. 12.

[22] *Jus Canonicum Universum editio novissima cui accessit Tractatus de Regulis Iuris* (6 vols., Romae, 1831–1834), lib. III, tit. 48, nn. 38, 39. (Hereafter this work will be referred to as *Jus Canonicum Universum.*)

[23] *Tractatus de Jure Regularium,* I, 254.

On the other hand Schmalzgrueber (1663–1735), arguing solely on the authority of the latter decree, held that the permission of the Holy See was universally required.[24] This opinion was also championed by Ferraris (1687–1763).[25] Pope Benedict XIV (1740–1758) declared that the Council of Trent had not detracted anything from the authority of the Holy See as established by the decree of Pope Boniface VIII, but had only imposed the additional obligation that, besides the permission of the Holy See, episcopal approbation and permission was required.[26] Wernz (1842–1914) does not approve of such argumentation. His argument is that the decree of Pope Boniface VIII (1294–1303) was solely for the mendicants and cannot be rightly applied to all regulars.[27]

Up to the year 1864 the practice of the Supreme Tribunals of the Church was not uniform in all instances, as was observed by one of the consultors of the Sacred Congregation of Bishops and Regulars. The regulars customarily sought the permission of the Holy See, but this in no way proved the necessity of seeking such permission. It was the best procedure, for thereby they precluded any possible difficulties that could have arisen in regard to the establishment of their monasteries and homes.[28] Pope Leo XIII (1878–1903) in his Constitution "*Romanos Pontifices*" of May 8, 1881 held as common opinion that besides the permission of the Bishop for the erection of houses of regu-

---

[24] *Ius Ecclesiasticum Universum,* III, tit. 36, nn. 28–30.

[25] *Prompta Bibliotheca Canonica, Iuridica, Moralis, Theologica necnon Ascetica, Polemica, Rubricistica, Historica* (8 vols., Romae, 1855–1892) ad v. "conventus," art. 1, nn. 13, 38. (Hereafter this work is referred to as *Bibliotheca.*)

[26] *Benedicti XIV Opera Omnia in XVII tomos distributa,* tom. XI, *De Synodo Dioecesana* (Prati, 1844), lib. 9, cap. 1, n. 9. Cf. also Monacelli, *Formularium Legale Practicum Fori Ecclesiastici* (4 vols., ed. 3 romana, Romae, 1844), Pars I, tit. 6, formula 19, adnot. 31. (Hereafter this work is referred to as *Formularium.*)

[27] *Ius Decretalium,* III, n. 616, note 149.

[28] Cf. S. C. Ep. et Reg., *"Americana votorum,"* 1 sept. 1864—*ASS,* I (1865–1866), 728; Bizzarri, *Collectanea in usum Secretariae Congregationis Episcoporum et Regularium* (Romae, 1863), pp. 781–785. (Hereafter this work is referred to as *Collectanea.*)

lars, papal permission was also required.[29] This was again confirmed in a declaration of the Sacred Congregation for the Propagation of the Faith in 1901.[30]

ARTICLE 2. LEGISLATION OF THE CODE

Legislation previous to the present Code of Canon Law considered the term *religious house* generically as designating any legitimate *ecclesiastical foundation* erected by the authority of the bishop or some similar prelate.[31] The Code has given it a much more restricted and precise meaning. Today it has taken on the technical aspects of the word meaning: a house belonging to any religious institute in general.[32] In the strict canonical sense, by the term *religious house* is meant a permanent and canonically established foundation where the religious of the same institute practice the common life under the direction of a legitimate superior as prescribed by their rule and constitutions.[33] Because of the peculiar juridic importance of religious orders,[34] a specific term had been provided to indicate their houses, a *regular house* mean-

[29] ". . . Quare communis hodie sententia est, qui favet passim rerum iudicatarum auctoritas, non licere Regularibus, tam intra quam extra Italiam, nova monasteria aut conventus sive collegia fundare sola Episcopi venia impetrata, sed indultam quoque a Sede Apostolica facultatem requiri."—*Fontes,* n. 582.

[30] S. C. Prop. Fide, litt. encycl., 7 dec. 1901—*ASS,* XXXIV (1901-1902), 639; *Fontes,* n. 4938.

[31] Larraona, "Commentarium Codicis,"—*Commentarium pro Religiosis,* III (1922), 46. (Hereafter this periodical will be cited *CpR.*) Wernz-Vidal, *Ius Canonicum ad Codicis Normam exactum,* Tomus III, *De Religiosis* (Romae: Aedes Universitatis Gregorianae, 1933), n. 43. (Hereafter this work will be referred to as *De Religiosis.*)

[32] *Canon* 488, 5º.

[33] Flanagan, *The Canonical Erection of Religious Houses,* The Catholic University of America Canon Law Studies, n. 179 (Washington, D. C.: The Catholic University of America Press, 1943), p. 25; McManus, *The Administration of Temporal Goods in Religious Institutes,* The Catholic University of America Canon Law Studies, n. 109 (Washington, D. C.: The Catholic University of America, 1937), p. 48. (Hereafter this work is cited *Administration in Religious Institutes.*) Pejška, *Ius Canonicum Religiosorum* (3. ed., Friburgi Brisgoviae: Herder and Co., 1927), p. 49.

[34] Particularly the question of their exemption from the jurisdiction of the local ordinary. Cf. can. 497, §1; 615; 617; 621.

ing one belonging to a religious order.[35] It should be observed that the term *regular house* is applied to the houses of any and all orders whether they be of Canons Regular, monks, mendicants or of clerics regular.[36]

A. Canonical Erection of Houses of Regulars

In the strict sense canonical erection is described as " the concession of moral personality, that is, an act of competent ecclesiastical authority or a prescript of law by which an association or an institute is acknowledged as a moral person in the Church." [37] With reference, therefore, to a religious house, canonical erection is the act of granting moral personality to a place where a religious community wishes to establish a permanent residence.[38] The legislation of the Code, though demanding the observance of certain legal formalities in establishing religious houses, does not in any way deny to any legitimately established religious institute the right to provide for itself and erect religious houses. Thus for exempt religious institutes in canon 497, §1, it is ordered that before they proceed to the formal erection of any religious house the authorization of the Holy See and written consent of the local ordinary must be obtained.

The authorization of competent authority, the Holy See and the local ordinary, should not be confused as constituting the formal decree of canonical erection of the religious house. It is a necessary condition for validity, but the canonical erection of the house follows from the acceptance by competent authority of the religious institute, acknowledging the new foundation as part of the institute. Nowhere does the Code require a formal decree of acceptance. Competent exempt religious superiors, because they have jurisdiction in the external forum, could issue a formal decree of acceptance but it is not necessary that they do so.[39]

---

35 Canon 488, 5º.

36 Larraona, " Commentarium Codicis,"—*CpR,* III (1922), 50.

37 Flanagan, *The Canonical Erection of Religious Houses,* pp. 32, 33; cf. canon 100, §1; Larraona, " Commentarium Codicis,"—*CpR,* V (1924), 418 and XII (1931), 249.

38 Larraona, " Commentarium Codicis,"—*CpR,* III (1922), 47.

39 ". . . however . . . prudence and good business methods will demand

The law itself provides that once the conditions for legitimate erection are fulfilled, the religious house becomes a moral person.[40]

As has been noted, the first and primary effect of legitimate canonical erection of a religious house, exempt or non-exempt, is that it is endowed with a legal existence as a moral person. This moral personality carries with itself certain other juridic effects as determined by the Code of Canon Law. These may be summed up as follows:

1. The religious house becomes equal to a minor and is accorded the legal protection granted to minors.[41]

2. By its nature it becomes perpetual and therefore cannot become extinct except if it be suppressed by legitimate authority or fail to exist factually for a hundred year period because of the lack of members.[42]

3. It participates in the local privileges of the religious institute of which it is a part.[43]

4. The new foundation becomes entitled to acquire and possess temporal goods unless particular constitutions restrict or exclude this capacity.[44]

5. It acquires a place of precedence in relation to the other houses in the locality from the moment of its canonical erection.[45]

---

that the decision of the religious superiors to erect a new house and the acceptance of this house as a part of the institute be made in writing, and that a record be kept in the archives of the institute. This is a necessary precaution in order to prove in the external forum that the religious house has a true canonical status."—Flanagan, *op. cit.*, p. 35.

[40] Flanagan, *op. cit.*, pp. 34, 35; Larraona, "Commentarium Codicis,"—*CpR,* V (1924), 418 and nota 338, XII (1931), 249; Wernz-Vidal, *De Religiosis,* n. 76, nota 23; Vromant, *De Bonis Ecclesiae Temporalibus ad usum utriusque cleri, praesertim missionariorum* (ed. altera aucta et recognita, Louvain: Museum Lessianum, 1934), n. 227. (Hereafter this work is cited *De Bonis Ecclesiae Temporalibus.*)

[41] Canon 100, §3. Cf. canons 1511, §2; 1655, §2; 1687, §1; 1737.

[42] Canon 102, §1.

[43] Canon 63–65; 613–624.

[44] Canons 531; 532; 1495, §2; cf. McManus, *The Administration of Temporal Goods in Religious Institutes,* pp. 48, 49.

[45] Canon 106, 5o. Cf. Flanagan, *The Canonical Erection of Religious Houses,* p. 37; Pejška, *Ius Canonicum Religiosorum,* pp. 54, 55.

B. Necessary Formalities

> Canon 497, §1: Ad erigendam domum religiosam exemptam, sive formatam sive non formatam, aut monasterium monialium, aut in locis Sacrae Congregationi de Prop. Fide subiectis quamlibet religiosam domum, requiritur beneplacitum Sedis Apostolicae et Ordinarii loci consensus in scriptis datus; secus satis est Ordinarii venia.

Canon 497, §1 establishes the necessity of observing certain legal formalities in the foundation of exempt religious houses. These legal formalities consist in obtaining the consent of competent ecclesiastical authority, which consent is determined as an act of ecclesiastical jurisdiction having the efficacy of a necessary condition in order that a religious house may obtain legal status as such before the law.[46] Thus for the erection of exempt religious houses the Code requires (1) a papal indult and (2) written consent of the local ordinary.

Requiring the indult or *beneplacitum* of the Holy See for the erection of all exempt religious houses, the Code introduced a notable change in ecclesiastical discipline. What had been considered previously as only " common opinion " for all except the Friars Minor and Capuchins, now became a universal law of the Church, comprehending all regulars. This disposition of the Code is in full accord and without prejudice to the concept of exemption.[47] Since it is part of common ecclesiastical law,

---

[46] Flanagan, *The Canonical Erection of Religious Houses,* p. 49.

[47] Exemption is a privilege whereby certain persons, places or things are withdrawn from the jurisdiction of a superior to whom they should have been subject. An outstanding case of exemption is that accorded to certain religious institutes either by law or by privilege. Canon 615 states that all regulars together with their houses and churches are exempt from the jurisdiction of the local ordinary except in cases provided for by ecclesiastical legislation. It is not only a privilege but it had been also canonized by the Code and became a part of the common law of the Church as expressed by the Code. Hence since it is both a law and a privilege it is to be regulated by the general norms for laws, tempered by the general norms for privileges.—Cf. O'Brien, *The Exemption of Religious in Church Law* (Milwaukee: The Bruce Publishing Co., 1943), pp. 8–11; Melo, *De Exemptione Regularium,* The Catholic University of America Canon Law Studies, n. 12 (Washington, D. C.: The Catholic University of America, 1921), p. 1.

derogation of the privilege of exemption can only be effected by special action on the part of the Holy See.[48] A further limitation on the exemption rights of religious has been placed in the second formality which requires the written consent of the local ordinary. This, too, is in perfect accord with canon 615 which determines the jurisdiction from which the religious are to be considered as exempt adding however, " except in cases provided for by law." [49]

These two formalities constitute the authorization necessary for the canonical erection of an exempt religious house. Included under the scope of this canon are all religious houses of exempt orders, be they formal [50] or non-formal. Non-formal houses in the law of the Code are made subject to the vigilance of the local ordinary,[51] but in the matter of their foundation they are made equal to the formal house and consequently the same formalities must necessarily be observed previous to their canonical erection.[52]

Since these formalities of authorization are strictly required by law, their fulfillment is necessary to the validity of the act of canonical erection of a religious house. This is the common and unqualified opinion held by most canonists.[53]

---

[48] Melo, *De exemptione Regularium*, pp. 35–37; O'Brien, *op. cit.*, pp. 18, 19; Pejška, *Ius Canonicum Religiosorum*, p. 50.

[49] Canon 615:—Regulares, novitiis non exclusis, sive viri sive mulieres, cum eorum domibus et ecclesiis, exceptis monialibus quae Superioribus regularibus non subsunt, ab Ordinarii loci iurisdictione exempti sunt, praeterquam in casibus a iure expressis.

[50] Can. 488: . . . veniunt nomine: . . . 5º . . . *domus formatae*, domus religiosa in qua sex saltem religiosi professi degunt, quorum, si agatur de religione clericali, quattuor saltem sint sacerdotes.

[51] Can. 617, §2.

[52] Larraona, " Commentarium Codicis "—*CpR*, V (1924), 420.

[53] Beste, *Introductio in Codicem* (Collegeville, Minn.: St. John's Abbey Press, 1938), p. 322; Chelodi, *Ius de Personis iuxta Codicem Iuris Canonici* (ed. altera a Bertagnolli recognita et aucta, Tridenti: Libr. Edit. Tridentum, 1927), n. 249, b (hereafter this work will be cited *Ius de Personis*); Fanfani, *De Iure Religiosorum ad normam Codicis Iuris Canonici* (2 ed., Taurini-Romae: Marietti, 1925), n. 21 (hereafter this work will be referred to as *De Iure Religiosorum*); Flanagan, *The Canonical Erection of Religious Houses*, pp. 49, 50; Gerster, *Ius Religiosorum in Compendium redactum pro Iuvenibus Religiosis* (Taurini: Officina Libraria Marietti, 1935), p. 26; Larraona, " Consultationes "—*CpR*, I (1920), 113.

Vromant,[54] however, proposes a partially different conclusion as to the exact efficacy of the authorization of the local ordinary as compared with the *beneplacitum* of the Holy See. He, together with the rest of the authors, maintains that whenever the *beneplacitum* of the Holy See is required for the erection of a religious house, it is necessary for the validity of the canonical erection. The consent of the local ordinary, however, is not required for the existence of the house but rather for its legal stability (*firmitas*).

The consent of the local ordinary, argues Vromant, is not required to the extent that its omission would render the act of canonical erection completely invalid. It is commonly agreed that if the consent of the local ordinary had been omitted before the erection, his grant of the consent *after the fact* is sufficient for validating the foundation.[55] He draws proof from pre-Code doctrine as supported by Fagnanus[56] and from a letter of Pope Pius IX (1846–1878) to Archbishop Darboy of Paris which stated that the proper, natural and juridic effect of convalidation is the sanation of the defect of an act that should have been previously posited.[57]

An act that is completely invalid, null in Canon Law,[58] requires the placing of a new act together with all the conditions required by law under pain of nullity. This power of validating or sanating an act which by universal law of the Church is considered invalid rests only with the supreme legislator of the

---

[54] "*De Licentiis Requisitis ad Erigendam Domun Religiosam*"—*Jus Pontificium,* VIII (1928), 213–215.

[55] Coronata, *Institutiones Iuris Canonici ad usum utriusque Cleri et Scholarum* (5 vols., Vol. I, Taurini, Italia: Ex Officina Libraria Marietti, 1928), n. 523, note 8 (hereafter this work is cited *Institutiones*); Melo, *De Exemptione Regularium,* p. 123; Vermeersch-Creusen, *Epitome Iuris Canonici cum Commentariis ad Scholas et ad Usum Privatum,* I (ed. altera, Mechlinae-Romae: H. Dessain, 1924), n. 560. (Hereafter this work is referred to as *Epitome.*)

[56] *Commentaria,* lib. III, tit. *de institutionibus,* c. 1, n. 58.

[57] ". . . Nam te minime latet hunc esse proprium, naturalem et iuridicum omnis ratihabitationis . . . effectum, sanandi scilicet defectum illius actus qui praecedere debuisset . . ."—*ASS,* XI (1878), 218.

[58] Canon 1680, §1.

entire Church, the Roman Pontiff, who alone possesses the fullness of power and jurisdiction in the Church.[59] Thus, if the sanation or ratification of an invalid erection which is given by the local ordinary after the fact of the foundation of a religious house is sufficient to bring about the effects required by common law, it must necessarily follow that the lack of the ordinary's consent will not make the act of establishing the house completely invalid. Were it to be completely invalid, mere ratification on the part of the local ordinary would not suffice. He would have to either repeat the entire act or decree of foundation, or he would have to seek sanation from the Holy See, or at least request and receive from the Holy See proper delegation for sanation.[60]

This conclusion of Vromant seems to be founded upon sound juridical principles if it considers, as it does seem to do, cases where the consent of both, the Holy See and the local ordinary, is required by law.[61]

C. MODE OF PROCEDURE

Concerning the method of procedure in obtaining the necessary consent for the foundation of a new exempt religious house, the Code of Canon Law is silent. The person who is to draw up the petition, is not determined, and it is not established by law as to whom the petition should be directed first, the Holy See or the local ordinary.

With regard to the drawing up of the petition, the very nature of the matter would seem to indicate that the petition be formulated and directed to the proper authority by the religious superior who is competent to act in behalf of the institute re-

[59] Canon 218; cf. also Harrigan, *The Radical Sanation of Invalid Marriages,* The Catholic University of America Canon Law Studies, n. 116 (Washington, D. C.: The Catholic University of America, 1938), pp. 2, 112, 113; S. C. C. *Albiganen et aliarum,* 17 maii, 1919—*Acta Apostolicae Sedis, Commentarium Officiale* (Romae, 1909—), XI (1919), 386; cf. also canon 586, §1 and 1141.

[60] Vromant, "*De Licentiis Requisitis ad Erigendam Domum Religiosam*" —*Jus Pontificium,* VIII (1928), 215.

[61] Flanagan, *The Canonical Erection of Religious Houses,* pp. 50–52. As to the question as to who is to be considered as competent local ordinary cf. Flanagan, *op. cit.,* pp. 56–61.

questing a new house. However, there is nothing that would forbid the local ordinary the right to formulate the petition to be sent to the Holy See, specially if he is the founder of the new religious house.[62]

Considering the question of precedence in requesting the consent, nothing certain can be deduced from canon 497, §1. Pejška,[63] on the basis of a response of the Congregation of the Propagation of the Faith, issued on December 7, 1901,[64] believes that the permission of the Holy See should be obtained first. The Congregation ordered that local ordinaries should abstain from granting permission for the erection of religious houses in territories subject to that Sacred Congregation without first obtaining the approval of the Congregation. From this Pejška concludes that it seems to be the mind of the legislator that even in other regions as well, the ordinaries should refrain from granting formal approval and definite consent until the consent of the Holy See has been obtained. They could however perform necessary preparatory acts with the religious superiors.

Wernz-Vidal,[65] and Larraona,[66] on the contrary, assert that to avoid useless ambiguity the consent of the local ordinary be obtained first. They state that the Holy See does not give its consent unless the bishop or ordinary was first interrogated and after he had given his written permission.

In essence there is not much difference of opinion among canonists. Though some assert that the consent of the Holy See must be obtained first, they do not deny that the preparatory acts can be perfomed by the ordinary together with the competent local superior. It is logical that proper investigation be made before petitioning authorization. The assurance of sustenance for the new foundation as required by canon 496 is a necessary condition before proceeding to the formality of establishing the house.

---

[62] Flanagan, *The Canonical Erection of Religious Houses*, pp. 75, 76; Pejška, *Ius Canonicum Religiosorum*, p. 51.

[63] *Ius Canonicum Religiosorum*, p. 51.

[64] S. C. Prop. Fide, *litt. encycl.* 7 dec. 1901—*ASS*, XXXIV (1901-1902), 639; *Fontes*, n. 4938.

[65] *De Religiosis*, n. 71.

[66] " Commentarium Codicis "—*CpR*, V (1924), 425.

Documentary evidence of proper sustenance would certainly be required by the Sacred Congregation before the granting of definite consent.

In practice, therefore, as it is pointed out by Flanagan,[67] the proper method of procedure requires that (1) prudent conferences between the religious superior and the local ordinary be had to estimate the sources and means of support for the proposed religious house; (2) the local ordinary gives his consent in the form of a "*Nihil obstat,*" subject to the approval of the Holy See; (3) this tentative consent is enclosed with the petition which is sent to the proper Congregation of the Roman Curia.[68]

D. EFFECTS OF AUTHORIZATION

Competent authorization to erect a religious house of an exempt religious institute carries with it the effects delineated in canon 497, §2.[69] For all clerical institutes it implies authorization to have a church or public oratory annexed to the house and to exercise the functions of the sacred ministry in conformity with the requirements of law. The use of this right, however, is restricted by the clause referring to canon 1162, §4 which requires special approval by the local ordinary of the site for a church or public oratory.

For all religious institutes the canon provides the right to exercise the works of piety which are proper to the rule and constitutions of the institute. The text of this canon also permits the local ordinary to attach certain conditions, possibly limiting the exercise of the works of the institute. These conditions however

---

67 *The Canonical Erection of Religious Houses,* p. 77.

68 The Sacred Congregation of Religious is the competent Congregation for the erection of exempt religious houses. In territories subject to the Sacred Congregation of the Propagation of the Faith one petition for erection must be directed to it and another to the Sacred Congregation of Religious. Cf. can. 7, 251, 252. Also Larraona, "Commentarium Codicis" —*CpR,* V (1924), 423.

69 Canon 497, §2.—Constituendae novae domus permissio facultatem secumfert pro religionibus clericalibus habendi ecclesiam vel publicum oratorium domui adnexum, salve praescripto can. 1162, §4, et sacra ministeria peragendi, servatis de iure servandis; pro omnibus religionibus, pia opera exercendi religionis propria, salvis conditionibus in ipsa permissione appositis.

cannot be contrary to the rights and privileges of the religious given in common or in their particular law as approved in their constitutions by the Holy See.[70] Conditions and limitations should be placed only for a reasonable and just cause. These, in turn, are chiefly those which have as their underlying principle, on the one hand, the desire of providing for all fairly and in an equal manner, and, on the other hand, the avoidance of contentions and rivalry among the religious themselves and between the religious and the secular clergy.[71] Larraona points out that this holy desire should not be too greatly exaggerated and should be confined within certain limits. Some contentions and rivalries are unavoidable. It would help therefore, he continues, to consider before God whether or not it is better to permit these contentions rather than fearing them to impede the great good that is ordinarily derived from religious houses.[72]

[70] Beste, *Introductio in Codicem,* p. 323; Larraona, "Commentarium Codicis"—*CpR,* V (1924), 430; Schäfer, *De Religiosis,* n. 84.

[71] Blat, *Commentarium Texus Codicis Iuris Canonici,* Vol. II, *De Personis* (ed. altera, Romae: Libreria del Collegio "Angelico," 1921), p. 541, n. 551. (Hereafter this work is referred to as *De Personis.*) Flanagan, *The Canonical Erection of Religious Houses,* p. 94; O'Brien, *The Exemption of Religious in Church Law,* p. 104; Wernz-Vidal, *De Religiosis,* n. 76.

[72] "Commentarium Codicis"—*CpR,* V (1924), 430, note 379.

CHAPTER II

Conditions for the Erection of a House of Regulars

Article 1. Pre-Code Legislation

A. Consent of Persons Concerned

Long before the Council of Trent the approval of the local ordinary for the erection of monasteries and homes by religious in any diocese had been an established law. This Council simply restated the old law.[1] The Tridentine provision could not be interpreted as if it gave the bishops power to permit or not permit the construction of monasteries at their own fancy. Such procedure would certainly have been detrimental to religion and the Church. In the opinion of most authors, this legislation was to be so understood that thereby a right had been granted to the bishop to determine whether such a foundation would be expedient or detrimental to the needs of the territory under his care. Consequently, if no reasonable cause existed, the bishop could not deny his permission. If he did, an appeal could be made to the Sacred Congregation of Bishops and Regulars.[2]

The grant or denial of this permission was not left to the bishop at will, i.e. without observing certain formalities. It was his duty, when approached for the permission for the erection of a monastery, to call and hear those concerned and then issue his decree of approval or denial. By those concerned, Pope Clement VIII, in his constitution "*Quoniam,*" of July 23, 1603,[3] meant the

[1] ". . . nec de cetero similia loca erigantur sine episcopi, in cuius dioecesi erigenda sunt, licentia prius obtenta."—Conc. Trident., sess. XXV, *de regularibus,* c. 3.

[2] Bouix, *Tractatus de Jure Regularium,* I, 261–264; Ferraris, *Bibliotheca,* ad v. "conventus" art. 1, n. 28; Pignatelli, *Consultationes Canonicae,* I, consultatio 179, n. 45.

[3] *Bullarum Diplomatum et Privilegiorum Sanctorum Romanorum Pontifi-*

priors and procurators of other communities who may have some interest in the proposed erection of the new monastery. The statement "*et aliis interesse habentibus*" gave rise to the question as to whether the local pastor was included.

Pignatelli,[4] Schmalzgrueber,[5] Leurenius (1646–1723),[6] and Reiffenstuel[7] contended that if the pastor is not called and permission is given, the grant is invalid. This, because of the words: "*aliis interesse habentibus.*" The pastor, they claimed, had a great interest in the matter, for the building of a new monastery could bring about a condition whereby offerings and other parochial rights might possibly become so diminished as to endanger his sustenance. Others, like Passerinus and Pasqualigius, referred to by Bouix,[8] whose opinion he follows, on the contrary, claim that the words "*aliis interesse habentibus*" do not include the pastors or any other persons but refer only to other superiors and procurators. They base their position on the fact that there are many convents which are not governed by priors but by superiors of diverse names, such as Abbots, Provincials, Guardians, etc. Also many convents did not have procurators taking care of their goods. The followers of this opinion, though they did deny the necessity of citing and hearing the pastor before the granting of such permission, did not deny that the pastor had a right to appeal to the bishop if he foresaw any loss threatening him from such a foundation. The bishop, in turn, was obliged to hear his case.

The constitution "*Quoniam*" of Clement VIII referred only to the erection of houses by mendicant orders. Pope Gregory XV, by his decree, "*Cum alias*" of August 17, 1622, extended this to all religious orders under whatsoever name they be called.[9] As

---

cum Taurinensis Editio (24 vols. et Appendix, Augustae Taurinorum, 1857–1872), XI, n. 320. (Hereafter this work is referred to as *Bull. Rom. Taur.*)

[4] *Consultationes Canonicae,* I, consultatio 179, nn. 52–58.

[5] *Ius Ecclesiasticum Universum,* III, tit. 36, n. 35.

[6] *Forum Ecclesiasticum* (5 vols., Venetiis, 1729), III, tit. 48, q. 997, n. 3.

[7] *Jus Canonicum Universum,* III, tit. 48, n. 33.

[8] *Tractatus de Jure Regularium,* I, 272–279. Cf. also Reiffenstuel, *l.c.;* Petra, *Commentaria ad Constitutiones Apostolicas* (5 vols. in 2, Venetiis, 1729) I, const. 2, sec. 1, n. 31.

[9] *Fontes,* n. 1715.

regards the consent of superiors of orders already existing in the locality, the Pope added that the ordinary could forego such consent and permit construction if he was certain that the new house could properly sustain itself in a manner that would not be prejudicial to the sustenance of the monasteries already in existence in that locality.[10]

Pope Urban VIII (1623–1644) by the Constitution "*Romanus Pontifex*," of August 28, 1624,[11] strictly reaffirmed the binding force of the two previous constitutions and abrogated all contrary privileges and exemptions.[12]

B. *Number of Religious to a House*

The number of religious that would live in any house was of especial concern to the Holy See and the Sacred Congregations. The Council of Trent in general terms stated: "But in the aforesaid monasteries and houses of men as well as of women, whether they do or do not possess immovable properties, only such a number of persons shall be determined upon and retained in the future as can be suitably maintained either from the revenues of the monasteries or from the customary alms." [13]

Pope Gregory XV (1621–1623) by the constitution "*Cum alias*" of August 17, 1622,[14] determined that the Tridentine legislation decreed that henceforth convents, houses, congregations or societies of religious or regulars of whatever order, even mendicants, should not be built unless in such a house at least twelve brothers or monks or religious would reside and be conveniently sustained from the income and customary alms.[15] The Sacred Congregation of the Council on June 21, 1625, on the

---

[10] Ferraris, *Bibliotheca,* ad v. "conventus," art. 1, nn. 21, 22; Leurenius, *Forum Ecclesiasticum,* III, tit. 48, q. 997, n. 3.

[11] *Fontes,* n. 389.

[12] Ferraris, *Bibliotheca,* ad v. "conventus," art. 1, nn. 22, 23; Lauretus de Franchis, *Controversiae inter Episcopos et Regulares atque Observationes Zacharii Pasquarigii* (Romae, 1656), p. 139, additio nn. 420, 421; Wernz, *Ius Decretalium,* III, n. 621.

[13] Conc. Trident., sess. XXV, *de regularibus,* c. 3;—transl. from Schroeder, *Canons and Decrees of the Council of Trent,* p. 219.

[14] §3—*Fontes,* n. 1715.

[15] Reiffenstuel, *Jus Canonicum Universum,* Lib. III, tit. 48, n. 34.

authority of Pope Urban VIII stressed the necessity for the observance of the constitution of Gregory XV, adding also that the monasteries or other such places already erected in which twelve religious do not actively reside or are not sustained, must be subject to the visitation, correction and jurisdiction of the local ordinary.[16]

Under these constitutions, the construction of monasteries or homes was not absolutely forbidden even if the number of religious residing therein was less than twelve. The constitution of Gregory XV simply prohibited the construction of a house if twelve religious would not reside or be sustained there. However the decree published by the authority of Pope Urban VIII did not prononuce such a foundation invalid but stated that if the conditions of the previous decrees were not fulfilled and verified, the regulars would then lose their privilege of exemption.[17]

The Popes,[18] and particularly the Sacred Congregation of Bishops and Regulars, insisted upon the number of twelve members if and when monasteries were to be erected.[19] Those not conforming were to be deprived of their privilege of exemption. However, the Sacred Congregation of Bishops and Regulars did not always urge the bishops to use their power of visitation of the smaller religious houses of exempt orders, unless the number of religious was notably small or special circumstances demanded such a procedure. On the contrary, says Wernz,[20] it expressly asked the bishops to abstain from exercising their right of visitation.[21] This can also be inferred from the consti-

[16] §14—*Fontes*, n. 2460.

[17] Bouix, *Tractatus de Jure Regularium*, I, 304, 305; Wernz, *Ius Decretalium*, III, n. 620.

[18] Cf., e.g., Innocentius XII, const. "*Nuper*," 23 dec. 1697, §10—*Fontes*, n. 260.

[19] S. C. Ep. et Reg., *Lisbonen.*, 4 iul. 1594—*Fontes*, n. 1511; *Aversana*, 11 iul. 1594—*Fontes*, n. 1512; decr. 22 aug. 1814—*Fontes*, n. 1893; *Sorana*, 20 iun. 1851—*Fontes*, n. 1960; *Montisvidei*, 22 febr. 1856—*Fontes*, n. 1974; also S. C. C., decr. 21 iun. 1626—*Fontes*, n. 2460, §14.

[20] *Ius Decretalium*, III, n. 260.

[21] Cf. S. C. Ep. et Reg., 20 mart. 1857 et 16 mart. 1866—*ASS*, II (1866–1867), 155–157; *Minorum conventualium*, 12 maii 1741—Bizzarri, *Collectanea*, pp. 396, 397; also S. C. C., 23 aug. 1873—*ASS*, VII (1872), 626, 629, 630.

tution of Pope Leo XIII, "*Romanos Pontifices*" of May 8, 1881. Although it speaks primarily of houses in mission countries, it states that, by common law, religious houses in which at least six religious do not reside must be subject to the jurisdiction of the bishop.[22]

C. *Sustenance*

One of the most important of considerations that had to be taken into account by the authorities who were to grant permission for the construction of religious houses was the question of their proper sustenance. That is why the Holy See had been so very insistent upon both the proper authorization and the determination of the number of religious that were to live in the monastery, convent or house.

The General Council of Trent insisted that only such a number of persons be retained in such monasteries and houses of religious as could be suitably maintained from either the revenues of the monasteries or from customary alms.[23] This disposition, generally proposed, was intended more as a general norm regulating the building of monasteries and houses rather than as a strict law.[24]

In like manner the Constitutions of Popes Clement VIII ("*Quoniam*"), of Gregory XV ("*Cum alias*") and of Urban VIII ("*Romanus Pontifex*"), previously referred to, insisted upon the possibility of a proper sustenance for such new monasteries without prejudice to the sustenance of the monasteries already existing in the locality. The Sacred Congregation of the Council, in a decree issued on June 21, 1625, by the authority of Pope Urban VIII, ordered that, in the future, all superiors of religious in Italy and the adjacent islands give an account of their temporal property to this Sacred Congregation.[25] This was ordered to determine the advisability of having religious houses

---

[22] *Fontes,* n. 582, §8; cf. also Wernz, *Ius Decretalium,* III, n. 620, note 159; Mocchegiani, *Iurisprudentia Ecclesiastica* (3 vols., Ad Claras Aquas [Quaracchi], 1904–1905), III, 393.

[23] Conc. Trident., sess. XXV *de regularibus,* c. 3.

[24] Pejška, *Ius Canonicum Religiosorum,* p. 54.

[25] *Fontes,* n. 2460.

which did not have twelve religious and which could not sustain themselves. In answering a doubt as to whether this decree was intended to be binding also outside of Italy, the response was in the affirmative.[26] Pope Innocent XII in his constitution "*Nuper*" of December 12, 1697, reiterated *ad verbum* the decree of the Sacred Congregation of the Council of June 21, 1625.[27] Identical was the practice of the Sacred Congregation of Bishops and Regulars. It did not permit the foundation of a new house unless it could be assured of proper sustenance for its members.[28]

These decrees and decisions stressed the fact that it did not suffice that the religious be sustained in any manner that they would wish. Their sustenance was to be "*commoda*" *et* "*congrua.*" This did not refer only to new monasteries but also to the possible effects upon the "*commoda*" and "*congrua*" sustenance of the monasteries already existing in the locality.[29]

ARTICLE 2. LEGISLATION OF THE CODE

A. Omission of Pre-Code Requirements

> Canon 496.—Nulla religiosa domus erigatur, nisi iudicari prudenter possit vel ex reditibus propriis vel ex consuetis eleemosynis vel alio modo congruae sodalium habitationi et sustentationi provisum iri.

Before proceeding to grant any religious the permission to erect a religious house, the authorities concerned must see to the possible fulfillment of certain prerequisite conditions established by law in reference to the means of supporting and sustaining the prospective foundation. These conditions are set down in canon 496. The canon directs that no religious house may be established unless it can be prudently estimated that a proper livelihood and sustenance will be assured the members. This

---

[26] *Ad ultimum—Fontes,* n. 2460.

[27] *Ad ultimum—Fontes,* n. 260, §15.

[28] Cf. *Fontes,* nn. 1315, 1490, 1511, 1512, 1960. Cf. also Matthaeucci, *Officialis Curiae Ecclesiasticae* (Venetiis, 1734), cap. 16, nn. 2–6.

[29] Lauretus de Franchis, *Controversiae inter Episcopos et Regulares,* pp. 139, 140, additio nn. 421, 422; Reiffenstuel, *Jus Canonicum Universum,* Lib. III, tit. 48, n. 46.

is to be determined by the consideration of its coming from either the fixed income of the community or from the usual alms given it or from other means. All religious houses are included, be they exempt or non-exempt, formal or non-formal, mendicant or non-mendicant. The canon simply states: "*nulla religiosa domus.*"

In the present law of the Code the former formalities so precisely required in pre-Code legislation are evidently no longer necessary for they are not repeated in the Code and consequently they do not retain their force as law.[30] It must be noted, too, that from the wording of the canon, greater freedom is given in establishing houses, leaving the capacity to found houses to the prudent judgment of the competent authorities. With this in mind the solemnities required by pre-Code law should not be overlooked completely. They may serve as useful norms in determining and guaranteeing the proper observance of canon 496.[31]

Pre-Code law required that the bishop before proceeding to give his consent for the erection of a religious house was to call and hear those interested, particularly the superiors and procurators of other religious communities already in the locality.[32] Prümmer, however, contends that although the Code does not treat of the conditions under which the ordinary should give his consent, it would seem that pre-Code papal ordinations still retain their force since they are founded upon the very nature of the act of foundation.[33] This position, although it cannot be denied as having great value in practice, cannot be sustained in law by virtue of canon 6, 6°. It ought to be used as a norm in determining the true necessity and feasibility of having a new religious house in a locality where there already exist a number of religious houses. The requirement of prudent judgment in

---

[30] Canon 6, 6°.

[31] Larraona, "Commentarium Codicis"—*CpR*, V (1924), 332, IV; Wernz-Vidal, *De Religiosis*, n. 75.

[32] Cf. const. "*Quoniam,*" 23 iul. 1603—*Bull. Rom. Taur.*, XI, n. 320; const. "*Cum alias*" 17 aug. 1622—*Fontes*, n. 1715.

[33] *Manuale Iuris Canonici in usum scholarum* (ed. 4. et 5. aucta, Friburgi Brisgoviae: Herder and Co., 1927), q. 181, p. 241. (This work is hereafter cited *Manuale Iuris Canonici.*)

canon 496 tends to give support to such a contention. It is perfectly in compliance with present discipline to safeguard the rights to a proper sustenance of other religious houses canonically erected in the place where the location of a new house is being contemplated. However, it is not a condition demanded by common law, but rather it is one of natural equity. Such procedure is certainly not opposed to the prescript of Canon Law and would certainly tend to assure the proper fulfillment of the conditions laid down in the Code.[34]

For the protection of the rights of already existing communities in the place of the proposed erection of a new religious house, a legal action of "*Nuntiatio Novi Operis*" may be instituted in accord with canon 1676. Should the superiors of already existing houses in the vicinity of the newly authorized foundation feel that their own rights to a proper sustenance will be prejudiced, they may seek an injunction against the proposed foundation until the rights of both parties be determined by judicial sentence.[35] Pejška, noting this right in accord with canon 1676, §2, holds that the injured parties may have recourse to the bishop or the Holy See with suspensive effect unless adequate steps arc taken to insure that matters will be restored to their original status if an adverse sentence will be given to the party convened.[36] Should the parties injured forego their *legal* right of action, but foresee that their rights could be prejudiced because of the new foundation, Chelodi maintains that the superiors concerned may have recourse to the Holy See instead of the legal action, but with devolutive effect.[37]

The question as to whether the consent of the pastor in whose territory the new religious house was to be erected was needed or not was disputed by pre-Code canonists. The present discipline removes him from all consideration as far as the religious house

---

[34] Flanagan, *The Canonical Erection of Religious Houses*, p. 41; Schäfer, *De Religiosis*, n. 83; Wernz-Vidal, *De Religiosis*, n. 75.

[35] Flanagan, *The Canonical Erection of Religious Houses*, p. 53.

[36] *Ius Canonicum Religiosorum*, p. 52; cf. also Sipos, *Enchiridion Iuris Canonici* (3. ed., Pécs: Typographia "Haladás R. T.," 1936), p. 340, b.

[37] *Ius de Personis*, n. 249, note 4. This opinion is repeated by Schäfer (*De Religiosis*, n. 83, h), Larraona ("Commentarium Codicis"—*CpR*, V (1924), 332, IV) and O'Brien (*The Exemption of Religious in Church Law*, p. 101).

itself is concerned. However it requires that the local ordinary should consult the pastors when a church or public oratory is to be opened together with the religious house.[38] The pastor can also seek a legal injunction in conformity with canon 1676, as has been determined above in regard to other religious superiors.[39]

Another formality of the former law required that before proceeding to the granting of a formal consent for the erection of a religious house, definite assurance was to be had that at least twelve religious would reside and be conveniently sustained therein.[40] The present legislation does not require any determined number of religious necessary to constitute a religious house. However canon 488, 5° may serve as a norm in determining the mind of the Holy See in reference to the required number of religious needed before proceeding to the formality of establishing a new foundation. The canon speaks only of the number required to constitute a formal house, the number being six professed religious. For non-formal houses there is no law. However in order to form and possess the privileges of a community the group must consist of at least three members.[41] Fanfani [42] states that ordinarily it would be wise and prudent, before proceeding to the foundation of a new monastery or convent, to have moral certitude that the proposed house would, if not immediately then shortly after its erection, become a formal house. It is the common opinion among authors that the Holy See is opposed to the foundation of establishments which would not be capable of housing and conveniently sustaining at least four religious. As to the maximum number canon 496 implies that no community be so numerous as to prejudice the rights of its members to a proper sustenance.[43]

---

[38] Canon 1162, §3; 1191, §1.

[39] Fanfani, *De Iure Religiosorum,* n. 21, quaest. II; Larraona, "Commentarium Codicis"—*CpR,* V (1924), 332, 333; Pejška, *Ius Canonicum Religiosorum,* p. 52. Wernz-Vidal (*De Religiosis,* n. 75, note 22) observe that a recourse by the pastor to the Holy See rarely obtains a happy ending.

[40] Cf. const. "*Cum alias*" 17 aug. 1622—*Fontes,* n. 1715 ad par. 3.

[41] Canon 100, §2.

[42] *De Iure Religiosorum,* n. 21, quaest. IV.

[43] Flanagan, *The Canonical Erection of Religious Houses,* pp. 26, 27, 41; Pejška, *Ius Canonicum Religiosorum,* p. 54.

B. Obligation of Prudent Judgment

Of vital importance to the establishment of a religious house in any locality is the obligation of exercising prudent judgment in selecting and approving the site of the new foundation. This prudent judgment should be concerned with a proper estimate as to the sufficiency of temporal support that will be forthcoming to the new religious house. In conformity with the prescript of canon 496, this prudent judgment should be chiefly centered upon the possibility of the new religious house supporting itself from its proper income, the usual alms and other means. Though a prerequisite condition for the erection of a religious house, the obligation of exercising prudent judgment pertains only to the licitness of the act of giving requisite consent for the establishment. It is not required for validity, for canon 496 does not contain any clause which would expressly or equivalently make the act null and void.[44]

Prudent judgment is the consideration of circumstances that are necessary in order to obtain a certain end,[45] in our case, the proper temporal sustenance of the prospective religious house. The person or persons that are to exercise and fulfill the obligation of prudent judgment are not determined in the Code. Considering canon 497, §1, the obligation would seem to devolve upon one or the other of the parties whose consent is required, either the Holy See or the local ordinary in the case of a house of exempt religious. Then again it is certain that the religious superior of the institute should be considered. The practice of the Holy See itself would seem to exclude the necessity of prudent judgment as being obligatory upon itself. Before granting its consent it is certain that documentary evidence of proper future sustenance would have to be sent together with the petition to the Holy See. The obligation would therefore have to be of necessity discharged previous to the petitioning of the Holy See.

---

[44] Cf. canon 11; also Flanagan, *The Canonical Erection of Religious Houses*, p. 43; Coronata, *Institutiones*, I, n. 523.

[45] Thomas, S., *Summa Theologica* (emendata a De Rubeis, Billuart et Aliorum Notis Selectis Ornata, 6 vols., Taurini [Italia]: Marietti, 1937), *Ia IIæ*, q. 47, art. 2, *corpus; IIa IIæ*, q. 49, art. 9, *corpus*.

Fanfani,[46] basing his opinion on pre-Code legislation which reserved the judgment as to proper sustenance to the bishop,[47] asserts that in the new law too it is the obligation of the local ordinary. Likewise Wernz-Vidal,[48] in determining the practical aspects of prerequisite formalities before the concession of consent, seem to imply that the obligation of prudent judgment rests with the bishop.

The more common opinion, however, places the obligation of formulating prudent judgment as common to both the local ordinary and the competent religious superior.[49] There can be no doubt that the local ordinary remains the competent judge in determining the prospects for a proper sustenance of the proposed house in the locality of his jurisdiction. In virtue of his position he can prudently determine the opportunities and the possibility of meeting not only the needs of the new foundation but also the advisability of establishing a new religious house. On the other hand it is also prudent procedure to solicit the advice of the competent religious superior to determine the particular needs and aims of the proposed religious house. Lacking one or the other a necessary element of prudent judgment is missing—the consideration of all circumstances in order to attain a certain end. Without doubt it is the bishop who makes the final decision as to the suitability of temporal means for the proper livelihood and sustenance of the religious. In accord with canon 496 he may not proceed with the grant of authorization for the erection of a religious house unless he has the assurance of suitable provision for a proper sustenance. The assurance in turn need not be absolutely and mathematically certain. That does not seem

[46] *De Iure Religiosorum*, n. 21, quaest. I.

[47] Cf. const. "*Quoniam*" 23 iul. 1603—*Fontes*, n. 190; const. "*Cum alias*" 17 aug. 1622—*Fontes*, n. 1715.

[48] *De Religiosis*, n. 75.

[49] Farrell, *The Rights and Duties of the Local Ordinary Regarding Congregations of Women Religious of Pontifical Approval,* The Catholic University of America Canon Law Studies, n. 128 (Washington, D. C.: The Catholic University of America Press, 1941), p. 58; Flanagan, *The Canonical Erection of Religious Houses*, p. 43; Coronata, *Institutiones*, I, n. 523, a; Larraona, "Commentarium Codicis"—*CpR,* V (1924), 332.

to be required by the concept of prudent judgment.[50] Neither is it necessary that the funds for proper sustenance be immediately on hand before the permission is given. A reasonable assurance that they will be forthcoming is sufficient.[51]

In formulating this prudent judgment the bishop, together with the competent religious superior, should consider: (1) The needs to be met and the opportunities offered in the locality; (2) The amount of temporal aid that the house will require and the guaranteed possibility of the religious house to obtain the required aid; (3) The purpose and special work of the institute.[52]

1. *Needs and Opportunities of the Religious House*

Prudence certainly demands that before proceeding to the erection of a religious house all means must be taken definitely to establish the needs of the particular institute and the opporunities that are or will be offered toward the fulfillment of these needs without prejudice to the religious houses already existing in the locality. The determination of the needs of the proposed religious house can be made after a consultation with the competent religious superior of the institute. He certainly may be considered as a capable judge of the actual needs in accord with the rule and constitutions professed by the religious order and possibly he too can be a judge as to the possible opportunities in the place selected. The local ordinary on the other hand is in a position to establish whether or not the locality in question is in need of another religious house if there are religious already existing there.

The superiors of other religious institutes in and about the territory of the proposed religious house, though their consent in the matter of erection is no longer needed, may be consulted by the local ordinary, if he wishes to do so. The same may be said as to the members of the secular clergy. These, having, so to say, a prior claim on the locality for the means of their sustenance by

[50] Flanagan, *The Canonical Erection of Religious Houses,* p. 44.

[51] Larraona, "Commentarium Codicis"—*CpR,* V (1924), 333, 334; O'Brien, *The Exemption of Religious in Church Law,* p. 101.

[52] Farrell, *The Rights and Duties of the Local Ordinary Regarding Congregations of Women Religious of Pontifical Approval,* p. 59.

reason of being there first, should be adequately provided for. Their right to a proper sustenance cannot be compromised or their means of support lessened without a proportionate benefit in return.[53] Too many religious houses in a limited locality may well be a detriment not only to the material support of one or the other, but also to the progress of religion itself. Rivalries, contentions and competition among religious institutes may well destroy the aims and purpose of religious institutes in general.[54]

2. *Amount of Temporal Aid and Guarantee of Required Aid*

Second to be considered, is the certainty of the amount of funds the institute has on hand and the guarantee of its future income. Pre-Code law was very definite in its requirement of proper provision for the convenient and suitable shelter and sustenance of the members of the religious house. This law had been left practically intact in the requirement of canon 496. In the formation of a prudent judgment for establishing a religious house the temporal means of its support cannot be overlooked. Hence an investigation of the material condition as to expenses and income must be made.

The consideration of expenses to be met and the income available is of prime importance in the process of eliciting a prudent judgment for the sustenance of the religious house. The expenses of construction and furnishing, of equipment and materials needed to carry on its proper works, of food, clothing and medical care, should be weighed against the possible income upon which the community will depend.[55]

Foremost in the mind of the local ordinary should be the assurance of suitable (*congrua*) lodging and sustenance for the religious in the community. The Code does not specify in any way just what would constitute suitable lodgings. Canon 594, §3, referring to the equipment of the religious house, states that it

[53] Flanagan, *The Canonical Erection of Religious Houses,* p. 44; Schäfer, *De Religiosis,* n. 83, h; Wernz-Vidal, *De Religiosis,* n. 75.

[54] Augustine, *A Commentary on the New Code of Canon Law,* III, *Religious and Laymen* (3. ed., St. Louis, Mo.: B. Herder Book Co., 1922), p. 85. (Hereafter this work will be referred to as *Religious and Laymen.*)

[55] Flanagan, *The Canonical Erection of Religious Houses,* p. 45.

should be in conformity with the poverty that they profess.[56] The prescript of suitable lodging and sustenance permits a rather flexible interpretation, depending, to a very great extent, upon the rule and the constitutions of the order and also upon the place where they live. It is quite certain that standards of living differ in different localities. Prospects in mission territories and poor localities should not be judged on par with the more prosperous city neighborhood.[57] Augustine,[58] referring to what should be considered as decent lodging, tries to establish a general norm according to which the authorities may formulate a prudent judgment. Thus, he states that a suitable lodging would be one with which a man of modest aspirations, of the middle class, would be content. The same may be said of material support. The vow of poverty should be held uppermost in the mind of the bishop and superiors. Luxuries and delicacies should not be sought after in religious houses. Neither, however, should extreme want be found there. Moderate living, in accord with the amount and type of work and the ordinary comforts due to a self-respecting human being should be the norm of guiding competent authorities in eliciting a prudent judgment.

The consideration of material aid should not be the prime factor in the establishment of a religious house. It should certainly be tempered with the consideration of the peace of the institute in its future relations with other institutes and the secular clergy in the territory.

3. Purpose and Special Work of the Institute

The specific manner for the practice of poverty, counselled by our Divine Saviour, was left to the particular interpretation of the founders of religious orders. These individual conceptions of the vow of poverty necessarily led to a difference in its practice.[59] The Code fully acknowledged these individual conceptions by

---

[56] Canon 594, §3.—Religiosorum supellex paupertati conveniat quam professi sunt.

[57] Flanagan, *op. cit.*, p. 45.

[58] *Religious and Laymen*, p. 86.

[59] Larraona, "Commentarium Codicis"—*CpR*, V (1924), 334, note 336; Turner, *The Vow of Poverty*, p. 91.

prescribing a general law. It obliges all superiors and subjects to observe faithfully and integrally the vows that they have professed, regulating their lives in accord with their rule of life and constitutions.[60]

With this in mind the local ordinaries in evincing prudent judgment must of necessity consider the purpose and the special work of the institute. This in turn must be judged together with the needs of the place where the religious house is to be established,[61] and also the facilities of the territory in supplying sufficient material aid to the new community to carry on its work. A consultation with the competent religious superior would certainly be indicated to determine exactly the nature and scope of the work the members of the proposed institute would undertake. The means of this support would need to be studied. Canon 496 enumerates these as fixed income, usual alms and a source practically unlimited designated by the term *other means.*

Should the institute be a mendicant community, bound by the law of strict cloisture and about to be established in a very poor locality, it cannot be expected that alms alone would suffice for a proper sustenance of its members. Adequate guarantees would have to be made that suitable support would be provided by other means, as, e.g., income from property, if the institute be capable of possessing such, or from possible revenues in return for sacred ministerial work.[62] The respective constitutions of particular orders would certainly determine the degree of their dependence upon alms, and the extent of their activities, if they could not suitably sustain themselves because of the lack of alms.[63]

Of vital importance is the consideration of the character of the proposed religious house. Houses, for example, of postulancy, novitiate, studies, etc., are usually provided for and supported by either the province or the order itself. If such a house is being

[60] Canon 593.—Omnes et singuli religiosi, Superiores aeque ac subditi, debent, non solum quae nuncuparunt vota fideliter integreque servare, sed etiam secundum regulas et constitutiones propriae religionis vitam componere atque ita ad perfectionem sui status contendere.

[61] Flanagan, *The Canonical Erection of Religious Houses,* p. 45.

[62] Larraona, "Commentarium Codicis,"—*CpR,* V (1924), 333.

[63] Augustine, *Religious and Laymen,* p. 84.

established, nothing more is required than the assurance that the province or order will be capable of bearing the burden of properly sustaining such a house in keeping with its character.[64]

C. Means of Support

Suitable support and sustenance of the religious houses has been and is considered of grave importance to the Holy See. The insistence of pre-Code law upon obtaining the consent of the superiors of other institutes and the guarantee of a suitable maintenance of the members of the religious house bears this out. Foremost in the mind of ecclesiastical legislators before proceeding to authorize the foundation of a religious house was an appropriate (*commoda*) and suitable (*congrua*) sustenance for not only the convents or monasteries to be erected but also for that of the monasteries already in existence in the locality.[65] The Code, though eliminating some of the formalities of the old law in canon 496, insists that no religious house should be founded unless suitable lodging and sustenance be provided. This sustenance should in turn be derived from either its fixed income, the usual alms, or from other means. These means, therefore, are to be considered as general norms and are to serve as guides for the ordinary before authorizing the erection of a new religious house. They are also prime factors in the continuous sustenance of the convent or monastery after its canonical erection. Particular attention is to be given to them so that they would in no way be detrimental to the suitable sustenance of other monasteries or of the clergy living in the territory who have an equal right in being assured funds for their proper livelihood.[66]

1. Fixed Income

Moral personality that is granted to religious houses following legitimate canonical erection carries with itself, as one of its

---

[64] Flanagan, *op. cit.*, p. 46; Larraona, "Commentarium Codicis"—*CpR*, V (1924), 333.

[65] Cf. Lauretus de Franchis, *Controversiae inter Episcopos et Regulares*, pp. 139, 140, additiones, nn. 421, 422; Reiffenstuel, *Jus Canonicum Universum*, III, tit. 48, n. 46.

[66] Schäfer, *De Religiosis*, n. 83, h.

effects, the right to own property. This is the common law of the Church.[67] To further emphasize the existence of the right of property ownership by a religious house, the Code clearly indicates in canon 531 that not only the institute, but also the province *and the house* have the right to possess temporal goods together with fixed incomes and endowments, unless this right is excluded or restricted in their rule and constitutions.[68]

In determining the means of sustenance of a religious house, the Code requires in canon 496 at least a well-founded hope that the proposed house will have some fixed and permanent revenues. It prescribes a traditional mode of sustenance, namely, *proper revenues*. The term *proper revenues* includes the income from fixed assets that are proper to the particular convent or monastery. To this may be added also the revenues derived from the industry of the members of the religious house.[69]

Dependability and permanence of the income should be the guiding force in effecting the canonical establishment of a new religious house. This permanence of income is assured to a great extent from the revenues accruing from the immovable and movable property which is capable of producing income. It may also be derived from safely invested capital, stocks and bonds.

The industry of the members may also contribute to a very great extent to the assurance of a proper and dependable sustenance. It is very often the purpose of the local ordinary in permitting religious to settle in his territory, that they obtain for themselves suitable support in return for their work, be it in the exercise of the sacred ministry, as, for instance, the administration of the Sacraments, and preaching, or in some work particular to the institute such as teaching, the care of hospitals, etc.

In providing proper sustenance for a religious house various possibilities involving the use of convent property and the results

---

[67] Canon 1495, §2.

[68] The Friars Minor and the Capuchins are not allowed even common ownership of property.—Cf. Conc. Trident., sess. XXV, *de regularibus*, c. 3. For other examples cf. McManus, *The Administration of Temporal Goods in Religious Institutes*, p. 38.

[69] Augustine, *Religious and Laymen*, p. 83; Flanagan, *The Canonical Erection of Religious Houses*, p. 46.

of the industry of its members must be considered in light of canon 142. This canon prohibits clerics from exercising commercial business or trading (*negotiatio et mercatura*) through themselves or others, whether for their own or for the utility of others.[70] In virtue of canon 592 these strictly negative obligations also bind religious.[71] To determine a prudent judgment as to the future sustenance of a religious house, some of the practical applications of canon 142 must be considered. Certain activities, though they also have a commercial aspect, are not forbidden to religious by the common law of the Church.[72]

The possession or use of property by a religious house implies the right to the income coming from that property. Thus it is licit for religious to cultivate their own fields, even with the aid of hired labor, and sell, for profit, the superfluous harvest. Authors commonly agree that they may even cultivate their fields with the intention of gaining profit from the sale of the harvest.[73] Should they purchase a field with a ripe harvest they may sell what is superfluous. Religious may also rent their fields or animals for profit.[74] These transactions seem licit because they do not come directly under the concept of commercial trading but rather they are a result of an abundance of crops or personal industry applied to the cultivation or proper use of the fields or animals in the possession and care of religious.

---

[70] Canon 142.—Prohibentur clerici per se vel per alios negotiationem aut mercaturam exercere sive in propriam sive in aliorum utilitatem.

[71] Canon 592.—Obligationibus communibus clericorum, de quibus in can. 124–142, etiam religiosi omnes tenentur, nisi ex contextu sermonis vel ex rei natura aliud constet.

[72] One must also bear in mind that not all transactions which are not comprehended under canon 142 and permitted to secular clerics by general ecclesiastical law can be permitted to religious on the basis of that general law. For them there is the added obligation of the observance of the rule and constitutions of the particular institute.

[73] Brunini, *The Clerical Obligations of Canon 139 and 142,* The Catholic University of America Canon Law Studies, n. 103 (Washington, D. C.: The Catholic University of America, 1937), p. 85 (hereafter this work is cited *Clerical Obligations*); Fanfani, *De Iure Religiosorum,* n. 328, B, 10º; Schäfer, *De Religiosis,* n. 312, g.

[74] Reiffenstuel, *Jus Canonicum Universum,* III, tit. 1, n. 136; Schmalzgrueber, *Ius Ecclesiasticum Universum,* III, tit. 50, n. 17.

Religious institutes, provinces and houses also have the right to benefit from their members' mechanical or technical abilities as evidenced in their writings, exercise of art, inventions and the production of goods from their own possessions. This benefit may also take on the form of material profit by the sale of such products. Personal industry may be shown, for example, in conducting magazines, making wine from the grapes of their own vineyards, wool from their own flocks of sheep, etc. The sale of these products does not constitute any forbidden form of trading. The point to be considered is whether such activities are becoming to the clerical or religious state.[75] It is also commonly admitted that hired labor may be used to convert one's own products and sell them for profit. It is well to remember that even though they be licit, certain transactions may not be carried on on a large scale, as for example the construction of a factory or mill for the purposes of canning fruit, or making cloth from the wool of their own sheep, etc. Such practice would hardly be justified under the provisions of canon 139, §1, which enjoins clerics and religious to sedulously avoid acts unbecoming to the clerical state in life,[76] and which might bring discredit to themselves and occasion scandal among the people.[77]

2. *Usual Alms*

The existence of religious orders depends largely upon the good will of the people. This good will is usually manifested by their care of the people for the temporal needs of the religious communities in compensation for the benefits that they derive from the various activities of the religious, both spiritual and temporal. As such, this good will becomes a very important factor to the religious house in its quest for proper sustenance. Attention is brought to it also by canon 496 in its use of the term ***usual alms.***

---

[75] Cf. canon 139, §1.

[76] Canon 139, §1.—Ea etiam quae, licet non indecora, a clericali tamen statu aliena sunt, vitent.

[77] Brunini, *Clerical Obligations,* p. 89. However it must be noted that reference is made only to the general requirements of the common law of the Church as expressed in the Code. Particular rules and constitutions should be consulted and consideration made for particular indults.

The *usual alms* referred to in this canon are not necessarily comprehended under canons 621–622. The latter govern the right of religious to beg alms, while the former refers only to the possibility of the religious receiving alms, without the necessity of seeking them. Geser, on the contrary, states [78] that the term *usual alms* may be used only in reference to the mendicant orders strictly so-called as they alone have the privilege by law to collect alms. This opinion, as Flanagan points out,[79] seems to be an unwarranted restriction of the term *usual alms* as used by the Code. The begging of alms from door to door (*ius quaestuandi*) is restricted by the Code as a privilege of mendicants, but there is no restriction placed upon the capacity of the religious to accept alms. The word *usual* in the sense of canon 496 appears to denote alms that are " customary," " ordinary," " regular," that is, alms that are received regularly from special benefactors, without the necessity of soliciting their offerings. Such offerings, if they can be depended upon as regular contributions, become an assured source of income and are to be included in the term *usual alms*.

3. Other Means

To promote the spread of religious life, the Holy See establishing general norms of procedure for the erection of religious houses, insists upon sufficient guarantees that the prospects of a suitable sustenance be uppermost in the minds of the authorities responsible for the foundation of a religious house. This insistence was not to be governed by too rigid criteria. The Code, therefore, in canon 496, while demanding a suitable sustenance for the members of the house, presents besides the two acceptedly traditional modes of income, a third: *vel alio modo*. This means of support, as is apparent, is general in its nature and indicates a practically unlimited source of income. The traditional forms, fixed income and usual alms, are characterized by their permanence or regularity while this mode would seemingly embrace all other means of income that are of a somewhat irregular and uncertain character.

---

[78] *The Canon Law Governing Communities of Sisters* (St. Louis, Mo.: B. Herder Book Co., 1938), p. 138.

[79] *The Canonical Erection of Religious Houses*, p. 47.

Under the term *other means* can be comprehended such sources of income as free-will offerings and donations that cannot be considered as a regular and assured source. Possible support coming from the offerings of those entering the institute is apparent in the Code itself.[80] The individual efforts of the members of the community in labor, either mental or physical, or in the exercise of an art or a profession, are to be considered also.[81] Pious foundations,[82] legacies and endowments [83] are also suggested in the legislation of the Code.

This enumeration is by no means exhaustive. An exact determination of the sources of revenue coming under the term *alio modo* does not seem necessary. It is important to note that the sources referred to above are of an irregular and uncertain nature and in themselves may or may not be sufficient for proper sustenance. It must be conceded that they do aid in assuring the religious a livelihood that is due them. The extent of this assurance should be estimated by prudent judgment.[84]

---

80 This however is to be understood as payment of expenses for food and clothing of the member himself, if it be so regulated by the constitutions of the institute or by an express agreement. Cf. canon 570, §1; Turner, *The Vow of Poverty*, p. 117.

81 Cf. canon 580, 2.

82 Cf. canon 1544–1550.

83 Cf. canon 1513, 2348.

84 Flanagan, *The Canonical Erection of Religious Houses*, p. 47.

PART TWO

SOURCES OF SUSTENANCE

CHAPTER III

Common Possessions

ARTICLE 1. PRE-CODE LEGISLATION

A. Legislation to the Council of Trent

Though almost all founders of religious institutes originally deplored the possession of temporal goods, yet in order to obtain a proper livelihood for all their religious, they soon found it necessary to permit the common ownership of temporal goods. This became particularly evident when the religious increased in numbers. Two pseudo-Isidorian decretals [1] one ascribed to Pope Clement I (c. 91–c. 100) and the other to Pope Urban I (222–230), ordered that those who had taken up a common life and vowed not to have anything as their own, should live a common life. Though these documents are spurious and cannot be used as an argument for establishing the existence of a law, they shed some light upon the question as to just how religious were expected to regulate their lives in regard to the various possessions that might come into their hands—a life in common with common ownership of all property.

[1] C. 2, 9, C. XII, q. 1; Jaffé, *Regesta Pontificum Romanorum ab Condita Ecclesia ad Annum post Christum Natum, 1198* (2. ed., 2 tom. in 1 vol., correctam et auctam auspiciis Gulielmi Wattenbach curaverunt S. Loewenfeld, F. Kaltenbrunner, P. Ewald, Lipsiae, 1885–1888), nn. †14, †87. (Hereafter the letters L, K and E will be joined with the letter J in designation of the editor of the document cited from Jaffé's work in its second edition. The pseudo-Isidorian decretals stand designated thus: JK, nn. †14, †87.); Hinschius, *Decretales Pseudo-Isidorianae et Capitula Angilramni* (Lipsiae, 1863), pp. 65, 143–144.

In no uncertain terms does St. Augustine (354–430) urge, in one of his sermons, that those living a common life have everything in common, keeping, owning or accepting nothing without the permission of the superiors.[2] Gratian, referring to a *Novella* of Justinian, states that if any woman or man without children chose the monastic life and entered a monastery, he or she lost all right to the things that he or she personally owned and their possessions belonged to the monastery which he or she entered.[3]

Pope Gregory I (590–604) vigorously opposed all private ownership by monks. In April, 591, writing to Anthemius, a subdeacon, he ordered that monks should not have anything as their own.[4] In his dialogues, as attested to by Pope Innocent III, he showed himself very severe to a certain monk who at his death was found to have money in his possession. This monk was to be buried together with his money outside of the monastery as a sign of perdition.[5] Similarly Pope Clement III (1187–1191), writing about a certain canon regular who did not renounce the private possession which he held contrary to the rule of St. Augustine, decreed[6] that the monk should be deprived of Christian burial and, if it could be done without great scandal, he should be excluded from the Church.[7]

Canon 26 of the II General Lateran Council (1139), under Pope Innocent II (1130–1143) denounced the pernicious and detestable custom of some women, who desired to be considered religious by the people, even though they followed no definite rule of life and even, on the contrary, built for themselves private

---

[2] C. 11, C. XII, q. 1.

[3] C. 9, C. XIX, q. 3; Nov. 123, C. 38.

[4] C. 5, X, *de regularibus et transeuntibus ad religionem,* III, 31; JE, n. 1110.

[5] C. 6, X, *de statu monachorum et canonicorum regularium,* III, 35; Potthast, n. 1734; cf. also Turner, *The Vow of Poverty,* p. 62.

[6] C. 4, X, *de statu monachorum et canonicorum regularium,* III, 35; JL, n. 16606.

[7] Hostiensis, *Commentaria in Quinque Libros Decretalium* (5 vols., in 3, Venetiis, 1581), *Lectura* in lib. III, tit. *de statu monachorum et canonicorum regularium,* c. 2, n. 3 (hereafter this work will be referred to as *Lectura*); Hostiensis, *Summa Aurea,* lib. III, tit. *de statu monachorum et canonicorum regularium,* n. 2.

domiciles in which, under the pretense of hospitality, they privately entertained guests. This procedure was prohibited and interdicted under the pain of excommunication.[8] The Third General Lateran Council (1179) in canon 10 particularly stressed the prohibition against religious' possession of a *peculium.*[9] He who had retained a *peculium* in spite of the fact that he was not permitted its administration by his abbot, was to be deprived of the Sacraments. If one would be found with private possessions upon his deathbed, and if he did not repent properly, he was to be deprived of the last Rites; neither was he to be buried among his confreres. An abbot acting contrary to this provision should be deprived of his office.[10]

Pope Innocent III, in a letter written on March 19, 1198, ordered the Archbishop of Aux to warn those religious who have any private property to resign it into the hands of their superiors, so that it may be converted toward the necessities of the house.[11] Again in 1202, in a letter to the abbot of Subiaco, he forbade to regulars the private ownership of anything and declared that if any religious was apprehended as having something he was to be

[8] C. 25, C. XVIII, q. 2; Mansi, XXI, 532, 533.

[9] C. 2, X *de statu monachorum et canonicorum regularium,* III, 32; Mansi, XXII, 224.—The *Glossa Ordinaria* ad v. *peculium* brings to attention the fact that *peculium* and private possessions are synonymous by simply stating: *peculium,* i.e. *proprium.*

[10] An interesting note is added in the Glossa ad v. *permissis.* The Glossator, stating that it is evident that a religious cannot have anything as his own, sets down two opinions as to the effect of a condition by which one, upon entering monastic life, stipulates the retention of private property. Does the monastic vow destroy the condition or does the condition destroy the monastic vow? The Glossator follows the former opinion because abdication of property, just as the safeguard of chastity, is of the substance of monasticism, so much so that even the Pope cannot grant a contrary permission, as it is stated in c. 6, X, *de statu monachorum et canonicorum regularium,* III, 36. Cf. also Hostiensis, *Lectura* in lib. III, tit. *de statu monachorum et canonicorum regularium,* c. 1, n. 3 and c. 6, n. 30; Raymundus de Peñafort, *Summa Iuris Canonici* (Veronae, 1744), pp. 76, 77; St. Thomas (*Summa Theologica,* II:II, q. 88, art. 11) confirms this latter statement. However, Garcias (*Tractatus de Beneficiis* [2 vols., Genevae, 1685], II, pars. 7, c. 10, nn. 38-87) proves at length that the Pope can and does dispense in such cases.

[11] C. 7, X, *de officio iudicis ordinarii,* I, 31; Potthast, n. 57.

expelled from the monastery and not received again unless he repented according to monastic discipline. If, upon the death of a regular it was discovered that he had privately retained property, the Pope then applied the punishment meted out by Pope Gregory I. If anything be given to a religious, he was not to presume to take it as his own, but was obliged to assign it to his superiors.[12]

Pope Clement V, at the Council of Vienne (1311–1312), in a decree giving detailed direction governing the entire exterior and interior life of the Benedictine monks, forbade religious and canons regular, under the pain of excommunication *ipso facto* to go to the palaces of secular princes to obtain their aid in forcing their superiors to give them pensions or other personal aid. The superiors in turn were ordered diligently to check such procedure and severely punish any such attempts.[13]

B. *Legislation of the Council of Trent*

In their quest for proper sustenance, it was very important that religious should act in conformity with their vow of poverty. Thus the question of the observance of poverty was always of particular interest to the Holy See. Consequently the Council of Trent, carrying out a general reform of regulars " to the end that the old and regular discipline be more easily and promptly restored where it has collapsed and may be the more firmly maintained where it has been preserved," decreed that:

> All regulars, men as well as women, adjust and regulate their life in accordance with the requirements of the rule which they have professed and especially that they observe faithfuly whatever pertains to the perfection of their profession as the vows of obedience, poverty and chastity, and any other vows and precepts peculiar to any rule and order and belonging to the essence thereof as

---

[12] C. 6, X, *de statu monachorum et canonicorum regularium,* III, 35; Potthast, n. 1734.

[13] C. 1, *de statu monachorum et canonicorum regularium,* III, 10, in Clem. —Schroeder, in his comment on this decree (*Disciplinary Decrees,* pp. 428, 429), states that " though it does not contain the formula of conciliar approval, there can be no doubt that its main provisions are based on conciliar material."

well as the preservation of common life, food and clothing.[14]

As a fundamental norm, common to all religious, the vow of poverty meant that the religious bound himself not to dispose of things independently of his superiors.[15] Thus common life, the aim of all religious founders, formed the basis of the truly religious life. Common ownership of temporal goods, in itself, was not contrary to the concept of the vow of poverty. With the exception of the Capuchins and the Friars Minor *de observantia* there was no universal law prohibiting such ownership. On the contrary, the Council of Trent ordered common ownership of immovable goods for all religious with the exception of the two mentioned branches of the Franciscan Order.[16]

The idea of a common life in religious orders meant primarily the exclusion of the possession of the *peculium,* i.e., a portion of temporal goods given to a religious for his own particular use and not for the use of the monastery.[17] The Council of Trent vigorously opposed private possessions by regulars. It decreed:

> To no regular therefore, whether man or woman, shall it be lawful to possess or to hold as his own or even in the name of the convent any movable or immovable property, of whatever nature it may be or in whatever manner acquired; but the same shall be handed over immediately to the superior and be incorporated in the convent. Neither shall it in the future be lawful for superiors to grant immovable property to any regular, not even the usufruct or use, or the administration thereof or as "commendam" . . . But should anyone

[14] Conc. Trident., sess. XXV, *de regularibus,* c. 1; transl. from Schroeder, *Canons and Decrees of the Council of Trent,* p. 218.

[15] Bouix, *Tractatus de Jure Regularium,* II, p. 538; Ferraris, *Bibliotheca,* ad v. "votum" art. 2, n. 45; Ojetti, *Synopsis Rerum Moralium et Iuris Pontificii* (3. ed., 4 vols., Romae, 1909–1914), ad v. "paupertas" n. 3086; Schmalzgrueber, *Ius Ecclesiasticum Universum,* III, tit. 35, n. 1.

[16] Conc. Trident. sess. XXV, *de regularibus,* c. 3. Cf. Ferraris, *Bibliotheca,* ad v. "dominium" art. 2, n. 21; Turner, *The Vow of Poverty,* pp. 21–45, 98, 195.

[17] Bouix, *Tractatus de Jure Regularium,* II, 540; Ferraris, *Bibliotheca,* ad v. "regulares" n. 15; Schmalzgrueber, *Ius Ecclesiasticum Universum,* III, tit. 35, n. 11.

> be discovered or convicted of possessing something in any other manner, he shall be deprived for two years of his active and passive voice and shall be also punished in accordance with the prescriptions of his rule and order.[18]

Navarrus,[19] Barbosa,[20] and Rodericus,[21] claim that this decree did not constitute any new law but only expressed more clearly what had been already expressed before,[22] namely that a religious could have a *peculium* but only with the permission of the superior and for a just cause. However, St. Alphonse held that it is more probable that the Tridentine decree was a new law whereby regulars could not have any *peculium* whatsoever.[23] The latter position seems to have been substantiated by later decrees of the Supreme Pontiffs. Thus Pope Clement VIII by the decree "*Nullus omnino*" of July 25, 1599 [24] prohibited all *peculia*. This was approved and renewed by the decree of the Sacred Congregation of the Council on September 21, 1624, on the authority of Pope Urban VIII.[25]

These decrees prohibiting *peculia* seemed to have been tempered by custom. St. Alphonse notes that [26] at his time in almost all religious orders, except those reformed, the use of the *peculium* with the consent of the superiors had been permitted to each religious, with the restriction that they be ready to give it up at the

---

18 Conc. Trident., sess. XXV, *de regularibus*, c. 2; transl. from Schroeder, *Canons and Decrees of the Council of Trent*, pp. 218, 219.

19 *De Regularibus* (*Opera Omnia*, 6 vols., Romae, 1618–1621), II, commentarium 2, n. 15.

20 *Pastoralis Solicitudo seu de Officio et Potestate Episcopi* (3 parts in 2 vols., Lugduni, 1656), Allegatio 103, n. 6. (Hereafter this work is referred to as *Pastoralis Solicitudo*.)

21 *Quaestiones*, III, q. 29, art. 10.

22 C. 2, X, *de statu monachorum et canonicorum regularium*, III, 35.

23 *Theologia Moralis* (cura et studio Leonardi Gaude, 4 vols., Romae, 1905–1912), II, lib. IV, c. 1, n. 15; cf. also Reiffenstuel, *Jus Canonicum Universum*, III, tit. 35, par. 1, nn. 7–10; Schmalzgrueber, *Ius Ecclesiasticum Universum*, III, tit. 35, n. 14; Bouix, *Tractatus de Jure Regularium*, II, 544.

24 *Fontes*, n. 187.

25 *Fontes*, n. 2454; cf. Ferraris, *Bibliotheca* ad v. "votum" art. 2, n. 45.

26 *Theologia Moralis*, II, lib. IV, c. 1, n. 15. Cf. also Schmalzgrueber, *Ius Ecclesiasticum Universum*, III, tit. 35, n. 14.

superior's wish and whenever they had satisfied the need for which it had been given. St. Alphonse reluctantly admits the validity of such a custom and warns that though superiors permitting the *peculium* are excused from grave sin in respect to the vow of poverty, they can hardly be excused from relaxation of the obligations of their respective rules in regard to common life.

The strict legislation in regard to the prohibition of private possessions was meant chiefly to provide for the common life among religious to be properly sustained from the goods of the monasteries, whether the latter be capable of possessing common goods or only the use of these goods as is the case with the Capuchins and the Friars Minor *de observantia.* Such had been the mind of the Popes and the Sacred Congregation of Bishops and Regulars when it, in many instances, forbade bishops and superiors to permit the ownership of private possessions to individual religious for the purpose of providing for their own necessities. It had been ordered that money or other income coming to the individual religious should be incorporated into the common fund and from that fund they were to be first provided for and the rest of the fund was to be turned over for common necessities.[27]

ARTICLE 2. LEGISLATION OF THE CODE

It is without doubt that foremost in the mind of the Church in admitting the right of religious institutes to acquire and retain the ownership of possessions was the provision of the means for the proper livelihood and sustenance of the members of the institute, province or house. The solemn vow of poverty, inasmuch as it excludes all private ownership of temporal goods by the individual members of the religious institute, in no way prohibits their ownership by the religious community itself. The right to common ownership of possessions is emphasized in the concept of the moral juridic personality, which is granted to canonically

[27] Clement VIII, const. "*Nullus Omnino,*" 25 iul. 1599—*Fontes,* n. 187; S. C. C. decr. 21 sept. 1625 iussu Urbani VIII—*Fontes,* n. 2454; S. C. Ep. et Reg., decr. 22 apr. 1851 auctoritate Pii IX—*Fontes,* n. 1959; Cf. also *Fontes,* nn. 1358, 1365, 1372, 1438, 1534, 1577, 1598, 1706, 1739, 1746; also Barbosa, *Iuris Ecclesiastici Libri Tres* (Lugduni, 1650), I, tit. 43, n. 77.

erected institutes, provinces or houses and which carries with it the right to possessions.[28] The Code of Canon Law recognizes this right when it ordains that not only the institute itself but also provinces and houses are capable of acquiring and owning temporal goods providing permanent income, unless this right be excluded or limited by their rule and constitutions.[29] This is an embodiment of pre-Code legislation as expressed in the Tridentine decrees.[30]

The outstanding example of the privation of the right to possessions on the part of the religious institutes in ancient pre-Code law was the special law for all the mendicants and, after the Council of Trent, that for the Capuchins and Friars Minor *de observantia.* Alluded to in canon 582, §2, these two branches of the Franciscan Order, because of their total renunciation of possessions, are incapable of acquiring property. Temporalities given them are acquired by the Holy See, which in turn gives these religious only the use of them.[31] Limitation of the right to own possessions by a religious house may involve a variety of restrictions, dependent upon the particular rule and constitutions of the religious institute. Thus, for example, in the Society of Jesus, the *domus professae* are incapable of ownership, while novitiate houses and colleges enjoy the right; by exception with the Discalced Carmelites, houses not destined for missions may have their own income.[32]

This privation of the right of ownership or its limitation by particular law of the individual institute argues for the general capability of the religious to acquire possessions. Total or partial restriction for and by religious institutes provided for by general or particular law does not deny this right but proportions it to

---

[28] Cf. *supra,* pp. 8–9.

[29] Canon 531.

[30] Conc. Trident. sess. XXV, *de regularibus,* c. 3.

[31] Cf. const., "*Exiit qui seminat,*" 14 aug. 1279—c. 3 *de verborum significatione,* V, 12 in VI°; const. "*Exivi de paradiso*" 6 maii, 1312—c. 1 *de verborum significatione,* V, 11 in Clem; const. "*Amabiles fructus*" 1 nov. 1428—*BF,* VII, 1838; Conc. Trident. sess. XXV, *de regularibus,* c. 3; Wernz-Vidal, *De Religiosis,* n. 342, note (30).

[32] Larraona, "Commentarium Codicis,"—*CpR,* XII (1931), 251 note 464; Wernz-Vidal, *De Religiosis,* n. 343.

the particular aim and circumstances of the institute. This right in turn is to be exercised primarily for the purpose of assuring proper maintenance and sustenance of the members of the institute, province or house. These possessions, however, are not to be held in private ownership but rather as common funds available to all. A common life and common ownership is and should be the aim of all religious bodies.

A. Common Ownership of Property

The ideal and aim of all founders of religious institutes has been without doubt the preservation of the common life both in reference to a definite plan of exercises and as regards temporal goods. This common life can be described as consisting not only in the fact that the religious live under a common rule but also in the fact that, because of the incorporation of the individual religious into the community, all necessities of the members are provided for by the community from the common goods in the possession of and under the administration of legitimate authority representing the institute.[33]

Common ownership of possessions actualizes the ideal of common life. The individual member of the religious community in taking upon himself the obligation of advancement in Christian perfection is entitled to the removal of solicitude and anxiety for the maintenance of his physical life in order to have more time for the perfecting of his spiritual life. Toward this end the individual entering the institute renounces all his claims to temporalities and places at the disposal of the community all the property that may come to him following his incorporation as a member of the community.[34]

This characteristic, the ownership of common goods, is not contrary to the ideals of Christian perfection, as some would possibly contend.[35] They reason that since Christ, the ideal of

---

[33] Aertnys-Damen, *Theologia Moralis secundum Doctrinam S. Alphonsi de Ligorio* (9. ed., 2 vols., Galopiae: Typis M. Alberts Filii, 1918), I, 1198; Fanfani, *De Iure Religiosorum,* n. 300; Schäfer, *De Religiosis,* n. 337.

[34] Turner, *The Vow of Poverty,* p. 195.

[35] This contention was rampant at the time of the institution of the mendicant orders in the thirteenth century. St. Thomas in his treatise

Christian perfection, possessed nothing at all, neither in His individual capacity, nor in common with others, neither should those who tend toward the realization of Christian perfection have possessions or the administration of temporalities privately or in common. This would be true if we could completely remove from mankind the necessity of providing for the necessary needs of the body, chief among which is its sustenance. Persons entering religious life cannot divest themselves of this requisite. A certain degree of solicitude is necessary for the acquiring and the conserving of goods which provide a decent maintenance of physical life. This solicitude in no way distracts the mind from that which pertains to spiritual perfection.[36]

We must further admit that solicitude for the needs of the body takes up much time in the life of all people. Religious would certainly be no exception to this rule. The sum total loss of time that would of necessity have to be given by them in providing individually for their needs would be too great a diversion from their aim of individual perfection. To eliminate as much of this purposeless waste of precious time the expedient of common ownership of goods, or at least the common administration of them, is of tremendous importance. Again, individual initiative on the part of the members of the institute for their own sustenance could well give cause to the rise of competition, selfishness and scandal among the members of the community and others. Thus, the time saved through common possessions and the elimination of possible contentions on the part of the members can be turned directly toward the purpose of personal sanctification or indirectly to the same end, through other activities in keeping with the rule and constitutions of the religious body in which the members have made profession.

It must be noted that the common life, with its consequences, is of the essence of religious life. This requisite is not derived from the very concept of religious life, but rather from the positive law of the Church. It cannot be denied that the Church,

---

Contra pestiferam doctrinam retrahentium homines a religionis ingressu (*Opera Omnia,* tomus XVII [Venetiis, 1587], Opusculum XVII, c. 15, 16), contributed greatly to its downfall.

[36] S. Thomas, *Summa Theologica,* IIa IIæ, q. 188, art. 7 *corpus.*

which has supreme authority in regulating the lives of the religious, can provide that there be no religious state without the common life. This prohibition of pre-Code law [37] is enjoined in the present Code. Canon 487 in defining the religious state refers to it as a permanent (*stabilis*) mode of common life.[38] In canon 594, §1 all religious institutes are ordered carefully to observe the common life not only in regard to actual dwelling in a place adapted to the performance of spiritual exercises but also as regards food, clothing and furniture.[39]

Obviously the purpose of this prescript is binding upon all religious institutes, and is intended for a proper assurance of the maintenance due a religious after entering a community. Coronata [40] divides the common life into that which is *perfecte communis* and that which is *minus rigorosa.* The former demands a complete submission to a common fund of the income, offerings and all other things that may come to an individual religious by whatsoever means, while the latter permits some relaxation either through the medium of a *peculium* or some other means.

In the history of the use of the *peculium* by most religious institutes it is apparent that the ideal of the perfectly common life was not reached in all religious institutes. Controversies were rife at the very promulgation of the Tridentine legislation.[41] Pre-Code law, expressly adverse to its use, apparently tolerated its usage because of custom.[42] In view of the controversy a distinction must be made. The *peculium* is twofold, independent and dependent. The independent or perfect *peculium* is one which

---

[37] C. 9, X, *de religiosis domibus,* III, 36; c. un. *de religiosis domibus,* III, 17 in VIº; Goyeneche, "De Transitu ad Aliam Religionem"—*CpR,* I (1920), 73, 74; Pejška, *Ius Canonicum Religiosorum,* p. 129; Wernz-Vidal, *De Religiosis,* n. 8, III.

[38] Canon 487.—Status religiosus seu stabilis in communi vivendi modus. . . .

[39] Canon 594, §1.—In quavis religione vita communis accurate ab omnibus servetur etiam in iis quae ad victum, ad vestitum et ad supellectilem pertinent.

[40] *Institutiones,* I, n. 604.

[41] A more detailed treatment of the use of the *peculium* in religious institutes may be had in Turner, *The Vow of Poverty,* pp. 68, 78–82, 202–208; Schäfer, *De Religiosis,* n. 338; Wernz-Vidal, *De Religiosis,* nn. 352, 353.

[42] Cf. *supra,* pp. 42–44.

carries with itself the full right of administration to the extent that the superior cannot revoke or restrict it. The dependent or improper *peculium* is one whereby some temporal goods, in most instances money, is given to a religious for his particular use, subject to the disposition of the superior. It must be fully noted that there had never been any doubt that the independent *peculium* was prohibited. The dispute was concerned with the permissibility of the dependent *peculium*.[43] Since the use of the dependent *peculium* was considered probably licit in pre-Code law, authors commonly hold that it remains so after the Code.[44]

The Code in prescribing the common life would seem to indicate reference to its less rigorous form. Though it is certainly the mind of the legislator that the perfect common life be introduced and observed where it had been relaxed, the possibility of exception to the common life cannot be denied. This is particularly borne out by the fact that there exists a probable opinion permitting a dependent *peculium*. Complete interpretation of the common life required for the religious state therefore devolves into the interpretation of the existence or non-existence of customs, indults and privileges.[45] Thus immemorial or centenary customs, since they are not expressly reprobated in the canon, may be tolerated.[46] Neither are the special indults and privileges acquired and enjoyed in pre-Code law revoked.[47]

The obligation of the common life is incumbent upon all the

---

[43] Gearin, "The Confessor and the Vow of Religious Poverty,"—*The American Ecclesiastical Review* (Philadelphia, 1889–1943, Baltimore, 1944—), LXI (1919), 152 (hereafter this periodical will be referred to as *AER*); Goyeneche, "Consultationes"—*CpR*, XI (1930), 261, 262; Schäfer, *De Religiosis*, n. 338; Wernz-Vidal, *De Religiosis*, n. 352.

[44] Beste, *Introductio in Codicem*, p. 404; Gearin, *l.c.;* Goyeneche, *l.c.;* Augustine, *Religious and Laymen*, p. 307; Fanfani, *De Iure Religiosorum*, n. 225, dubium 1; Pejška, *Ius Canonicum Religiosorum*, p. 122; Turner, *The Vow of Poverty*, pp. 207, 208; Schäfer, *De Religiosis*, n. 338; Wernz-Vidal, *De Religiosis*, n. 352; Coronata, *Institutiones*, I, n. 605; Prümmer, *Manuale Iuris Canonici*, q. 223, 2, p. 298; Sipos, *Enchiridion Iuris Canonici*, p. 384.

[45] Chelodi, *Ius de Personis*, n. 276, p. 461, note 4; Coronata, Institutiones, I, n. 604, p. 766, note 4; Sipos, *Enchiridion Iuris Canonici*, p. 384.

[46] Canon 5.

[47] Canon 4.

members of the religious community, superiors as well as subjects. No distinctions are to be permitted. From the date of religious profession the community incurs the obligation of providing for the necessities with maternal care.[48] Under ordinary circumstances all religious are to lead a more or less uniform life. The Code requires moral uniformity as to food, clothing and furniture.[49]

Moral uniformity is required because of the possibility of the occurrence of circumstances which may not only merit but also demand that the individual religious be given extra care. This is occasioned particularly in time of sickness when special attention must be paid to diet.[50] Pre-Code law insisted on and provided for this.[51] It is in no way contrary to the common life that members of the community, who are unfortunate in some way or other, should be treated in accord with their particular needs. It is the mind of the Church that all particular necessities of the religious be provided for.[52] This was particularly emphasized in the law's insistence that specially in the time of sickness nothing should be lacking that would promote the recovery of health. Medical treatment and health trips cannot be overlooked if they are prescribed by physicians. This conclusion however should be considered in the light of a response of the Sacred Congregation of Bishops and Regulars which insisted upon uniformity of treatment and procedure in cases of similar sicknesses,[53] and the avoidance of superfluities.[54] Restoratives, such as trips for this

---

[48] Pejška, *Ius Canonicum Religiosorum,* p. 130; Schäfer, *De Religiosis,* n. 337.

[49] Vermeersch-Creusen, *Epitome,* I, n. 696.

[50] Augustine, *Religious and Laymen,* p. 304; Gearin, "The Confessor and the View of Religious Poverty"—*AER,* LXI (1919), 151; Turner, *The Vow of Poverty,* p. 198.

[51] Cf. c. 6, X, *de statu monachorum et canonicorum regularium,* III, 35.

[52] Conc. Vaticanum, "Schema constitutionis super perfecta Vita Communi"—Mansi, LIII, 790, 792 (hereafter this Schema will be referred to as Concil. Vatic., *De Vita Communi*); Gearin, *l.c.,* Schäfer, *De Religiosis,* n. 337; Turner, *The Vow of Poverty,* p. 198.

[53] S. C. Ep. et Reg., decr. 22 aug. 1814, §X—*Fontes,* n. 1893.

[54] Augustine, *Religious and Laymen,* p. 304; Turner, *The Vow of Poverty,* p. 198.

purpose, would not be denied to the religious if as Turner points out [55] it had been demonstrated already by the example of superiors and the exemplary members of the institute, that such means are not foreign to the spirit of the institute. The rule and constitutions of the particular order would probably indicate the extent to which these means should be employed.

In the determination of proper sustenance, food and drink hold a prominent position. No distinction among the members should be tolerated in this regard. Pre-Code law was expressly adverse to the practice whereby superiors or some few religious dined outside the refectory on specially prepared foods denied to the rest of the community.[56] It should be noted that this is prohibited as a practice. Occasions may arise, and often do, when certain individual religious may be asked to dine outside the community, as, e.g., at some banquet commemorating an ecclesiastical or even a national event. It is certainly wholly contrary to the mind of the Church that the individual religious should be permitted to have, as a practice, quantities of food and drink for their own personal and arbitrary use. Such is not the sustenance referred to in can. 496.[57]

To the proper maintenance of the religious may be referred also the question of their clothing. The common life requires that this also be procured for the individual by the community.[58] Under normal conditions no differences are to be tolerated. Practices permitting the contrary can cause grave disorders in religious discipline. If the members of the community be permitted indiscriminately to accept clothing that is greater than the quantity and superior to the quality permitted by the standard set in the individual rule and constitutions, destructive tendencies are sure to arise in the observance of the poverty professed by the

[55] *L.c.*

[56] Cf. const. Clementis VIII, "*Nullus omnino*" §4, 25 iul. 1599—*Fontes,* n. 187; S. C. Ep. et Reg., decr. 22 aug. 1814—*Fontes,* n. 1893; also c. 6 X, *de statu monachorum et canonicorum regularium,* III, 35.

[57] Cf. Aertnys-Damen, *Theologia Moralis,* I, n. 1200, 1°, p. 468; Turner, *The Vow of Poverty,* p. 197.

[58] Const. "*Nullus Omnino*" §3, 25 iul. 1599—*Fontes,* n. 187; Concil. Vatic., *De Vita Communi,*—Mansi, LIII, 792.

members of the order.[59] In all institutes the quality of the clothing is not to be excessively refined, nor should it be too menial. It should rather be of the type that befits the position of the religious. The general norm to be followed is that religious be comfortably clothed in accord with the conditions of time and place. Therefore, the quality, as well as the quantity, of the goods should be judged by it. Comfort, and not niceties, should be the standard guiding the interpretation of what constitutes proper clothing for religious. Uniformity of clothing in its design and material is specially demanded.[60]

Proper furnishings are also to be provided the religious. By furnishings is meant all the movable goods that are given to the members of the community for their own personal use.[61] These, in accord with common life, are to be uniform for all persons. The rooms should be identical in the quantity and quality of the furniture. However the purpose and aim of the institute or even the position of office of the individual religious cannot be overlooked in the assignment of personal equipment. The tools, such as furniture, instruments, books, etc., which tend to the proper discharge of an office are not to be considered as being contrary to common life.[62] It must, however, be pointed out that the acquisition and retention of such seemingly individual necessities must be obtained by the permission and under the supervision of legitimate authority in the community.

Proper provision as to the necessities of food, clothing and furniture cannot be denied to the members of the community. Nevertheless a certain measure of comfort and relaxation in line with the spirit of the institute may be permitted.[63] The spirit of poverty which they have professed should ever be in the minds of both the superiors and the subjects. The Code in para-

---

[59] Cf. canon 594, §3; Turner, *The Vow of Poverty*, pp. 198–199.

[60] Beste. *Introductio in Codicem*, p. 404; Turner, *The Vow of Poverty*, pp. 198, 199.

[61] Beste, *op. cit.*, p. 404; Vermeersch-Creusen, *Epitome*, I, n. 696.

[62] Turner, *The Vow of Poverty*, p. 199; Vermeersch-Creusen, *Epitome*, I, n. 696.

[63] Aertnys-Damen, *Theologia Moralis*, I, 1202; S. Alphonsus, *Theologia Moralis*, II, lib. IV, c. 1, n. 30; Concil. Vatic., *De Vita Communi*—Mansi, LIII, 792.

graph 3 of canon 594 commends to religious the standard that their furnishings be compatible with the poverty that they professed.[64] It is desired that religious be faithful not only to the general requirements of poverty common to all religious but also to the specific idea of poverty that is demanded by the rule and constitutions of the order of which they are members.[65]

B. *Income of Religious*

One of the main sources of sustenance in a religious community is that guaranteed by the industry of the members of the community. The common life requires that the religious himself contribute to the proper sustenance of the members of the community as much as it is in his power and inasmuch as it is his duty to do so. All professed religious have the obligation of applying all their strength and faculties for the institute according to the mode which may be determined by the superiors. This is implied in the contract of religious profession by which the religious takes upon himself the obligation of service for the institute.[66]

The Code of Canon Law is expressly specific in its attention to the industry of the members of the religious community. Canon 580, §2, speaking of the religious with simple vows, states that whatever he acquires by his industry in respect of his institute or by reason of his being a religious he acquires for the institute.[67] Canon 582 declares that whatever property a regular in any way acquires, after his solemn profession, belongs to the order, province or house, in orders that are capable of possessing goods, and if the order be incapable of possessions it is acquired in ownership by the Holy See.[68]

---

[64] Canon 594, §3.—Religiosorum suppellex paupertati conveniat quam professi sunt.

[65] Gearin, "The Confessor and the Vow of Religious Poverty"—*AER*, LXI (1919), 151; Vermeersch-Creusen, *Epitome*, I, n. 696.

[66] Pejška, *Ius Canonicum Religiosorum*, p. 130; Schäfer, *De Religiosis*, n. 337.

[67] Canon 580, §2.—Quidquid autem industria sua vel intuitu religionis acquirit, religioni acquirit.

[68] Canon 582.—Post solemnem professionem, salvis pariter peculiaribus Apostolicae Sedis indultis, omnia bona quae quovis modo obveniunt regulari:

It can readily be seen that the legislator does not wish that individual religious as such should retain possessions beyond that which the common life permits. All necessities are to be supplied from the common fund. The religious in turn are to contribute whatever is within their means to that common fund.[69] The personal industry of the religious referred to in the Code bears a very wide interpretation. The law itself does not distinguish or except any particular type of industry of the religious. It would seem to encompass all the personal activity of the religious which in any way is remunerative, be it of the nature of their vocation or not.[70] The Sacred Congregation for Religious, in a series of responses concerning the money coming to religious in connection with their military service during the war (1914–1918),[71] insisted that whatever the religious acquired during the time that he had been bound by vows, be they solemn or simple, must be turned over to the community. These responses approved by Pope Pius XI and promulgated on March 16, 1922, have the effect of universal law.[72] It is not evident that these responses were intended by the Sacred Congregation as a norm for all analogous cases. However there can be little doubt that the Sacred Congregation wished to demonstrate the guiding principle in this interpretation of the vow of religious poverty. In accordance with this all compensations,

---

1° In Ordine capaci possidendi, cedunt Ordini vel provinciae vel domui secundum constitutiones.

2° In Ordine incapaci, acquiruntur Sanctae Sedi in proprietatem.

[69] The Supreme Court of the United States indirectly recognizes the right of the religious institute to the compensation for the services, skill, labor and ministry resulting from the industry of its members.—Cf. Turner, *The Vow of Poverty,* p. 115, wherein he cites the case of Order of St. Benedict v. Steinhauser. Cf. also Order of St. Benedict v. Steinhauser, 234 U. S. 640.

[70] Goyeneche, "Consultationes"—*CpR,* I (1920), 340; Pejška, *Ius Canonicum Religiosorum,* p. 130; Schäfer, *De Religiosis,* n. 330.

[71] *AAS,* XIV (1922), 196, 197; cf. Bouscaren, *The Canon Law Digest* (2 vols., Milwaukee: The Bruce Publishing Co., 1934–1943), I, 311; *Periodica,* XI (1922), 32–34; *CpR,* IV (1923), 33, 34.

[72] Cf. *AAS,* XIV (1922), 197; Creusen, Garesché, Ellis, *Religious Men and Women in the Code* (4. English ed., Milwaukee: The Bruce Publishing Co., 1940), p. 186.

given for whatever services performed by religious, belong to the institute.[73]

1. *Gifts to Religious*

Under the classification as fruits of industry one can consider the offerings given to a religious as a religious or on behalf of the community. Concerning donations made as mere personal gifts a distinction is to be made in reference to the quality of the vows professed by the religious. A religious who professes solemn vows loses his juridic capacity to acquire temporal goods. Hence any donation coming to him from whatsoever source pertains to the religious house or to the Holy See.[74] A religious who professes only simple vows renounces only the administration of temporal goods but retains the ownership of them and the right to acquire new possessions. In view of this mere personal gifts are generally considered as accruing to his own possessions.[75] However the presumption is that these gifts are given to him as a religious on behalf of the institute and unless the contrary be proven they must be regarded as given to the institute.[76]

A question may be raised as to whether a religious is entitled to refuse a gift. It must be noted that the vow of poverty, either simple or solemn, denies the religious the right of alienating or disposing of the things already acquired and has no reference to the goods that have not as yet been acquired.[77] Non-acceptance of gifts does not constitute an act of dominion but rather it signifies some influence on the transformation of the intention of the donor. Refusal of a donation given to the religious as a religious or on behalf of the institute would not be contrary to the vow of poverty nor would it violate the principles of justice. It would be an offense against charity if such a refusal were made for no just reason or if the house would be in need of such an offering. There

---

[73] Goyeneche, "Annotationes"—*CpR,* IV (1923), 39; Turner, *The Vow of Poverty,* pp. 152–154.

[74] Canon 582. Cf. also Schäfer, *De Religiosis,* n. 329, a.

[75] Vermeersch-Creusen, *Epitome,* I, n. 683.

[76] Schäfer, *De Religiosis,* n. 329, b; Wernz-Vidal, *De Religiosis,* n. 327, III.

[77] S. Alphonsus, *Theologia Moralis,* II, lib. IV, c. 1, n. 20.

would also be a violation of the vow of obedience if the superior ordered that such gifts be accepted.[78]

2. *Writings of Religious*

The Code declares that the fruits of the industry of the religious exercised by him as a religious are not his own but come into the possession of the institute.[79] No distinction is made as to whether the industry be purely physical or intellectual. If it carries with itself material reimbursement it falls within the limits of the legislation. However the intellectual activities of religious have created difficulties. Are these, as set forth in the form of manuscripts or notes on, for example, inventions, to be included so as to become the property of the institute, or are they to be considered the property of the individual religious? In pre-Code law, the most common opinion, as held by St. Alphonse,[80] asserted that the religious had dominion over his manuscript or invention. The reasons advanced were that industry of this type pertained to the sciences and was intellectual rather than material property, which did not fall under the vow of poverty [81] and that such had been the common custom.[82]

Shortly before the promulgation of the Code, the Sacred Congregation for Religious had been asked whether a religious of either solemn or simple vows, who had produced a manuscript during the time of his profession, retained its dominion so that he could donate or alienate it under whatsoever title. The reply, approved by Pope Pius X, was negative.[83] The reason of the response seems to be that manuscripts though a product of in-

---

[78] Augustine, *Religious and Laymen*, p. 135; Gearin, "The Confessor and the Vow of Religious Poverty"—*AER*, LXI (1919), 147; Gerster, *Ius Religiosorum*, p. 172; Larraona, "Commentarium Codicis,"—*CpR*, II (1921), 40, 41; Turner, *The Vow of Poverty*, pp. 100, 101; Schäfer, *De Religiosis*, n. 329, g; Wernz-Vidal, *De Religiosis*, n. 327.

[79] Canon 580, §2; 582.

[80] *Theologia Moralis*, II, lib. IV, c. 1, n. 14.

[81] Turner, *The Vow of Poverty*, pp. 93, 94.

[82] Cf. also Suarez, *De Religione* (*Opera Omnia*, ed. nova a Carolo Berton, Parisiis: Apud Ludovicum Vives, 1856–1861, vol. XIII-XVI, *De Religione*), tract. VIII, lib. 3, c. 13, n. 10.

[83] S. C. Rel., 13 iul. 1913—*AAS*, V (1913), 366.

tellectual effort possess in themselves the possibility of material or market value.[84] This decision did not deprive the religious of the dominion of his manuscript; it only restricted the exercise of that dominion so that he could not alienate or donate it for these are acts which imply proprietorship. Hence, writings and inventions of religious come under the vow of poverty only in respect to their possible alienation.[85]

In another respect the production and use of manuscripts, inventions and the like, may come under the obligations of the vow of obedience.[86] There certainly can be no question as to the right of the religious community to the writings and inventions of religious who are specially assigned to provide toward a common sustenance through their intellectual activity. Such efforts are meant primarily to provide needed revenues and as such fall under the concept of the industry of religious and become the property of the community as to ownership, use and alienation.[87] It is not doubted that the community which by reason of profession provides the religious the necessities to life and work, possesses also the right to his labor and its fruits, if they can be measured materially. The possibility of material emoluments accruing to a professed religious in return for any of his efforts, in this case for his writings or his inventions, gives the right to these effects to the institute.[88]

Manuscripts or notes of a religious because they are something personal to the religious, a complement of intellectual endeavor, in accord with the decision referred to above, are property of the

---

[84] Manuscripts that are solely for personal use, as notes or aids of the memory, are not to be included under the terms of this decision.—Pejška, *Ius Canonicum Religiosorum,* p. 124. Cf. Prümmer, *Manuale Iuris Canonici,* q. 223, p. 297.

[85] Augustine, *Religious and Laymen,* pp. 305, 306; Goyeneche, "Studia Canonica"—*CpR,* II (1921), 141, 142; Prümmer, *Manuale Iuris Canonici,* q. 223, p. 297; Salsmans, "Annotationes"—*Periodica,* VII (1914), 166, 167; Schäfer, *De Religiosis,* n. 328; Wernz-Vidal, *De Religiosis,* n. 350.

[86] Pejška, *Ius Canonicum Religiosorum,* p. 124.

[87] Goyeneche, "Studia Canonica"—*CpR,* II (1921), 141; Schäfer, *De Religiosis,* n. 328; Voltas, "Consultationes"—*CpR,* I (1920), 278.

[88] Augustine, *Religious and Laymen,* p. 340; Voltas, "Consultationes"—*CpR,* I (1920), 278; Wernz-Vidal, *De Religiosis,* n. 350.

religious institute only in so far as they may be alienated. Every man has the natural right to conserve his knowledge and everything that leads to it. Religious profession does not deny him that right. Hence it follows that the religious may do anything with his manuscripts that does not savor of acts of proprietorship. Though poverty and justice do not seem to demand it, charity toward the community must be considered if and when a religious would destroy a manuscript that would be sufficiently well elaborated to be of value. Such procedure would show ingratitude toward the institute which cares for him and provided the opportunities for study.[89]

Similar to the question of manuscripts are the objects of art wrought by religious. Paintings, sculptures, etc. in themselves are not considered as material things but rather spiritual as determined by the exercise of one's ingenuity or art. As such they do not come under the obligations of the vow of poverty. The right to ownership and to the material gain, if any, rests with the monastery or convent.[90] However, with regard to the source of the materials authors draw up a distinction. They assert, with St. Alphonse,[91] that if the community furnished the materials, or if the religious produced the object of art with the intention of retaining it, ownership was acquired by the institute. If the professed religious acquired the materials from a source outside the institute and produced a painting or a piece of sculpture by his own industry, for the person furnishing the material, the object belongs to that person and not to the institute. However, if the latter be done without the permission of the superior obedience and justice would then be violated.[92] Obedience would be violated in virtue of his religious vows; justice in virtue of canons 580, § 2 and 582.

---

[89] Prümmer, *Manuale Iuris Canonici,* q. 223, pp. 297, 298; Schäfer, *De Religiosis,* n. 328.

[90] Cf. canon 580, §2; 582.

[91] *Theologia Moralis,* II, lib. IV, c. 1, n. 14.

[92] Augustine, *Religious and Laymen,* p. 306; Pejška, *Ius Canonicum Religiosorum,* p. 124; Turner, *The Vow of Poverty,* p. 97; Wernz-Vidal, *De Religiosis,* n. 351.

CHAPTER IV

Almsgathering

Article 1. Pre-Code Legislation

A. Legislation to the Council of Trent

The origin of the idea of collecting alms did not come with the rise of religious orders, but had been in practice long before. The first monastic institutes, professing a poverty which permitted the common ownership of property, did not of necessity depend upon the reception of alms for their sustenance. However, examples can be found of persons who professed a life of absolute poverty, although they did not belong to any particular religious community. They lived in complete reliance upon alms and frequently begged the necessities of life.[1]

The idea of collecting alms by going from place to place was practiced universally in the early centuries of the existence of the Church. It received great impetus at the time of the Crusades, when the term *quaestores* came into use. These *quaestores,* gathering alms either for themselves or for others, upon request obtained various privileges for those who generously responded to their call for alms. Notable among these was the concession of indulgences to the contributors. This gave rise to various abuses particularly in regard to the claiming and publishing of fabricated and fictitious indulgences.

In a letter to the Archbishop of Lyons, dated December 9, 1198, Pope Innocent III[2] severely condemned the practice of the Hos-

[1] Meyer, *Alms-gathering by Religious* (Licentiate dissertation in Canon Law, Catholic University of America, Washington, D. C., 1940), pp. 13–15; Roth, "Zbieranie Jałmużn przez Osoby Zakonne"—*Ateneum Kapłanski* (Włocławek, 1914—), XXXVIII (1936), 279, 280.

[2] C. 11, X, *de privilegiis et excessibus privilegiatorum,* V, 33; Potthast, n. 468.

pitallers of St. John, who not being able to go in quest of alms themselves, selected as collectors, priests, suspended by their own bishops, and uneducated and irreligious lay people, who through their irresponsible activities caused great scandal to both the clerics and lay people. Severe penalties were to be inflicted upon those found collecting alms, falsely wearing the garb of religious.[3] Those sending them were to be prohibited to preach and those that were sent by such means, if they were lay people, were to be excommunicated, and if clerics, suspended, contrary privileges notwithstanding.

At the IV General Lateran Council (1215), under Pope Innocent III, definite legislation on the matter of collecting alms was set forth. In canon sixty-two it forbade the admission of the seekers of alms (*quaestores*) into a diocese for this purpose without a letter permitting them to do so from the Apostolic See or from the respective diocesan bishops. In which case they were not to do anything but what was expressly permitted them in these letters. Those who have been assigned to collect alms must be upright and discreet; they must not seek lodgings in unbecoming places, incur useless or extravagant expenses, and they must avoid above all the fraudulent wearing of the habit of a religious.[4]

Condemnation of certain practices of some collectors was especially emphasized at the General Council of Vienne (1311-1312) by Pope Clement V.[5] It had been brought to the attention of the Pope that some of these *quaestores* with great audacity and deceitfulness, of their own accord, granted indulgences; dispensed from vows; absolved from perjury, homicide and other sins, those confessing to them; declared the latter free from the obligation of paying back stolen goods; released them from a third or fourth part of the penance prescribed by law; claimed the liberation from Purgatory of three or more souls, as of the parents or

---

[3] Cf. glossa ad v. *signatos;* Hostiensis, *Lectura* in lib. V, tit. *de privilegiis et excessibus privilegiatorum,* c. 11, n. 2.

[4] C. 14, X, *de poenitentiis et remissionibus,* V, 38; Mansi, XXII, 1050, 1051; Schroeder, *Disciplinary Decrees,* p. 287; Hostiensis, *Lectura* in lib. V, tit. *de poenitentiis et remissionibus,* c. 14, nn. 12, 14.

[5] C. 2, *de poenitentiis et remissionibus,* V, 9 in Clem.

friends of those who give them alms; granted to benefactors a plenary remission of sins, and, to use their own words, absolved *a poena et culpa.*

These abuses were forcefully condemned by Pope Clement, who, to counteract any possibility of recurrence, revoked all privileges which might have been in any way granted to any places or orders or persons. The *quaestores* were forbidden to enter dioceses for the purpose of collecting alms without first obtaining apostolic letters either from the Holy See or the respective bishops. In the process of soliciting alms they could do nothing but what had been expressly stated in these letters. The local bishops were to watch over this and punish with ecclesiastical penalties and censures any violations in this matter.[6]

B. *Post-Tridentine Legislation*

The Fathers of the Church at the Council of Trent, mindful of the necessity of regulating the solicitation of alms which heretofore, despite the regulations of the IV General Lateran Council[7] and the Council of Vienne,[8] caused scandal to and complaint from the faithful, forbade those soliciting alms, commonly known as *quaestores,* to preach either personally or by proxy.[9] In another decree this same Council, because of the very little hope of amendment of the practices of the questors, aimed at and abolished the name and function of these, notwithstanding any contrary privileges, even though they were immemorial.[10]

This Tridentine legislation speaking generally in reference to all religious institutes caused difficulties in regard to the mendicant orders which possessed no common property. These, deriving their chief means of sustenance through almsgathering, were denied, by some, the privilege of collecting alms. Pope Pius V, realizing the difficulties, declared in his constitution "*Etsi mendi-*

---

[6] C. 2, *de poenitentiis et remissionibus,* V, in Clem.; McVann, *The Canon Law on Sermon Preaching* (New York, N. Y.: The Paulist Press, 1940), pp. 21, 22.

[7] C. 14, X, *de poenitentiis et remissionibus,* V, 38.

[8] C. 2, *de poenitentiis et remissionibus,* V, 9 in Clem.

[9] Conc. Trident. sess. XXV, *de ref.* c. 2 *in fine.*

[10] Conc. Trident. sess. XXI, *de ref.* c. 9.

cantium" of May 16, 1567, that the decrees of the Council of Trent could not and should not apply to the mendicants, since their very existence depended upon alms.[11] Apparently this did not settle the question. On June 12, 1608, the Sacred Congregation of the Council stated that the Sacred Congregation of Cardinals, interpreters of the Council of Trent, declared that the mendicants had been in no way prohibited from seeking alms, provided, however, that they did not authorize others to collect in their name. If other religious or seculars were used, then explicit permission was required from the bishop.[12]

The Sacred Congregation of Bishops and Regulars, in a number of decrees issued to various bishops on the question of alms-gathering by mendicants, decreed that these orders did not need the permission of the local ordinary in their quest for alms in the dioceses where they had established monasteries and that they were not to be taxed in any way for the exercise of this privilege, particularly when they had the faculty to gather alms from their superiors.[13] This privilege was approved and confirmed by Pope Clement XI in his constitution "*Exponi nobis*" of July 8, 1717.[14] The basis for this privilege was found in the fact that when once a convent had been established in a diocese that convent had the right to provide for its sustenance by means approved in its rule.[15]

The collecting of alms in time caused abuses which took on a serious character. This had been brought about by the lack of a definite and uniform norm of procedure, regulating this privilege. Because of the peculiar circumstances of the times and to avoid abuses and a departure from the religious spirit, bringing discredit upon the orders themselves, the Sacred Congregation for Religious was moved to set down norms controlling the col-

---

[11] *Fontes,* n. 121, §2, n. 15.

[12] *Fontes,* n. 2373; cf. Ferraris, *Bibliotheca,* ad v. "eleemosyna" n. 38; Pignatelli, *Consultationes Canonicae,* VIII, consultatio 12, nn. 2, 18; Fagnanus, *Commentaria,* in lib. V, tit. *de privilegiis,* c. 11, n. 3.

[13] Cf. *Fontes,* nn. 1391, 1514, 1532, 1643, 1779, 1820; *decr.* 1 oct. 1586—Bizzarri, *Collectanea,* p. XXV; cf. also Ferraris, *Bibliotheca,* ad v. "eleemosyna" n. 35.

[14] *Bull. Rom. Taur.,* XXI, 763.

[15] S. C. Ep. et Reg., 6 oct. 1595 as referred to by Ferraris, *Bibliotheca,* ad v. "eleemosyna" n. 35.

lection of alms.[16] On November 21, 1908, by the authority of Pope Pius X, this Sacred Congregation in a decree "*De eleemosynis colligendis*" [17] prescribed the method to be followed in seeking alms and the discipline to be observed by the collectors in religious institutes of men. In two sections the norms given are: (1) For mendicant orders; (2) For non-mendicant orders and other religious institutes of men. The norms governing mendicant [18] orders are:

1. Regulars who are and are called mendicants may by apostolic privilege collect alms with only the permission of their superiors in the diocese in which they have a convent. The bishop's permission is necessarily presumed to be included in his consent and approval for the erecting of the convent.

2. If these regulars wish to collect outside of the diocese in which they have a convent, they must obtain written permission through their superior, from the bishop of that diocese.

3. The ordinaries should not deny such permission without grave and urgent cause when some convent cannot adequately sustain itself through almsgathering in the diocese where it had been erected.

4. Permission once granted is understood to endure until expressly revoked.

5. In order that the mendicant enjoy this right they must collect alms themselves and not through persons outside their order.

6. Regulars collecting alms must always have with them an authentic letter testifying to their faculty and office as almsgatherers. This letter must be shown to the pastors and bishops whenever they may request it.

7. Regular superiors should entrust this office only to religious

---

[16] Cf. Meyer, *Alms-gathering by Religious*, pp. 70, 71; Roth, "Zbieranie Jałmużn przez Osoby Zakonne"—*Ateneum Kaplanskie,* XXXVIII (1936), 281.

[17] *Fontes*, n. 4391.

[18] The name *mendicant* is applied in general to orders which in their original constitutions were forbidden to own property either personally or in common, and therefore derived their support through alms.—Taunton, *The Law of the Church* (St. Louis, Mo., 1906), ad v. "mendicantes" p. 427; Pejška, *Ius Canonicum Religiosorum,* pp. 7, 8; Schäfer, *De Religiosis,* pp. 52, 53.

of mature age and judgment, and never to those who are still pursuing their studies.

8. Except on account of grave necessity, the collectors of alms should not go about alone but in pairs.

9. Those collecting alms outside the locality of their convents are to reside with the pastors or other secular or regular clerics; lacking these, with some pious benefactor, known for his Christian integrity and virtue.

10. The collectors should not remain outside their own house for more than a month, if they are collecting in their own diocese, or more than two months, if they are collecting outside their diocese. When they return they must not be sent out again unless they first lead the community life for a month or two months respectively.

11. Those collecting alms in the place where their convent is located may not remain outside their own house overnight.

12. Almsgatherers should always be mindful of their state in life and go about with a zeal, humility, modesty and neatness as befits a religious.

13. Regular superiors have a grave obligation to prescribe for their collectors of alms norms of procedure as dictated by prudence.

14. If regular collectors notoriously fail to adhere to these provisions and cause scandal among the faithful or dare to act contrary to a legitimate prohibition in collecting alms, the local ordinary should order them back to their own homes and, as delegates of the Holy See, enjoin their superiors to correct and punish them according to the gravity of the scandal given. If the superiors neglect to do so the bishop should have recourse to the Holy See as soon as possible.[19]

ARTICLE 2. LEGISLATION OF THE CODE

A. Meaning of Almsgathering

Almsgathering or begging, a privilege accorded to religious in the present ecclesiastical legislation, has been and still remains one of the important methods of bringing about a proper sustenance to the members of a religious community and the ful-

[19] Meyer, *Alms-gathering by Religious,* pp. 72, 73.

fillment of the aims peculiar to the institute. The Code in treating the question retains in substance the special provisions established by the decrees of the Sacred Congregations.[20]

The term almsgathering (*quaestuatio, stipem cogere*) as used by the Code is to be accepted in its canonical sense and cannot be predicated to other methods of seeking financial support. To seek alms is to make a personal appeal to the charity of the people by seeking offering from door to door.[21] Three things contribute to the canonical concept of the term: (1) The appeal should be personal and contain the idea of going from house to house; (2) It should be a general quest, not limited to a few individuals; (3) It should be made for the purpose of obtaining offerings either for the religious himself, for other persons or for some pious cause.[22] Hence almsgathering as provided for by the Code has reference to only a particular type of endeavor and does not embrace all the modes of seeking temporal aid. Cases of appeal for funds not coming under the concept of almsgathering in the canonical sense do not come under its laws but must be judged by general or particular law given for that particular type of appeal.[23]

In particular the following modes of seeking financial aid are not to be considered under the term almsgathering:

1. If one seeks only the aid of persons known to him.[24]

---

[20] S. C. Ep. et Reg., decr. "*Singulari*," 27 martii, 1896—*Fontes*, n. 2029 (for women religious) and S. C. Rel., decr. "*De eleemosynis colligendis*," 21 nov. 1908—*Fontes*, n. 4391 (for men religious).

[21] Chelodi, *Ius de Personis*, n. 283; *Cocchi, Commentarium in Codicem Iuris Canonici ad usum Scholarum*, Lib. II (2. ed., Augustae Taurinorum: Officina Libraria Marietti, 1926), *De Personis*, pars. II *De Religiosis*, p. 222 (hereafter this work is referred as *De Religiosis*). Fanfani, *De Iure Religiosorum*, n. 358; O'Brien, *The Exemption of Religious in Church Law*, p. 247; Pejška, *Ius Canonicum Religiosorum*, p. 67; Roth, "Zbieranie Jałmużn przez Osoby Zakonne"—*Ateneum Kaplanskie*, XXXVIII (1936), 281; Schäfer, *De Religiosis*, n. 428; Wernz-Vidal, *De Religiosis*, n. 408.

[22] Roth, *ibid.* 281; Wernz-Vidal, *De Religiosis*, n. 408.

[23] O'Brien, *The Exemption of Religious in Church Law*, p. 247; Papi, *Religious in Church Law* (New York: P. J. Kenedy and Sons, 1924), ad v. "collecting" p. 36.

[24] O'Brien, *op. cit.*, p. 247; Vermeersch-Creusen, *Epitome*, II (Mechlinae-Romae: H. Dessain, 1925), n. 283; Vromant, *De Bonis Ecclesiae Temporalibus*, n. 76.

2. If one seeks aid by visiting some or a few homes, even though some of these persons are not acquaintances.[25] In reference to the above points it must be noted that it is immaterial whether the person in quest of alms does so with the permission of his superior or on his own initiative. The canonical concept of almsgathering requires that it be a general and not a quest limited to a select few, be they acquaintances or not.

3. Begging donation in a church or from some society or organization is not almsgathering but takes on the form of voluntary offerings.[26]

4. Appeals at homes of single benefactors to which one had been invited or to which one comes of his own initiative even though these visits be regular and made with the intention of receiving some benefaction.[27]

5. Appeals to the public through the medium of some publication cannot be considered almsgathering.[28]

6. Requests for alms made by written appeals, e.g., through circular letters, are not considered as almsgathering in the canonical sense.—Since legislation on almsgathering had not deviated from the requirements of pre-Code law, its discipline is retained. In view of canon 6, 3° and 4° the decree " Singulari " [29] merits special attention regarding written appeals. It states expressly that superiors may seek alms through letters without the permission of the local ordinary.[30] Hence alms obtained in this manner are to be considered as customary or usual alms or voluntary offerings. Commentators on the Code commonly agree to this interpretation.[31]

---

[25] O'Brien, *l.c.; Prümmer, Manuale Iuris Canonici,* q. 248, p. 333; Schäfer, *De Religiosis,* n. 428; Vromant, *l.c.*

[26] O'Brien, *l.c.;* Roth, Zbieranie Jałmużn przez Osoby Zakonne"—*Ateneum Kaplanskie,* XXXVIII (1936), 281; Schäfer, *l.c.;* Vromant, *l.c.*

[27] Cf. n. 26.

[28] Pejška, *Ius Canonicum Religiosorum,* p. 67; Roth, *l.c.,* p. 282.

[29] S. C. Ep. et Reg., 27 martii, 1896—*Fontes,* n. 2029.

[30] " Superiorissae . . . nulla petita licentia . . . possint eleemosynas . . per litteras impetrare ab honestis ac benevolis personis quibuscumque."—ad n. IV.

[31] Creusen, Garesché, Ellis, *Religious Men and Women in the Code,* n. 319, p. 240; Fanfani, *De Iure Religiosorum,* n. 357; Coronata, *Institu-*

The modes of appeal for material aid referred to above are not almsgathering in the canonical sense. Hence for their use there is no necessity of obtaining special permission of the local ordinary in institutes which by common law require the ordinary's permission to collect alms. As such there is no question of the use of these types of appeal for the mendicants strictly so-called, since they possess the privilege of begging alms. However, it does not follow that these means may be employed indiscriminately. Though general law would seem to permit them, particular law of the diocese or of the institute may restrict them.[32] The decree "Singulari" expressly states that superiors may accept alms requested and offered from whatsoever source unless a legitimate superior for a reasonable cause prohibits such action.[33]

In the matter of collecting alms by members of religious orders a distinction must also be made as to the type of order. Regulars are to be considered as mendicants and non-mendicants. Mendicants in turn are grouped as mendicants strictly so-called, mendicants in the wide sense and mendicants improperly so-called.

From the standpoint of the type of vow of religious poverty, regulars are divided into mendicant and non-mendicant. The latter permit possessions in common while the former, generally speaking, do not. In reference to the mendicant orders the following is to be noted:

1. Mendicants strictly so-called. These are regulars who on the strength of their earliest institution and by their rule and constitutions are forbidden acquisition or possession of temporal goods with stable income either as physical or moral persons.[34]

---

tiones, I, n. 628; Papi, *Religious in Church Law,* ad v. "collecting," p. 36; Prümmer, *Manuale Iuris Canonici,* p. 248, p. 333; Roth, *l.c.,* p. 281; Schäfer, *De Religiosis,* n. 428; Vromant, *De Bonis Ecclesia Temporalibus,* n. 76.

[32] Creusen, Garesché, Ellis, *op. cit.,* p. 240.

[33] "Nihil tamen impedit, quominus Superiorissae, nulla petita licentia possint eleemosynas undequaque oblatas accepto habere vel etiam per litteras impetrare . . . usquedum a legitimo Superiore rationabili ex causa non prohibeantur."—ad n. IV.

[34] Maroto, "Annotationes"—*CpR,* I (1920), 170; O'Brien, *The Exemption of Religious in Church Law,* p. 246; Papi, *Religious in Church Law,* ad v. "Mendicant Orders," p. 167; Roth, "Zbieranie Jałmużn przez Osoby

Not only are they prohibited individual proprietary ownership, but also common ownership. Their main source of sustenance is to be derived from alms. To this classification belong the Friars Minor and the Friars Minor Capuchins,[35] Jesuits and the Discalced Carmelites.[36]

2. Mendicants in the wide sense. These are regulars who from their pristine rule did not hold possessions even in common and were originally mendicants in the strict sense, but have availed themselves of the Tridentine dispensation regarding the vow of poverty.[37] To these are numbered Friars Preachers, Hermits of St. Augustine, Friars Minor Conventual, etc.[38]

3. Mendicants improperly so-called. These are religious to whom had been conceded the enjoyment and communication of the privileges of the mendicants. Among these are the Cistercians, Camaldolese, Theatines, etc.[39]

B. Requisite Permission

The Code of Canon Law in canon 621 legislates on the matter of collecting alms by regulars who bear the name of mendicant and are so in fact. Members of these orders may with the sole permission of their superiors collect alms in the diocese in which their religious house is established. Outside that diocese they need the written permission of the local ordinary of the diocese in which they desire to seek alms.[40] The local ordinaries, especially those of adjoining dioceses, unless for grave and urgent reasons may not refuse or revoke this permission, if the religious

---

Zakonne,"—*Ateneum Kaplanskie,* XXXVIII (1936, 282; Schäfer, *De Religiosis,* n. 51, 5; Wernz-Vidal, *De Religiosis,* n. 25.

[35] Cf. Conc. Trident., sess. XXV, *de regularibus,* c. 3.

[36] Cf. p. 116, note.

[37] Conc. Trident., sess. XXV, *de regularibus,* c. 3.

[38] Cf. *supra,* p. 67, n. 34; also *CPI,* 16 Oct. 1919—*AAS,* XI (1919), 478, n. X.

[39] O'Brien, *op. cit.,* p. 246; Schäfer, *op. cit.,* n. 51; Wernz-Vidal, *op. cit.,* n. 25.

[40] Canon 621, §1:—Regulares, qui ex instituto mendicantes vocantur et sunt, eleemosynas in dioecesi, ubi eorum religiosa domus est constituta, quaerere valent de sola Superiorum licentia; extra dioecesim vero indigent praeterea licentia scripto data ab Ordinario loci in quo eleemosynas colligere cupiunt.

house possibly cannot subsist solely on the alms collected in the diocese in which it is established.[41]

The exemption of mendicants strictly so-called from the jurisdiction of the local ordinary in the matter of almsgathering is dependent upon their vow of very strict poverty. Because of their incapacity to obtain and withhold ownership of goods even in common, their sustenance has to be provided through other channels, chiefly through the alms given them. Incapability of ownership gives to these, as if inborn and natural, the right to sustain themselves not only from alms that are offered voluntarily but also from those that they beg.[42] This is the right that is acknowledged to them in canon 621.

The intercession of the local ordinary in the question of gathering alms by mendicants in the strict sense is unnecessary and excluded. Bishops, in granting permission to erect a religious house, agree that the religious regulate their lives internally and externally in accord with their rule, constitutions and particular privileges.[43] Thus giving mendicants, strictly so-called, the right to establish a religious house in his diocese implies also their privilege to obtain a proper sustenance by almsgathering.[44] The entire question of gathering alms in regard to permission rests with the superiors of the institute, local or major, as determined by its particular rule and constitutions.[45] Encroachment of this right by the local ordinary in the form of certain limitations to, for example, only certain places or parts of the diocese would overreach his competence. Should the local ordinary judge that the mendicants of any house in his diocese are proceeding far in

---

[41] Canon 621, §2:—Hanc licentiam Ordinarii locorum, praecipue dioecesium finitimarum, nisi gravibus et urgentibus de causis, ne denegent neve revocent, si religiosa domus ex mendicatione in sole dioecesi, in qua est constituta, vivere nullo modo possit.

[42] Schäfer, *De Religiosis*, n. 428.

[43] Cf. *supra*, pp. 15-16.

[44] Canon 497, 2; cf. S. C. Rel., decr. "*De Eleemosynis colligendis*," 21 nov. 1908, 1, 1o—*Fontes*, n. 4391; Schäfer, *De Religiosis*, n. 429; Vromant, *De Bonis Ecclesiae Temporalibus*, n. 79.

[45] Clancy, *The Local Religious Superior*, The Catholic University of America Canon Law Studies, n. 175 (Washington, D. C.: The Catholic University of America Press, 1943), p. 68; Blat, *De Personis*, n. 697, p. 689.

excess of proper measures in their zeal in the quest of alms, he may have recourse to the superiors of the institute or to the Congregation for Religious.[46]

The right of exemption of mendicants, strictly so-called, is limited to only the diocese in which they have established a religious house. Should they wish to extend their activities outside the diocese, they would have to obtain, besides the permission of their own superiors, the written permission of the ordinary of the place in which they wish to collect alms. Canon 621, §2 enjoins the local ordinary not to deny or restrict his permission unless for grave and urgent reasons. The gravity or urgency of these reasons are to be prudently determined by the local ordinary. He should weigh the potentialities of the people of his jurisdiction in regard to their contributions with the needs of the community or pious work for which the quest is being arranged.[47] After an objective judgment, the ordinary may also limit the quest to a certain time, or to certain places or parts of his diocese. Special consideration should be had for mendicants who cannot obtain a proper sustenance in the diocese in which they have a house either because the diocese is small or because of the poverty of the people therein.[48]

Concerning almsgathering by mendicants in the wide sense, those improperly so-called and other regulars, the Code is silent. Canon 621, §1 makes no mention of them. Hence apparently its provisions could not be applied to regulars who are not mendicants strictly so-called. The Pontifical Commission for the Authentic Interpretation of the Code was asked: Whether can. 621, §1 is to be understood as applying only to religious who are mendicants in the strict sense; or also to those who are called such in a broader sense, as, for example, the Order of Preachers. The answer was in the affirmative to the first part; in the negative to the second part.[49] The reason for this decision rests mainly on

[46] Roth, "Zbieranie Jałmużn przez Osoby Zakonne,"—*Ateneum Kaplanskie*, XXXVIII (1936), 282.

[47] Roth, *l.c.*, p. 283.

[48] Cf. S. C. Rel., decr. "*De eleemosynis colligendis*" 21 nov. 1908, I, n. 3—*Fontes*, n. 4391.

[49] *CPI*, 16 oct. 1919, n. 10—*AAS*, XI (1919), 478; transl. from Bouscaren, *The Canon Law Digest*, I, 323.

the fact that all regulars, except mendicants in the strict sense, possess common goods with fixed and regular incomes. They lack the basic legal foundation due to which canon 621, §1 grants mendicants, in the strict sense, the right to collect alms with solely the permission of their own superiors. There can be no doubt that by the common law of the Church as expressed in canon 621, and the reply of the Pontifical Commission, all other regulars require the permission of the local ordinary even when they would wish to beg alms in the diocese in which their house is established. Notwithstanding the common law of the Church, particular privileges for almsgathering granted to mendicants in the wide sense have not been revoked. Consequently, if they possess such privileges,[50] they need not the permission of the local ordinary if they wish to beg alms in the diocese wherein they have a convent.[51]

Regarding mendicants improperly so-called and other regulars, such as the Benedictines, no mention is made in the Code, or decisions of the Holy See. Positing a just cause there is no doubt that they could collect alms. However, owing to their status as possessors of common property with fixed revenues, a question may be raised as to the source of requisite permission to be obtained by them. Would the permission of the local ordinary suffice or must they also obtain a special privilege from the Holy See? Canon 621, §1 speaks only of mendicants in the strict sense. The response of the Pontifical Commission of October 16, 1919, adds reference to mendicants in the wide sense. Canon 622, §1, beginning with the words *Alii omnes religiosi*—all other religious—undoubtedly gives the idea that the legislator might wish to regulate the question of almsgathering by the religious not mentioned in the preceding canon. However, canon 622 speaks only of religious congregations of either pontifical (paragraph 1) or diocesan (paragraph 2) approval. In accord with canon 488, 2° the legislator would not seem to include non-mendicant regulars into any of the classes mentioned in canon 622. It is also difficult

[50] Granted, for example, in the constitution of Pius V, "*Etsi mendicantium*" of May 16, 1567—*Fontes,* n. 121.

[51] Coronata, *Institutiones,* I, n. 628; Prümmer, *Manuale Iuris Canonici,* q. 248, nota 117; Roth, *l.c.,* p. 284; Schäfer, *De Religiosis,* n. 249.

to presume, points out Roth,[52] that the legislator, formulating *ex professo* the question of almsgathering by religious, would overlook such a large group of them. It would seem therefore that canon 621 includes not only the mendicant but all regulars. The consequence would be that non-mendicant regulars need not the special permission of the Holy See to seek alms. They have this privilege in virtue of canon 621, §1. It is sufficient for them to obtain permission of the local ordinary.

The interpretation of canon 621, §1, given above, and brought forth by Roth, is not contrary to the response of the Pontifical Commission of October 16, 1919. The response states that only mendicants in the strict sense can beg alms in the confines of the diocese in which their house is erected with the sole permission of their superiors. The sense of canon 621, §1 is therefore the following: Regulars, who are mendicants strictly so-called, can beg alms in the diocese in which their house is located with only the permission of their superiors. All other regulars must obtain the permission of their superiors and also that of the local ordinary, unless special privileges exclude the local ordinary.[53]

C. *Rules for Collecting Alms*

The begging of alms by religious may very often prove a danger to the individual religious collecting alms. The continual contact of the quaestors with the world and at times a prolonged absence from the monastery may well lead to worldly infection contrary to the spirit of the religious rule of life. To forestall the evil that could possibly arise from almsgathering, the Code requires on the one hand certain qualifications on the part of the person assigned to the task of seeking alms,[54] and, on the other hand, it orders that quaestors in seeking alms observe the norms given in the instructions of the Holy See.[55] In both instances

---

[52] *L.c.*, p. 284.

[53] Roth, "Zbieranie Jałmużn przez Osoby Zakonne"—*Ateneum Kaplanskie*, XXXVIII (1936), 287; Schäfer, *De Religiosis*, n. 430.

[54] Canon 623.—Non licet Superioribus stipem colligendam committere, nisi professis aetate animoque maturis, maxime si de mulieribus agatur, nunquam autem iis qui in studia adhuc incumbunt.

[55] Canon 624.—Quod vero attinet ad modum in quaeritand stipe servandum

special reference is made to the decrees, "*Singulari*" of March 27, 1896, for women religious [56] and "*De eleemosynis colligendis*" of November 21, 1908, for men religious.[57]

1. Qualifications of the collector. Canon 623 orders that it is not licit for the superior to entrust the collection of alms to any religious except to one of mature age and approved character, and never to those who are pursuing studies. Thus postulants, novices and professed religious who are occupied with studies, even though they be priests, cannot be sent.[58] It must be added that the privilege of collecting alms does not include the faculty of using persons, other than the members of the particular mendicant community, even though they be other regulars. The use of quaestors, who are not members of the religious community for whom the alms are begged, had been already forbidden in the decree "*De eleemosynis colligendis*" (I, 5). It is also implied in canon 1503 which, upholding the privileges of canons 621–624, states that private persons whether clerics or laymen are forbidden to collect alms (*stipem cogere*) for any pious or ecclesiastical institute or cause without the written permission of the Holy See or proper ordinary and the local ordinary of the place where the alms are to be collected.[59]

2. Method and discipline to be followed by the collectors of alms. As regards regulars, the Code in Canon 624 canonized, so to say, the method and discipline to be observed by collectors of alms as given in the rules of the decree "*De eleemosynis colligendis.*" [60]

---

et ad disciplinam a quaestuantibus custodiendam, religiosi utriusque sexus stare debent instructionibus a Sede Apostolica hac de re datis.

[56] *Fontes,* n. 2029.

[57] *Fontes,* n. 4391.

[58] Roth, "Zbieranie Jałmużn przez Osoby Zakonne"—*Ateneum Kapłanskie,* XXXVIII (1936), 287; Schäfer, *De Religiosis,* n. 430.

[59] Maroto, "Annotationes"—*CpR,* I (1920), 171; Papi, *Religious in Church Law,* ad. v. "collecting" p. 39; Roth, *l.c.,* p. 287; Schäfer, *De Religiosis,* n. 430.

[60] For the norms of this decree cf. *supra,* pp. 109, 110; cf. also Papi, *op. cit.,* ad v. "collecting" pp. 38, 39; Roth, *l.c.;* Schäfer, *op. cit.,* n. 431; Vromant, *De Bonis Ecclesiae Temporalibus,* n. 83.

CHAPTER V

Fluctuating Income

Article 1. Goods of Those Entering Religious Orders

A. Payment for Sustenance by Postulants and Novices

For the preservation of the liberty of aspirants to the religious life and to avoid the dangers of simony, the Code, except in two instances, prohibits any demand of compensation for expenditures toward the support of a postulant or novice. Canon 570, §1 orders that unless the constitutions or an express agreement made previous to entering into the postulancy or the novitiate stipulate the payment of a certain sum for food and clothing, nothing may be demanded to cover the expenses of the postulancy or the novitiate. Paragraph 2 of the same canon adds that everything the aspirant brings with himself into the order and which was not actually consumed by use, must be returned to him if he leaves the order without making his religious profession.[1]

The law as expressed in this canon is in complete harmony with the legislation previous to the Code as evidenced in the *Corpus Iuris Canonici.*[2] The Tridentine Fathers for the purpose of protecting the freedom of the applicants to religious life ordered that:

> Before the profession of a novice, whether male or female, nothing shall under any pretext whatever be

[1] Canon 570.—1. Nisi pro alimentis et habitu religioso in constitutionibus vel expressa conventione aliquid in postulatu vel novitiatu ineundo solvendum caveatur, nihil pro impensis postulatus vel novitiatus exigi potest.

2. Quae adspirans attulerit et usu consumpta non fuerint, si e religione, non emissa professione, egrediatur, ei restituantur.

[2] Cf. c. 2, 3, C. I, q. 2; c. 2, X, *de statu monachorum et canonicorum regularium,* III, 35; c. 8, 19, 25, 30, 40, X, *de simonia, et ne aliquid pro spiritualibus exigatur vel promittatur,* V, 3; c. 1, *de simonia,* V, I, in Extravag. com.

> given to the monastery from the property of the same, either by parents, relatives or guardians, except for food and clothing during the time of probation, lest the novice should be unable to leave for the reason that the monastery possesses the whole or greater part of his substance, and he would be unable easily to recover it in case he should leave. The Holy Council, therefore, commands under penalty of anathema, both givers and receivers, that this be in no wise done, and that to those who leave before profession everything that was theirs be restored.[3]

In like manner, the Sacred Congregation of Bishops and Regulars, on December 11, 1789[4] forbade regular superiors, or the convent, or any particular religious to demand anything from a novice for the purpose of receiving the habit or making the profession. The only exception was the cost of food and clothing for the time of probation. The postulant or novice however could of his own free will make a donation, provided it would be a small one and would not endanger his right to leave the order freely, if he thought it necessary.[5]

The aspirant, strictly speaking, was not obliged to take on the obligation of paying the expenses of his sustenance. This was provided in order that he should in no way be impeded from freely leaving the order during the time of probation. The freedom of returning to the world would be greatly lessened if the novice, when leaving, would be obliged to refund the expenses of maintenance, particularly if he would not have the means to do so. It should be noted that monasteries have been founded to sustain not only the professed but also the candidates for profession.[6] However a postulant or novice may donate something for his food and clothing if he wishes to do so. He may also under certain circumstances have the obligation in justice

---

[3] Conc. Trident. sess. XXV, *de regularibus,* c. 16; transl. from Schroeder, *Canons and Decrees of the Council of Trent,* p. 227.

[4] S. C. Ep. et Reg., *Carmelitarum,* 11 dec. 1789—*Fontes,* n. 1884. Cf. also S. C. Ep. et Reg., *Ordinis Minorum,* 30 mart. 1838—*Fontes,* n. 1915.

[5] Appeltern, *Compendium Praelectionum Juris Regularis Adm. R. P. Piati Montani* (2. ed., Parisiis, 1913), quaest. 80, resp. 1. (Hereafter this work is referred to as Appeltern, *Compendium Juris Regularis.*)

[6] Schmalzgrueber, *Ius Ecclesiasticum Universum,* III, tit. 31, n. 80.

of refunding the expenses of his sustenance if he leaves the order. The latter may occur in two instances: (1) If he entered the order fraudulently, i.e. without the intention of persevering and performed duties insufficient to have taken care of his food and clothing; (2) If the novice made a pact with the monastery for a refund, or if a legitimate custom existed of refunding if the aspirant left.[7] On the other hand, if the novice or postulant gave something to the monastery solely for the purpose of his maintenance during the time of his probation, the monastery was not obliged to refund the donation if he left the order.[8]

Under present legislation payment of expenses for food and clothing by applicants is regulated either by the disposition of the constitutions or by special agreement made prior to entering the community as an applicant to religious life. Lacking these, the institute cannot demand any refund. However, spontaneous donations by the applicants for the purpose of covering the expenses may be accepted.[9]

Concerning the fruits of a postulant's or a novice's industry the Code is silent. Turner states that " in practice, the novice will agree to perform a specific work or series of works for the Institute. Refusal to obey in a reasonable matter and especially when the work is not of a distracting nature would tend to form an unfavorable opinion of the candidate in the mind of the capitulars." [10] It is highly practical that all applicants before being admitted into the community sign an agreement that can be sustained in the civil forum, by which they give up any right to compensation for the work that they may perform during the time of the postulancy or the novitiate.[11] It is also very advisable that

[7] Schmalzgrueber, *op. cit.*, III, tit. 31, n. 81.

[8] Cf. Barbosa, *Iuris Ecclesiastici Universi Libri Tres*, I, tit. 42, nn. 226–228; Bouix, *Tractatus de Jure Regularium*, I, 591; Fagnanus, *Commentaria*, in lib. III, tit. *de regularibus*, c. 23, nn. 31–36; Ferraris, *Bibliotheca* ad v. "novitiatus" nn. 69, 70; Appeltern, *Compendium Juris Regularis*, quaest. 76. Mattheucci, *Officialis Curiae Ecclesiasticae*, c. 34, nn. 25–30; Blat, *De Personis*, n. 639; Gerster, *Ius Religiosorum*, p. 104; Pejška, *Ius Canonicum Religiosorum*, p. 101.

[9] Turner, *The Vow of Poverty*, p. 117.

[10] *Op. cit.*, p. 117.

[11] Beste, *Introductio in Codicem*, p. 381; Schäfer, *De Religiosis*, n. 257.

an inventory of the goods and money brought by a candidate be made and carefully filed. This should be done for the purpose of safeguarding the community against unjust petitions and incriminations should the postulant or novice leave the community.[12]

B. Donations Made to the Order in Cession of Property Rights by Novices

The canonico-juridical position of professed religious from the standpoint of the vow of poverty is established in the Code. The solemnly professed religious renounces all his rights to all private ownership and to all administrative acts of ownership. The simply professed retains the ownership of his property but cedes its administration, use and usufruct to another.[13] The professed religious in virtue of the vow of poverty, be it solemn or simple, is incapable of making donations without the permission of his superiors. Neither may superiors insist that he make them. However, by reason of the necessity of testamentary action in the form of cession of either ownership of his property or its administration before the vows are taken, a question can be raised as to whether the novice could in the disposition of his property rights favor the institute or community of which he is a member.

Canon 569, §1 imposes upon all novices who have property at the moment of their profession, the obligation of ceding the administration of it to whomsoever they wish and, unless the constitutions provide otherwise, of freely disposing of its use and usufruct.[14] The Code in reference to the cession of administration is very clear and precise. From the term "*cedere cui maluerit*" it is apparent that the intention of the legislator is the full enjoyment of total freedom by the novice in selecting persons to administer his property.[15] He may even cede total ad-

---

[12] Beste, *l.c.;* Schäfer, *l.c.*

[13] Cf. canon 569, 580–582.

[14] Canon 569, §1. Ante professionem votorum simplicium sive temporariorum sive perpetuorum novitius debet, ad totum tempus quo simplicibus votis adstringetur, bonorum suorum administrationem cedere cui maluerit et, nisi constitutiones aliud ferant, de eorundem usu et usufructu libere disponere.

[15] Hannan, *The Canon Law of Wills* (Philadelphia, Pa.: The Dolphin Press, 1935), n. 341; Maroto, "Annotationes"—*CpR,* I (1920), 166.

ministration to the institute or community should one or the other be willing or capable of accepting it.[16]

Concerning the use and usufruct, the phrase "*nisi constitutiones aliud ferant*" was not too clear. The Code Commission was asked: Whether the words of can. 569, §1, *nisi constitutiones aliud ferant* refer to the word *libere,* so that it is allowed to determine by the constitutions the end for which novices may dispose of the use and usufruct of their property. The reply was: The constitutions which were approved before the promulgation of the Code are to be observed, whether they deprive novices of the right to dispose of the use and usufruct of their property, or whether they restrict or define that right.[17] Hence the disposition of the use and usufruct of the property of a novice may be determined by the constitutions of the individual orders, even though they may be contrary to the prescript of the Code which requires a free disposition. In virtue of the authentic interpretation of the Code Commission, the particular law of the institute previous to the Code prevails over general law. The same is to be said of the constitutions approved since the Code.

Restrictions made by the constitutions may be various. They may, for example, require that there be made a partial or even a total transfer of the use and usufruct to the order, to the religious house, or to some pious cause, etc.[18] Should the constitutions be silent on the matter, the general law of the Church expressed by the Code is to be followed and the novice would be free to dispose of the use and usufruct in accord with his own wishes.[19]

In canon 580, §3 mention is made of modifications of the ces-

---

[16] Pejška, *Ius Canonicum Religiosorum,* pp. 64, 98; Schäfer, *De Religiosis,* n. 253; Turner, *The Vow of Poverty,* p. 124, note 21. The Constitutions of the Friars Minor (n. 77) state that the novice may cede administration, use and usufruct to whomsoever it pleases him, but not to the order.

[17] *CPI,* resp., 16 oct. 1919—*AAS,* XI (1919), 478; transl. from Bouscaren, *The Canon Law Digest,* I, pp. 304, 305.

[18] Gearin, "The Confessor and the Vow of Religious Poverty"—*AER,* LXI (1919), 140, 141; Maroto, "Annotationes"—*CpR,* I (1920), 166–168; Turner, *The Vow of Poverty,* pp. 128, 129.

[19] Maroto, *ibid.,* p. 166.

sions or disposition of property rights previously executed by the novice in accord with canon 569. The arrangement made by the professed religious in regard to his property is not immutable. It can be changed though only with the authorization of the General Superior of the order, unless the constitutions stipulate that the permission of some other superior is sufficient. As to the modification provided for in this section of canon 580, there is a special provision should the professed religious wish to favor the institute. The modification must not be in favor of the institute, particularly if a notable amount of property is involved.[20]

The monastery can accept the administration, use or usufruct freely entrusted to it by a novice or by a professed who has received new property after profession. It can also be the beneficiary to a certain extent, after permission to alter previous arrangements has been obtained. The extent is determined by the clause of canon 580, §3, prohibiting the transfer of a notable part. The determination of a notable part rests largely upon the amount of the property involved, regulated by standards of prudent judgment.[21] Canonists seem to favor the opinion that a third part of the total is certainly notable.[22] However, it is possible that, the larger the amount of property, the smaller will be the fraction required to constitute a notable part.[23]

ARTICLE 2. PIOUS FOUNDATIONS

Among the ordinary sources of acquiring temporal goods by religious Pejška lists, in the first place, pious foundations.[24] A

---

[20] Canon 580, §3 . . . dummodo mutatio, saltem de notabili bonorum parte, non fiat in favorem religionis; . . .

[21] Gearin, *ibid.*, p. 142; Fanfani, *De Iure Religiosorum*, n. 256; Larraona, "Commentarium Codicis"—*CpR*, II (1921), 44, 2o.

[22] Chelodi, *Ius de Personis*, n. 247; Cocchi, *De Religiosis*, n. 80, p. 167; Prümmer, *Manuale Iuris Canonici*, quaes. 217, resp. 3; Turner, *The Vow of Poverty*, p. 139, note 80. Coronata (*Institutiones* I, n. 593, 1o) states that certainly a notable part is half or even a third and certainly never a fourth. Augustine (*Religious and Laymen*, p. 280) states that a little over a half of the total income or revenues is a notable part.

[23] "Plerumque notabilis non erit quae quartam partem non superet, quamvis summa absolute notabilis sit."—Vermeersch-Creusen, *Epitome*, I, n. 683, 2 a.

[24] *Ius Canonicum Religiosorum*, p. 63.

pious foundation [25] is the sum total of temporal goods given to a moral ecclesiastical person on the condition of the fulfillment of some specified religious function in return for the annual income thereof. This obligation may be either perpetual or for a long time.[26] The extent of time included in the term *diuturnum tempus* —for a long time—is not determined in the Code. Diverse opinions of authors put it as a time extended as far as fifty years [27] and as low as ten years.[28]

In the law previous to the Code, pious foundations, being ecclesiastical in character, were subject to the laws of the Church. With this in mind the Tridentine Fathers ordered that bishops, as delegates of the Apostolic See, be the executors of all pious foundations notwithstanding any custom, even though immemorial, any privilege or statute whatsoever.[29] The administrators of pious foundations were bound to render an account of their administration to the ordinary. However, if because of custom or privilege an account was to be rendered also to others, this had to be done jointly with the rendering of the account to the bishop.[30] The decrees of the Council of Trent stressed the subjection of all to the local bishops in the question concerning the spiritual care of souls in his territory. Pious foundations, however, that were given over to the regulars enjoying the privileges

[25] Though the question is treated in the Code rather in its administrative than acquisitive character, it can and is here referred to as property producing income that is fluctuating.

[26] Canon 1544, §1. Nomine piarum fundationum significantur bona temporalia alicui personae morali in Ecclesia quoquo modo data, cum onere in perpetuum vel in diuturnum tempus ex redditibus annuis aliquas Missas celebrandi, vel alais praefinitas functiones ecclesiasticas explendi, aut nonnulla pietatis et caritatis opera peragendi.

[27] Prümmer, *Manuale Iuris Canonici,* quaest. 456, resp. 1.

[28] Vermeersch-Creusen, *Epitome,* II, n. 865. Cf. also Nebreda, "De loci Ordinariorum iuribus circa pia legata donationesve tum Religiosis tum eorum ecclesiis etiam paroecialibus facta"—*CpR,* VII (1926), 115; (Hereafter this article is referred to as "De Loci Ordinariorum juribus.") Hannan, *The Canon Law of Wills,* n. 753; Vromant, *De Bonis Ecclesiae Temporalibus,* n. 346.

[29] Conc. Trident. sess. XXII, *de ref.,* c. 8.

[30] Conc. Trident. sess. XXII, *de ref.,* c. 9.

of exemption were withdrawn from the jurisdiction of the local ordinary.[31]

On the basis of the privilege of exemption all goods of regulars whether they pertain to the institute, the province, the house, or their churches are withdrawn from the jurisdiction of the local ordinary.[32] As a consequence pious foundations in their temporal aspect are exempt also.[33] This is clearly indicated in canon 1550 which declares that the rights and duties of the local ordinary mentioned in canons 1545–1549 pertain exclusively to the major superior if the pious foundation is made in favor of an exempt religious institute.[34] This right is also safeguarded in a response of the Code Commission given on July 25, 1926,[35] in which the right of the local ordinary to demand an account of the administration of legacies and foundations in churches belonging to religious *pleno iure,* was affirmed but without prejudice to the prescriptions of can. 630 §4 and can. 1550.[36]

Although in canon 1550 mention is made only of churches, it is apparent, writes O'Brien,[37] from the nature of exemption and from canons 500 and 615 that pious foundations given in favor of other moral persons pertaining to exempt religious are withdrawn from the jurisdiction of and the vigilance of the local ordinary. An exception, however, must be made in cases where the fund established is a pious foundation for the promotion of an enterprise that does not come within the concept of exemption,

---

[31] Schmalzgrueber, *Ius Ecclesiasticum Universum,* III, tit. 36, n. 6.

[32] Cf. canon 500, 615, 1550.

[33] O'Brien, *The Exemption of Religious in Church Law,* p. 265.

[34] Secular Churches proper to the diocese but given over to the care of religious are not included in this canon. Hence pious foundations given to them are subject to the jurisdiction of the local ordinary. Cf. Miller, *Founded Masses according to the Code of Canon Law,* The Catholic University of America Canon Law Studies, n. 34 (Washington, D. C.: The Catholic University of America, 1926), p. 51. (Hereafter this work is referred to as *Founded Masses.*) Nebreda, "De loci Ordinariorum iuribus" *CpR,* VII (1926), 331, 332; Vromant, *De Bonis Ecclesiae Temporalibus,* n. 354; Hannan, *The Canon Law of Wills,* n. 769.

[35] *AAS,* XVII (1926), 393; Bouscaren, *The Canon Law Digest,* I, p. 699.

[36] Cf. *infra,* pp. 120–122.

[37] *The Exemption of Religious in Church Law,* p. 267.

but is, for example, proper to the diocese.[38] In exempt religious orders, only the major superior has the right of issuing and determining the norms relating to the substantial elements of and the acceptance of pious foundations. It is his right to establish a definite sum of money or a certain amount of temporal goods necessary before a pious foundation can be accepted. He can also prepare a plan for the proper distribution of the income derived therefrom.[39] Before a pious foundation can be validly acquired the written consent of the major superior must first be obtained.[40] The deposit of the money or the temporal good assigned to the fund must be made immediately in a safe place, pending its ultimate investment. Both the first deposit and the final investment must be done according to the direction of the major superior.[41] All the articles of the foundation, even though they were made orally, must be put in writing, and at least in two copies; one of which must be deposited in the provincial curia and another placed in the archives of the moral person to whom the fund had been entrusted.[42] A record of the obligation of the foundation and their fulfillment must be kept by the superiors of the moral person to whom the foundation had been given. An account of the fulfillment of these obligations must be sent to the major superior at determined intervals.[43]

The obligations of regulars in the matter of pious foundations for the most part take on the form of the duty of celebration of masses at stated times in return for the temporal aid rendered. The Sacred Congregation of the Council in a decree issued on June 21, 1626, upon the authority of Pope Urban VIII, ordered that pious foundations given to regulars were subject to the General or Provincial of the order.[44] It further required that all money or movable goods acquired with the obligation of celebrating mass *in perpetuum* be immediately deposited in a holy

[38] Cf. canon 1516, §3; Hannan, *The Canon Law of Wills*, nn. 758, 769.

[39] Canon 1545.

[40] Canon 1546, 1.

[41] Canon 1547.

[42] Canon 1548.

[43] Canon 1549.

[44] *Fontes*, n. 2460. Cf. also Wernz, *Ius Decretalium*, III, n. 204.

place or given to a faithful person and as soon as possible invested in immovable goods producing income. In the document of acceptance express mention was also to be made of the obligations annexed to these goods. Pope Innocent XII, by his constitution "*Nuper*" of December 23, 1697,[45] confirmed the previous decree but prohibited all future acceptance of foundations with the obligation of perpetual masses without the permission, previously obtained, of either the Minister General or the Provincial, and that in writing.

Because in the course of time the obligations arising from the foundation masses had been somewhat neglected, the Sacred Congregation of the Council in a decree, "*Vigilanti*" of May 25, 1893[46] ordered that an annual report on the manner of administration had to be sent to the proper ordinary, the local ordinary in the case of diocesan foundations and the major superior in the case of foundations of exempt religious orders. In order to avoid ambiguities, this same Sacred Congregation in another decree, "*Ut debita*" of May 11, 1904[47] prescribed that the time of the term "year" within which the report was to be made, is to run from the end of that year within which the duties of the foundation are to be fulfilled.

The Code too, in canon 1550, grants full authority over foundation masses to the major superior. A doubt would seem to arise concerning the question of stipends for the founded masses, in virtue of canon 813, §3. This canon requires that all religious, even exempt, conform to the decrees of the local ordinary or the diocesan custom of fixing the stipend for manual masses. This difficulty is only apparent, for neither canon 813 nor canon 1545 gives jurisdiction to the local ordinary over the founded mass stipends of exempt religious. Proper distinctions must be made. Canon 831 speaks only of manual stipends which are not to be confused with founded mass stipends. The former lack the element of perpetuity or long durability proper to the latter. Hence the founded mass stipend is distinct and must be determined by the canonical requirements for pious foundations as

[45] *Fontes*, n. 260.

[46] *ASS*, XXVI (1893–1894), 58.

[47] *ASS*, XXXVI (1903–1904), 673.

established in canon 1545 and modified by canon 1550. The major superior of exempt religious is therefore not bound by the local requirements as to the manual, or even founded stipends, because he has an exclusive right to determine the amount of money or property necessary to establish a pious foundation.[48]

ARTICLE 3. FREE-WILL OFFERINGS

The most popular and universally approved means of sustenance for religious have been the free-will offerings given them by those entering religion, by the founders of monasteries and by other benefactors. In the opinion of St. Thomas,[49] religious could and did receive offerings in a threefold manner: (1) As the poor, through the generosity of the faithful; (2) As ministers of the Altar; (3) As beneficiaries of contributions in their churches.

A. Offerings through the Generosity of the Faithful

The help thus given in time assumed large proportions, which had led to various abuses such as the vast enrichment of some monasteries and the desire of many bishops and clerics to take away the property from the religious under various pretexts. The canons found in the *Corpus Iuris Canonici* in this respect deal mostly with the possible eradication of these abuses. None challenged the right of the religious to this means of sustenance. Thus, for example, Pope Gregory I, on June 6, 591,[50] forbade the Archbishop of Naples and his priests from trying in any way to take from the religious any of the offerings given them by the faithful. This prohibition, according to the Glossator,[51] was issued because the monks did not have under their care any souls and therefore owed the bishops only a disciplinary obedience. If they had had any souls under their care they would have been obliged to render some portions of their offerings to the bishops

---

[48] O'Brien, *The Exemption of Religious in Church Law*, p. 267; Miller, *Founded Masses*, pp. 52, 53.

[49] *Summa Theologica*, IIa IIæ, q. 86, art. 2 ad 2.

[50] C. 1, X, *de statu monachorum et canonicorum regularium*, III, 35; JE, n. 1365.

[51] Glossa ad v. *disciplinae*. Cf. Hostiensis, *Lectura* in lib. III, tit. *de statu monachorum et canonicorum regularium*, c. 1.

because of these people, since these, in turn, were obliged to support their bishops. A marginal gloss states that bishops could not assume to take all the donations but only what was considered as the *pars canonica,* the sum of which did not seem to be determined. It was to be given for the purpose of maintenance and support of the bishop.

The right of religious to offerings is not expressly mentioned in the Code. The right is taken for granted. One can say that it is implied in canon 496 where the legislator demands a proper sustenance from fixed income, usual alms or other means. The term *usual alms,* as used in this canon, is to be understood in the sense of free-will donations as explained above.[52]

B. Offerings to the Religious in the Exercise of the Sacred Ministry

In the very beginning of religious life the undertaking of the sacred ministry for the benefit of the people outside of the order had not been intended by the founders of religious institutes. Originally communities of lay brothers they had among their members only a few clerics, and these were ordained to minister to the spiritual needs of the monks. As the numbers of religious increased, the numbers of religious privileged with Sacred Orders also increased. The increase opened the opportunity for the possible use of these priests as aids to the parochial clergy. The idea that the care and direction of souls could and should be given to them if grave reason existed, such as, for example, when suitable secular clerics could not be found, was accepted as early as the fourth century. Thus Pope Siricius, in a letter dated February 10, 385, wished to have pious and learned monks ordained to take upon themselves the works of the sacred ministry.[53]

---

[52] Cf. *supra,* pp. 35-36.

[53] C. 29, C. XVI, q. 1; JK, n. 255; cf. Hostiensis, *Lectura* in lib. III, tit. *de statu monarchorum et canonicorum regularium,* c. 2, n. 1; Hostiensis, *Summa Aurea,* lib. III, tit. *de statu monachorum et canonicorum regularium,* n. 4.—Gratian lists two other decrees, one attributed to St. Ambrose (c. 21, C. XVI, q. 1), and another to a Pope Innocent (c. 22, C. XVI, q. 1), by which clerical offices are permitted to the monks. However, Friedberg in *h. c.,* nn. 151, 156 lists these as of uncertain origin. To that of St.

In the thirteenth century special privileges were granted to the mendicant orders. Their vocation called for them to preach the word of God to all people everywhere. Pope Boniface VIII by the decree "*Super cathedram*" of February 18, 1300, to put an end to quarrels between parochial rectors and the Friars Preachers and the Friars Minor, permitted the Friars to preach freely in open squares and in their own places, except where the local bishop desired to preach himself or to have another preach for himself. To preach in parish churches they needed the permission of the local bishops.[54]

The Council of Trent strictly regulated the functions of the sacred ministry particularly that of the administration of the sacrament of penance and preaching.[55] The approval of regulars for these tasks was left to the judgment of the local ordinary for his own territory. Decrees of the succeeding Popes retained in full the Tridentine legislation.[56]

The present legislation does not deny the exercise of the functions of the sacred ministry to regulars but retains in substance the previous laws regarding the necessary authorization. Canon 874, §1 requires that all priests, even exempt, must have delegated faculties from the local ordinary to hear the confessions of the faithful subject to him.[57] Canon 1338, §2 insists that the re-

---

Ambrose, the *Correctores Romani* add that nothing of that sort is found in the works of St. Ambrose, but that the decree seems of a very recent authorship; that of Innocent probably refers to Innocent II (1130–1143).

[54] C. 2, *de sepulturis,* III, 6, in Extravag. com.; Potthast, n. 24913; *BF,* IV, n. 179; cf. also c. 2, *de sepulturis,* III, 7, in Clem; c. un. *de iudiciis,* II, 1 in Extravag. com.

[55] Conc. Trident. sess. V, *de ref.,* c. 2; sess. XXIII, *de ref.,* c. 15; sess. XXIV, *de ref.,* c. 4.

[56] Cf. Pius V, const. "*Ad exsequendum,*" 1 nov. 1567—*Bull. Rom. Taur.* VII, 629; Gregorius XV, const. "*Inscrutabili,*" 5 febr. 1622—*Fontes,* n. 199; Benedictus XIV, const. "*Ad Militantis,*" 30 mart. 1742—*Fontes,* n. 326; Benedictus XIV, const. "*Firmandis*" 6 nov. 1744—*Bullarii Romani Continuatio Summorum Pontificum* (19 vols., Prati, 1756–1883), I, 450–457 (hereafter this work is referred to as *Bull. Rom. Cont.*); Leo XIII, const. "*Romanos Pontifices,*" 8 maii, 1881—*Fontes,* n. 582.

[57] O'Brien, *The Exemption of Religious in Church Law,* pp. 177–180.

ligious, including the exempt, need the approval of the local ordinary to preach to the faithful in his diocese.[58]

The exercise or non-exercise of the various acts of the sacred ministry connected with the administration of the sacraments and the sacramentals, cannot in itself be dependent upon the amount of monetary contribution to be derived therefrom. The prime purpose of the performance of these functions is to render spiritual aid to the faithful. In return for this aid, it must be noted that certain material subsidies are justified for the support of those who have little or no time remaining to give to the quest for their proper temporal support by other kinds of activity. The obligation of this support falls upon those who benefit from the administration of the sacred ministerial functions, the faithful.[59] What is true of the clergy in general applies also, in this case, to regulars who are asked to perform sacred functions. Just what this temporal remuneration is to be is not determined in the Code, but is left, rather, to provincial Councils, diocesan Synods and, at times, to custom.[60]

The most common of the sacred functions exercised by religious, outside their own churches, is their assistance in parochial affairs (*parochiale aliquod officium*) as adverted to in canon 463, §3, and commonly referred to as " week-end work " in parishes. Lacking legislation in general ecclesiastical law, reimbursement for the services rendered is left to particular law and custom. In most instances priests assisting a pastor in such a manner are usually assigned a regular assistant's salary plus an extra *honorarium* for any of the special services they may render, e.g. preaching an extra sermon, Masses celebrated at an unusual hour, extra confessions, etc.[61]

---

[58] Cf. McVann, *The Canon Law on Sermon Preaching*, pp. 63-66; O'Brien, *op. cit.*, pp. 129, 130.

[59] Cf. c. 23, 26, 27, C. XII, q. 2; c. 16, X, *de praebendis et dignitatibus*, III, 5. Cf. also Piontek, " Pennies Collections and other Free Will Offerings in the Code of Canon Law "—*AER*, CIX (1943), 192.

[60] Cf. canon 463, 1410, 1502, 1507.

[61] Piontek, " A Gentleman's Agreement "—*The Jurist* (Washington, D. C.: The Catholic University of America, 1941—), III (1943), 300. In many instances diocesan statutes will determine how much should be given for such services.—Piontek, *ibid.*, p. 304. Lacking diocesan or episcopal pro-

The preaching of the Catholic Faith is principally committed to the Roman Pontiff for the universal Church, and to the bishops for their own dioceses. The bishops are bound to preach the Gospel in person unless they are legitimately excused. They should also employ, besides pastors, other qualified persons to aid in an effective discharge of their preaching office.[62] Thus, the bishops, the true doctors and teachers of their flock,[63] have the fullest responsibility for instructing their subjects and under ordinary circumstances must perform this duty in person. In their respective territories they are the pastors of the flock and should see to its proper spiritual nourishment. When they cannot cope with the needs of the people they must engage others, not excluding religious.[64] Complete freedom is given to bishops in choosing and approving preachers for the faithful of the territory under their supervision.[65]

Sermon preaching as referred to above comprehends not only the parochial homilies given on Sundays and the Holy Days of Obligation but also the various other forms of preaching such as occasional and special sermons, missions, retreats, lectures to non-Catholics, apologetical conferences, etc. All these types of sermons come under the requirements of the preaching office if they be delivered to the faithful. They are also subject to the approval of the local ordinary.[66]

Of particular interest is the material consideration given to religious, in our case regulars, in return for the exercise of the office of preaching. In most instances, it is important as a source of sustenance for the religious. Nowhere in the Code is there any mention made as to the amount and type of reimbursement to be offered. Its determination must be left to the local ordinary.

---

vision retribution ought to be determined by a practical application of canon 463, §3 as mitigated by what is known as a "gentleman's agreement" referred to as natural or canonical equity—Piontek, *ibid.*, p. 284.

[62] Canon 1327.

[63] Canon 1326.

[64] McVann, *The Canon Law on Sermon Preaching*, pp. 95–98; O'Brien, *The Exemption of Religious in Church Law*, pp. 129, 130.

[65] Cf. canon 1339, §1.

[66] McVann, *op. cit.*, pp. 148, 155.

Lacking this, it is left to the prudent judgment of the pastor who seeks the services of a special preacher. Though justice requires a proper compensation for the services rendered, the remuneration takes on the nature of a donation or offering, the amount of which is dependent upon the circumstances of time and place at which the sermons are to be delivered. Diocesan regulations could well determine this amount. More often a true form of "gentleman's agreement" will be resorted to.[67]

C. *Offerings Given to Religious in Their Churches*

As was the case with the exercise of the functions of the sacred ministry, it was not the mind of the founders of religious institutes that they should have churches or parishes under their care. After the exercise of priestly functions came to be permitted, the possibility of giving parishes to the care of religious was considered and accepted as early as the fifth century. A letter of Pope Gelasius written on March 11, 494,[68] stated that religious could through a dispensation have parishes under their care.[69] An Apocryphal decree,[70] attributed to a Pope John, states that abbots (superiors) could, solely on their own authority, appoint their own priests to parishes which belong to them *pleno iure*.[71]

---

[67] For the extent and consideration of the "gentleman's agreement" cf. Piontek, "A Gentleman's Agreement"—*The Jurist,* III (1943), 284–305.

[68] C. 1, D. LV; JK, n. 636.

[69] To this letter Hostiensis (*Lectura* in lib. III, tit. *de statu monachorum et canonicorum regularium,* c. 2, n. 1) adds that it is to be understood as of poor parishes.

[70] C. 1, C. XVI, q. 2. This decree is not listed in JK.

[71] In the early Middle Ages, with the advance of feudal thought, the system of proprietary churches developed. Parishes and other churches were considered subject to the private ownership of laymen, bishops, monasteries, collegiate or cathedral chapters, etc. The exercise of proprietary rights by the owners of such churches led, very often, to serious conflicts between the hierarchy of the church and these owners. While the reforms of Pope Gregory VII (1073–1085) and his successors tended toward the suppression of private lay-ownership—a goal reached only under Pope Alexander III (1159–1181), with the conversion of such ownership into patronage, by which a patron had only the right to present a candidate for a benefice, church, etc., subject to the approval of ecclesiastical authority—they favored possession by canons and monks, but construing this possession as

With the great increase in the numbers of the faithful, which caused a lack of their proper spiritual care, it became necessary to give some parishes over to the care of religious. Some were given "*Quoad temporalia tantum*" that is, those from which the religious could gain a temporal subsistence in return for the services they rendered. These parishes were supervised by the local ordinary in regard to the spiritual administration. Other parishes were given to them "*pleno iure*" that is, those in which both the temporal and spiritual administration was cared for directly by the major superior of the religious.[72]

At the Council of Clermont in 1095, Pope Urban II,[73] speaking of parochial churches which were in the hands of the monks, forbade the placing of priests there without the consultation of the bishop on the part of the abbots and on the part of the bishops, without consultation of the abbots. Subjection of religious parishes to episcopal control was again stressed at the Council of Faenza under the same Pontiff.[74] Similarly, the III General Lateran Council (1179) under Pope Alexander III forbade the reception of churches by religious without the permission of bishops and the appointment of their priests to parishes which do not belong to them *pleno iure,* without first presenting the candidates to the bishops. Those priests who had already been appointed could not be removed without the permission of the

---

unio or *incorporatio pleno iure,* i.e., giving the entire government of the church to the monks with the exception of the *cura animarum* for which they were obliged to render an account to the bishops. Cf. Barraclough, *Papal Provisions* (Oxford: Basil Blackwell, 1935), pp. 61-65; Tellenbach, *The Church, State and Christian Society at the Time of the Investiture Contest,* transl. by R. F. Bennet, Studies in Medieval History, n. 3 (Oxford: Basil Blackwell, 1940), pp. 69-71, 113, 117-119, 122-125.

[72] Barbosa, *Iuris Ecclesiastici Universi Libri Tres;* I, c. 43, n. 122; Bouix, *Tractatus de Jure Regularium,* II, p. 16; Reiffenstuel, *Jus Canonicum Universum,* III, tit. 37, nn. 2-6.

[73] C. 6, C. XVI, q. 2; Mansi, XX, 902.

[74] C. 7, C. XVI, q. 2; Gratian's *dictum* to this chapter states that this decree of Urban II is to be understood as pertaining only to those churches which the abbots have built on their own possessions and not to those which had been given to them by the bishop.

bishops.[75] The IV General Lateran Council (1215) under Pope Innocent III accepted in full the dispositions of the III General Lateran Council on this matter.[76]

The Fathers of the Council of Trent did not deny to religious the right to possess churches but regulated it as to the exercise of the *cura animarum* as it affected persons other than those belonging to the household of the monastery. All those who exercised the *cura animarum* were subject to the immediate jurisdiction, visitation and correction of the local ordinary in regard to that *cura* and the administration of the sacraments.[77]

This subjection of regular pastors was reemphasized by Pope Pius V in his constitution "*Ad Exsequendum*" of November 1, 1567 [78] by Pope Gregory XV in the constitution "*Inscrutabili*" of February 5, 1622,[79] by Pope Benedict XIV in two constitutions, "*Ad militantis,*" of March 30, 1742 [80] and "*Firmandis*" of November 6, 1744,[81] and by Pope Leo XIII in his constitution "*Romanos Pontifices*" of May 8, 1881.[82]

In the present legislation regulars, being clerical institutes, are entitled by common ecclesiastical law to open a church [83] of a

---

[75] C. 3, X, *de privilegiis et excessibus privilegiatorum,* V, 33; Conc. Lat. III, c. 9—Mansi, XXII, 223.

[76] C. 31, X, *de praebendis et dignitatibus,* III, 5: Conc. Lat. IV, c. 61—Mansi, XXII, 1047, 1050. Cf. Hostiensis, *Lectura,* in lib. III, tit. *de praebendis et dignitatibus,* c. 31, nn. 4–10.

[77] Conc. Trident. sess. XXV, *de regularibus,* c. 11. Excepted by this same chapter were 1. the monastery of Cluny with its territories; 2. parishes of religious situated in the places where the General of head of the Order ordinarily had his principal residence; 3. other monasteries or houses in which abbots or other regular superiors exercised episcopal and temporal jurisdiction over pastors and parishioners. Cf. Bouix, *Tractatus de Jure Regularium,* II, p. 139; Schmalzgrueber, *Ius Ecclesiasticum Universum,* III, tit. 37, n. 13.

[78] *Bull. Rom. Taur.,* VII, 629, §5.

[79] *Fontes,* n. 199.

[80] *Fontes,* n. 326.

[81] *Bull. Rom. Cont.,* I, 450–457.

[82] *Fontes,* n. 582.

[83] Canon 1161.—Ecclesiae nomine intelligitur aedes sacra divino cultui dedicata eum potissimum in finem ut omnibus Christifidelibus usui sit ad divinum cultum publice exercendum.

public oratory.[84] This right is given to them in virtue of canon 497, §2 which states that the permission given by the bishop to erect a house in the case of clerical institutes implies also the faculty of opening or constructing a church or public oratory adjacent to the house. But before selecting the site where the religious intend to build, a special approval of the local ordinary must be obtained as provided by canon 1162, §4. Though canon 497, §2 refers to only the fourth paragraph of canon 1162, the requirements of the preceding two paragraphs of that canon cannot be overlooked. Reasons for the special approval of the site for a church or public oratory may be found in paragraphs two and three. Without doubt the financial provisions required by paragraph two and the spiritual welfare of the faithful emphasized in paragraph three are important factors to be considered in determining the location of any church.[85]

The right of religious to a church in the locality where they have erected a house does not in any way give them the right to have a parish connected with the monastery. Parishes,[86] because of the care of souls connected with them, come under the jurisdiction of the local ordinary. The law of the Church though requiring subjection to the local ordinary in the question of the *cura animarum,* does not deny to religious the right to the possession of parishes. This is especially clear in the Code in its treatment of religious pastors and vicars.[87] The relationship between a parish and a religious community as provided by the Code may be effected:

1. In regard only to its temporalities. Such a union or incorporation is known as *incorporatio ad temporalia tantum* or *non pleno iure.* Through such an incorporation the religious com-

---

[84] Canon 1188, §1. Oratorium est locus divino cultui destinatus, non tamen eo potissimum fine ut universo fidelium populo usui sit ad religionem publice colendam.

§2. Est vero oratorium: 1o *Publicum,* si praecipue erectum sit in commodum alicuius collegiis aut etiam privatorum, ita tamen ut omnibus fidelibus, tempore saltem divinorum officiorum, ius sit, legitime comprobatum, illud adeundi.

[85] Flanagan, *The Canonical Erection of Religious Houses,* p. 84.

[86] Cf. canon 216, §1 and 3 with canon 415, §2.

[87] Cf. canon 630, 631, 471.

munity acquires a right to the income or revenues of the parish, but not to the office of pastor. The parish remains secular. The superior of the house to which it is attached must present to the local ordinary a priest of the secular clergy to be installed as pastor, who is to be assigned a portion of the revenues for his proper sustenance.[88]

2. In regard both to its temporalities and to the care of souls. Such a union or incorporation is known as *incorporatio pleno iure.* Through such a union the religious community acquires the right to both the revenues and the office of the pastor. The parish thus becomes a religious parish. The superior may present a priest of the institute to exercise the *cura animarum,* who is to be approved and installed as vicar by the local ordinary.[89] The incorporation of parishes with religious communities either *pleno iure* or *non pleno iure* cannot be effected without the authority of the Holy See.[90]

3. Parishes may be entrusted to religious without having been canonically incorporated with the community (*simpliciter concredita*). When this takes place the parish remains secular in character. The religious pastor, and the community through the pastor, acquire a right only to the revenues assigned to the office of pastor.[91]

Offerings and donations given to the religious in their own churches belong to the religious.[92] Papi [93] proposes the question

[88] Canon 1425, §1. Cf. Chelodi, *Ius de Personis,* n. 222, c; Fanfani, *De Iure Religiosorum,* n. 446; Nebreda, "De Loci Ordinariorum Iuribus"—*CpR,* VII (1926), 117, 118; O'Brien, *The Exemption of Religious in Church Law,* p. 121; Papi, *Religious in Church Law,* ad v. "parishes" p. 220; Vermeersch-Creusen, *Epitome,* II, n. 752; Wernz-Vidal, *De Religiosis,* n. 414.

[89] Canon 1425, §2; 452; 454, §5; 457. Cf. also authors referred to in preceding note (n. 88).

[90] Canon 1423, §2, 1425, §1.

[91] O'Brien, *The Exemption of Religious in Church Law,* p. 121; Papi, *Religious in Church Law,* ad v. "parishes" p. 222; Delgado, *De Relationibus inter Parochum Religiosum et Eius Superiores Regulares cum Respectu Particulari ad Ius speciale O. F. M.* (Roman Catholic Book Agency, 1940), 30.

[92] Ferraris, *Bibliotheca,* ad v. "oblationes" nn. 25, 26; Reiffenstuel, *Ius*

as to whether by virtue of incorporation *pleno iure* the religious community acquires the right to all the income or revenues of the parish or only to the revenues which belong to the office of pastor. Arguing from the canons treating of the investment of money given to a religious parish as dependent upon the disposition of the local ordinary (canon 533, §1, n. 4) and of the necessity of rendering an account of the administration of this source of income to the local ordinary (canon 535, §1, n. 2), Papi further states that the Code "has framed its canons in keeping with the view that by virtue of this union the right of the religious community does not extend to all the revenues of the parish." This is true in cases where there is no doubt that the offerings or donations have been given to the parish. Should the intention of the donor be doubtful, Turner [94] points out that a distinction must be made. Religious pastors in the question of doubt as to the purpose of offerings and donations can be considered as acting either in their official capacity as pastors or in their non-official capacity, as religious. Religious in their official capacity as pastors must be guided by the norm set in canon 1536, §1 stating that unless the contrary be proven it must be presumed that whatever is given to rectors of churches, including religious, is given to the church.[95] Thus, if a donation is given to a religious who is pastor, it is given to the church unless it appears that the gift was meant as a personal donation. If it was a personal donation the further problem arises as to whether it belongs to the community or to the personal capital of the religious. This problem is to be solved according to the principles of moral theology attending to the circumstances of the donation and the principles given in canon 580 §§1 and 2 concerning the ownership of tem-

Canonicum Universum, III, tit. 30, n. 195; Rodericus, *Quaestiones,* III, q. 20, art. 1.

[93] *Op. cit.,* p. 221.

[94] *The Vow of Poverty,* pp. 155, 156.

[95] Canon 1536.—§1. Nisi contrarium probetur, praesumendum est quae donantur rectoribus ecclesiarum, etiam religiosorum, esse ecclesiae donata.— It is evident that this canon is drawn up in the light of Pope Leo XIII's constitution "*Romanos Pontifices*" of May 8, 1881 (*Fontes,* n. 582) as interpreted by the *Tribunale Supremum Apostolicae Signaturae (AAS,* XII [1920] 258, 259).

poral goods by religious of simple vows and the earnings from the industry of religious. For religious of solemn vows the requirements of canon 582 must also be considered.[96]

ARTICLE 4. TESTAMENTARY ACQUISITION

Throughout the history of ecclesiastical law [97] there was never any doubt that religious orders, considered as moral persons, could receive temporal goods through donations "*inter vivos*" [98] or "*mortis causa.*" [99] This is made clear from early authors who give preference to religious in reference to dispositions of testaments made to the poor in general.[100]

The privilege of receiving subsidies through testamentary acts is not denied to religious by the Code. Canon 1513, §1 ordains that anyone not disqualified by natural or ecclesiastical law may make a bequest of his temporal goods to any pious cause either by an act "*inter vivos*" or "*mortis causa.*" In the consideration of the text of this canon the word "*actum*"—act—should be interpreted in the sense that it applies not only to the term "*inter vivos*" but also to the term "*mortis causa.*" In turn, the term "*actus mortis causa*" indicates a wider scope than the "*donatio mortis causa.*" It includes all testamentary dispositions, the most general form of which is the testament itself.[101] Thus canon

---

[96] Beste, *Introductio in Codicem,* p. 749; Pejška, *Ius Canonicum Religiosorum,* p. 66; Sipos, *Enchiridion Iuris Canonici,* p. 834.

[97] Under secular law the interests of beneficiaries may often be defeated either directly or indirectly. Concerning these direct and indirect disabilities depriving religious or charitable institutes of bequests to them, cf. Hannan, *The Canon Law of Wills,* pp. 320–386.

[98] That is the disposition of temporal goods made during the life of the donor and having effect prior to the donor's death.—Vermeersch-Creusen, *Epitome,* II, n. 834; Vromant, *De Bonis Ecclesiae Temporalibus,* n. 184.

[99] The technical "*donatio mortis causa*" may be defined as "a voluntary, revocable, executed transfer, intended as a gift, of a future interest, vesting at death, in any kind of property to any amount, accompanied by delivery and acceptance, made by one who possesses testamentary capacity."—Hannan, *The Canon Law of Wills,* n. 53.

[100] Ferraris, *Bibliotheca,* ad c. "legatarius" n. 50; Reiffenstuel, *Jus Canonicum Universum,* III, tit. 26, n. 815; St. Thomas, II:II, q. 32, art. 9.

[101] A testament may be defined as "a lawful and voluntary solemn juridical act, essentially revocable, valid without the acceptance of the beneficiary,

1513, §1 asserts the testamentary capacity of those making the testament and of the beneficiaries.[102] The canon is not limited to an act by which capacity is given to the donor to make a gift but also to an act by which a pious cause is made capable of receiving such a gift. For our purpose, it cannot be denied that among the various pious causes [103] a prominent place is held by religious orders and their houses. Being pious causes, religious institutes, provinces and houses, did and could benefit from testamentary acts.[104]

Temporal goods, unless given for a specific purpose, coming to regulars in accord with the provision of canon 1513, §1 are to be received and incorporated immediately into the common fund of the monastery, if the monastery is capable of possessing common goods.[105] As to those monasteries and convents incapable of common ownership, as the Friars Minor and the Capuchins, it must be noted in general that they are not entirely incapable of receiving bequests. They cannot accept legacies that transfer perpetual ownership or possession to the Friars, but they can receive those which come to them as pure and simple alms, even though they be considered as annual income, such as, for example, offering for the annual sacrifice of the Mass for the donor. In pre-Code law this was substantiated by decisions of the Sacred Congregation of Bishops and Regulars and was considered the common opinion of authors as recorded by Ferraris.[106]

---

by which a person enjoying due competence provides for what he wills to be done after his death with his estate, in whole or in part, determined fractionally or specifically."—Hannan, *op. cit.*, n. 67; cf. also nn. 58–60.

[102] Hannan, *op. cit.*, n. 173.

[103] "Causae piae sunt omnia opera quae finem religionis vel caritatis habent, et motivo supernaturali suscipiuntur, praesertim in favorem eorum qui tali auxilio indigent."—Vermeersch-Creusen, *Epitome*, III (Romae: H. Dessian, 1923), 548. Cf. Vromant, *De Bonis Ecclesiae Temporalibus*, n. 146.

[104] O'Brien, *The Exemption of Religious in Church Law*, p. 243; Pejška, *Ius Canonicum Religiosorum*, pp. 63, 64.

[105] Cf. can. 582. Also Ferraris, *Bibliotheca*, ad v. "legatarius" nn. 88–94; Fagnanus, *Commentaria*, in lib. III, tit. *de statu monachorum*, c. *monachi*, nn. 44–48; Rodericus, *Quaestiones*, II, q. 26, art. 6.

[106] *Bibliotheca*, ad v. "legatarius" nn. 95–118.

The Sacred Congregation of Bishops and Regulars on two occasions (September 2, 1870 and June 20, 1868) stated that the Friars Minor and the Capuchins were incapable of possessing legacies by way of perpetual conveyence, i.e. as if they were due them *in perpetuum* by civil enforcement of testamentary provisions. Neither can they accept the principal but only the annual income from interest or dividends. In addition such bequests could only be received as simple and pure alms, as a stipend for the celebration of Mass, with the solemn protestation that thereby they did not intend to acquire any right to the temporal goods in virtue of the legacy.[107] Rodericus argued that the capablity of the Friars to acquire such legacies was based upon the fact that a bequest which conferred an annual income to the Friars should not be considered as a single legacy but as a multiple legacy. Just as one can bequeath something for one year he can also do so for each succeeding year and thus provide for an annual bequest. It would certainly seem severe, continues Rodericus, to deny the testator the privilege of providing annually for the Friars after his death, when he could do so while living, giving them alms annually. Any benefactor as long as he lives can give alms annually if he so wishes. He can also oblige his heirs that after his death the heirs should, out of the goods left, give alms to the Friars for their necessities.[108]

---

[107] S. C. Ep. et Reg., *Romana se Minorum Observantium,* 2 sept. 1870—*Fontes,* n. 1999; *Minorum Capuccinorum,* 20 iun. 1868—*Fontes,* n. 1813; Fagnanus, *Commentaria,* in lib. V, tit. *de excessibus praelatorum,* c. *nimis parva,* nn. 47, 51.—The Constitutions of the Friars Minor (nn. 308–310) permit the acceptance of legacies as pure alms with the protestation by the competent superior that the Friars acquire no right to the alms nor do they obligate themselves strictly to the fulfillment of the requirements of the legacy. They could, if the heir or executor did not wish to give them alms due them from the legacy, appeal to them to consult their conscience for this would not be exacting a debt but rather seeking an alms, but they could not demand from them these annual offerings before any judge whatsoever.—Cf. Ilg, *An Explanation of the Rule of the Friars Minor* (2. ed., 1940), pp. 116, 117; Kazenberger, *The Book of Life,* transl. by a Father of the Province of the Most Holy Name (n. p., 1905), p. 174.

[108] Rodericus, *Quaestiones,* II, q. 127, art. 1; Kazenberger, *The Book of Life,* p. 174.

ARTICLE 5. ACQUISITION BY PRESCRIPTION

Prescription may be defined as a mode of acquiring a title to property by means of its continued and uninterrupted possession as established by positive law.[109] The right to acquisition by prescription is proper to all, moral and private persons, providing the requirements of positive law, civil and ecclesiastical, are fulfilled.[110] Consequently religious houses, mainly on the strength of their moral personality, granted them at the time of their canonical erection,[111] may acquire and be safeguarded by the laws of prescription. This right is expressly acknowledged in the Code. Canon 1508 declares prescription, as a mode of acquiring possessions or freeing oneself from certain obligations, to be regulated according to the norms set down in civil law of the respective nations, provided they do not conflict with exceptions and limitations made in Canon Law.[112]

On the strength of canon 1508 the particular points of prescription that are not considered in the Code must be determined from the requirements and conditions of civil legislation in the territory in which the application of prescriptive rights is intended.[113] Without doubt this provision refers to those temporal goods which of their nature or because of the purpose which they serve, are of a profane character. Regarding those that, because of their nature, are considered sacred [114] the Code has placed exceptions either by excluding them totally from the operation of prescription (those enumerated in canon 1509), or by limiting their acquisition to certain persons or for stated purposes (canon 1510). For goods that are properly ecclesiastical canon 1512 re-

---

109 Fanfani, *De Iure Religiosorum,* n. 333, 40; Prümmer, *Manuale Iuris Canonici,* q. 447, resp. 1; Vromant, *De Bonis Ecclesiae Temporalibus,* n. 115.

110 Chelodi, *Ius de Personis,* n. 83.

111 Cf. *supra,* pp. 8–9.

112 Canon 1508.—Praescriptionem, tanquam acquirendi et se liberandi modum, prout est in legislatione civili respectivae nationis, Ecclesia pro bonis ecclesiasticis recipit, salvo praescripto canonum qui sequuntur.

113 Beste, *Introductio in Codicem,* p. 730; Pejška, *Ius Canonicum Religiosorum,* p. 67; Sipos, *Enchiridion Iuris Canonici,* p. 816; Vroment, *De Bonis Ecclesiae Temporalibus,* n. 118.

114 Canon 1497. 2. Dicuntur *sacra,* quae consecratione vel benedictione ad divinum cultum destinata sunt; . . .

quires that good faith (*bona fides*) be had not only at the time of the beginning of the possession of the goods to be prescribed, but throughout the entire time required for their prescription.[115]

The time limit for the prescription of immovable goods, precious movables and real and personal actions is supplemented by canon 1511. For goods pertaining to the Holy See a space of 100 years is required and for goods belonging to other moral ecclesiastical persons a period of 30 years. The time limit for prescription of immovable goods or precious movables not belonging to the Holy See or to a moral ecclesiastical person, and other movable goods, is to be determined by the requirements of civil law.[116] Before the Code some religious orders enjoyed special privileges regarding the time limit for prescription of goods pertaining to the institute. Thus, for example, goods of the Benedictines could not be prescribed until after a period of 60 years. Goods of some mendicants and Cistercians could not be prescribed until after a space of 100 years. These privileges, not expressly revoked in canon 1511, remain in force in accord with canon 4.[117]

---

[115] Beste, *op. cit.*, p. 731; Vromant, *op. cit.*, n. 139. "A civil regulation derogating from this canon (1511) will have no binding force in the forum of conscience, but will have to be followed in the external forum before the court."—Heston, *The Alienation of Church Property in the United States*, The Catholic University of America Canon Law Studies, n. 132 (Washington, D. C.: The Catholic University of America Press, 1941), p. 139. (Hereafter this work will be referred to as *Alienation of Church Property.*)

[116] Beste, *op. cit.*, p. 731; Prümmer, *Manuale Iuris Canonici*, q. 447, resp. 2, c; Vromant, *op. cit.*, n. 134, 2.

[117] Capello, "De Praescriptione"—*Jus Pontificium*, IV (1924), 23, 24; Vromant, *De Bonis Ecclesiae Temporalibus*, n. 134, 4; Prümmer (op. cit., q. 447, resp. 2, c.) without qualification states that goods pertaining to mendicants cannot be prescribed until after a period of 60 years. Cf. also Vermeersch-Creusen, *Epitome*, II, n. 831.

PART THREE

ADMINISTRATION OF TEMPORAL GOODS BY REGULARS

CHAPTER VI

THE RIGHT TO OWN PROPERTY

ARTICLE 1. PRE-CODE AFFIRMATION OF THE RIGHT

A. From the Earliest Times to the XIII Century

THE right and means of acquisition and possession of temporal goods by the earliest religious institutes is not too clear in early Church law.[1] The earliest legislation is not definite. The rule of religious life of St. Benedict (480–543) which portrayed vestiges of the life of the earliest eastern monks as St. Anthony (251–356), St. Pachomius (292–346) and St. Basil the Great (329–379), and which was introduced and adopted as a norm of monastic life throughout the Western World, presupposed the possession of property by religious.[2] At the time of the *Decretum Gratiani* (c. 1140) the right of religious to acquire and possess temporal goods was an acknowledged fact. The *decreta* handed down by Gratian and the later decretals concerned themselves chiefly with secondary questions of ownership, special and individual instances which needed some particular interpretation or clarification.[3]

---

[1] For the extent of the affirmation of this right to own property by religious in Roman Law and later civil law cf. McManus, *The Administration of Temporal Goods in Religious Institutes,* pp. 10–13, 17-19, 25–33.

[2] McManus, *op. cit.,* p. 15; Turner, *The Vow of Poverty,* pp. 14–18; Schäfer, *De Religiosis,* n. 10; Wernz, *Ius Decretalium,* III, nn. 603, 604.

[3] Goodwine, *The Right of the Church to Acquire Temporal Goods,* The Catholic University of America Canon Law Studies, n. 131 (Washington, D. C.: The Catholic University of America Press, 1941), pp. 68-70.

In the *Decretum* we find a number of decrees of Pope Gregory I (590–604) establishing the right of religious to ownership of property. Because of their state in life they were acknowledged the right to certain property from which their temporal needs would be satisfied. Thus in a letter to the subdeacon Gratiosus, written in January, 593, the Pope declared it necessary to provide with considerable care for those who select for themselves the religious life. Describing in detail the property in question, the Pontiff commanded the subdeacon to give full right to it to the Abbess Flora so that she, together with her congregation and her successors, could possess it with a definite and stable right.[4] In another letter, written in September, 595, he exhorted the Bishop of Ravenna to confirm the donations that a certain John, his predecessor, had ordered to be given to the monastery near the Church of St. Apollinaris.[5] Then in April (598), writing to all the bishops, he prohibited them from presuming any right to the income, possessions or privileges of the monasteries. Nor could they in any way or on any occasion diminish, defraud, dispossess or commit any acts of violence upon the cells and small farms which pertained to the monasteries.[6] Then again in August, 598, to John, the Bishop of Squillace (Scyllaceno), he wrote that neither the laws of the world nor the statutes of the sacred canons permit under any title the taking of things that by right belong to the monasteries.[7]

Conciliar legislation noted in the *Decretum* also recognized this right. A decree, believed to have emanated from the Council of Mainz (796), made it unlawful for a bishop to take away any of the possessions of a monastery on the pretext of the misconduct of the abbot.[8] The fourth canon of the Second Council of Nicaea, known also as the *Synodus Septima,* held in 787, forbade the bishops, under any circumstances whatever, to demand anything

---

[4] C. 75, C. XII, q. 2; JE, n. 1221.

[5] C. 3, C. XII, q. 5; JE, n. 1380.

[6] C. 5, C. XVIII, q. 2; JE, n. 1504.

[7] C. 41, C. XVII, q. 4; JE, n. 1521.

[8] C. 7, C. XVI, q. 6. Friedberg (*Corpus Iuris Canonici,* editio Lipsiensis II [Richter-Friedberg] 2 vols., Lipsiae, 1879–1881, ed. anastatice repetita, 1928) n. 74, ad *h. c.* asserts this to be an uncertain chapter.

from other bishops, clerics or monks subject to their jurisdiction.[9] A decision of the Council of Altheim, held in the presence of the Emperor Conrad in 916, considered the case where an abbot was elected to the episcopacy. After becoming a bishop he inherited a large patrimony. Upon his death the monks requesting that patrimony were told by the Council that they had a right only to those possessions which had been given the abbot previous to his consecration.[10]

On November 16, 1198, Pope Innocent III, in a letter to the Archbishop and Chapter of Lyons, wrote that constitutions which had been observed for a long time and which an approved custom sanctioned should not be overruled. With this in mind he ordered that the possessions given to the cloistered and other religious places in accordance with a custom, without, however, the legally required solemnities, be considered as validly given with full right of ownership.[11] This same Pontiff on November 27, 1199, answering an appeal of the abbot and convent of St. Sylvester concerning possessions which had been taken from them, without citation, confession or conviction, by the Prefect of Rome and given to the Church of St. Mary, condemned the procedure and ordered the possessions to be restored to the monastery.[12]

B. *From the Thirteenth Century to the Code*

The thirteenth century witnessed a revival of religious zeal and a new concept of the religious vow of poverty. As Christianity progressed, the Church and religious orders, due to the generosity of the faithful, acquired wealth. With this wealth came also prestige and with prestige a relaxation of religious zeal and discipline. This gave rise to numerous attempts at reform, both orthodox and heretical, particularly in regard to the ideal of poverty.[13] Among the orthodox reformers, the most popular and

---

[9] C. 64, C. XVI, q. 1; Schroeder, *Disciplinary Decrees,* p. 146; Mansi, XIII, 749.

[10] C. 1, C. XVIII, q. 1; Mansi, XVIII A, 332.

[11] C. 2, X, *de consuetudine,* I, 4; Potthast, n. 424.

[12] C. 10, X, *de constitutionibus,* I, 2; Potthast, n. 879. Cf. Hostiensis, *Lectura* in lib. I tit. *de constitutionibus,* c. 10.

[13] McManus, *The Administration of Temporal Goods in Religious Insti-*

later the most influential were the mendicants, who chose to rely for their sustenance upon the uncertain income derived from mendicancy, and the liberality of the faithful.[14]

The eleventh and twelfth centuries had already witnessed many attempts at reform, so numerous that the IV Lateran Council (1215) in its thirteenth canon was led to forbid the founding of new religious orders and to command those wishing to enter religious life to choose an order already approved.[15] Despite this prohibition, it seems that new mendicant orders were founded whose manners and customs merited a condemnation at the II Council of Lyons (1274). In its twenty-third canon, this Council prohibited and abolished all orders, including mendicant, founded after the IV Lateran Council and lacking the approval of the Apostolic See.[16] "Those founded after that Council and confirmed by the Apostolic See, who by virtue of their profession, rule, or constitutions are dependent for their livelihood on the alms of the public, we decree that they observe the following rule: Those who have already made profession in them may remain in them if they wish, but these orders may not henceforth receive any more to profession, nor may they acquire new houses or other places, or dispose of houses or places that they have without special permission of the Apostolic See. These things we reserve to the disposition of the same See, . . . Any violation of these provisions invalidates the acts so performed, and those guilty shall incur excommunication. . . . The present constitution, however, we do not wish to be extended to the Order of Preachers and Friars Minor, whose eminent usefulness to the universal Church is apparent. The Order of Carmel and the Hermits of St. Augustine whose foundations antedate the aforesaid council, we permit to continue *in suo statu* till we ordain otherwise." [17]

---

tutes, p. 19; Meyer, *Almsgathering by Religious*, pp. 19-26; Turner, *The Vow of Poverty*, p. 23.

[14] Cf. Glossa in c. un. *de excessibus praelatorum et subditorum* V, in VI° ad. v. *mendicantes;* c. un. *de religiosis domibus*, III, 17 in VI°.

[15] Mansi, XXII, 1002, 1003.

[16] Pope Boniface VIII inserted this decree into the *Liber Sextus*, c. un., *de religiosis domibus*, III, 17 in VI°; Mansi, XXIV, 96, 97.

[17] Transl. according to Schroeder, *Disciplinary Decrees*, p. 351. In his

Of the mendicant orders, the Order of Friars Minor was particularly singled out by the Decretal *Collectors*.[18] The Order of Friars Minor is to be considered mendicant by the disposition of its rule. St. Francis set as his ideal of poverty the total renunciation of all earthly things according to the spirit of the Holy Gospel. This he emphasized in his rules.[19] The Rule of Life of the Friars Minor was formally approved by Pope Honorius III in 1223. Inculcating absolute poverty, it made special provisions for obtaining the necessities of life for the friars.[20] In the fifth chapter it enjoins " Those friars to whom the Lord has given the

---

comment on this canon, Schroeder (*op. cit.*, p. 352) states that "Pope Gregory (X) died before he could carry out his intention in regard to them (The Order of Carmel and Hermits of St. Augustine). Boniface VIII showed them special favor, so much so that when he inserted this decree in the *Liber Sextus,* he replaced the passage, *in suo statu manere concedimus, donec de ipsis fuerit aliter ordinatum,* by the words, *in solido statu volumus permanere.* A marginal annotator (glossa ad v. *in solido*) tells us that it was the intention of Gregory to abolish all mendicant orders except the Dominicans and Franciscans, and of the non-mendicant orders to retain only three, namely the Cistercians, Benedictines and the Templars and Hospitallers, which two he intended to unite."

[18] Inasmuch as the rule of the Order of Friars Minor was given special attention in the *Corpus Iuris Canonici* (cf. c. 3, *de verborum significatione,* V, 12 in VI°; c. 1, *de verborum significatione,* V, 11 in Clem.; C. 1, 2, 3, *de verborum significatione,* 14, in Extravag. Joan. XXII) emphasis is here placed upon that Order in determining the position of the mendicants in relation to the possession of temporal goods.

[19] Some authors claim that St. Francis compiled three distinct rules. The first was approved *viva voce* by Pope Innocent III in 1209; the second, perfected in 1221, was not approved; the third was approved by Pope Honorius III by the Bull "*Solet annuere*" issued on November 29, 1223.—Cf. Holzapfel, Heribert, O.F.M., *Manuale Historiae Ordinis Fratrum Minorum,* latine redditum a G. Haselbeck (Friburgi Brisgoviae: B. Herder Book Co., 1909) pp. 16–18. A difficulty arises in regard to the what some authors consider the second rule, written in 1221. Fr. Paschal Robinson calls this a misconception, " for the rule which they describe as dating from 1221 is not a new one, but the same that Innocent III approved (1209), not indeed in its original form which has not come down to us, but rather, in the form it had assumed in the course of twelve years, as a consequence of many changes and additions."—Robinson, *The Writings of St. Francis of Assisi* (Philadelphia, The Dolphin Press, 1906), p. 26.

[20] Robinson, *op. cit.*, pp. 64–74.

grace of working should labor faithfully and devoutly so that in banishing idleness, the enemy of the soul, they do not extinguish the spirit of holy prayer and devotion, to which all temporal things should be subservient. But for the recompense of their labor, they may receive for themselves and their friars the necessaries of the body, except coins or money; and this humbly, as becometh the servants of God and the followers of most holy Poverty." [21] If this did not suffice, in the sixth chapter the friars are reminded to "appropriate nothing to themselves neither a house nor a place nor anything. And as pilgrims and strangers in this world, serving the Lord in poverty and humility, let them go confidently for alms; nor should they be ashamed, because the Lord made Himself poor for us in this world." [22] This same idea is further emphasized in his Testament where we read: "And I labored with my hands [and] I wish to labor and I wish firmly that all the other friars labor in work that pertains to honesty. And those who do not know how, should learn, not with the desire of receiving the price of labor but for the sake of good example and to repel idleness. And when the price of labor is not given us, let us have recourse to the table of the Lord, begging alms from door to door." [23]

Because the question of the Franciscan idea of poverty as handed down by St. Francis was a constant issue for disputation, Pope Nicholas III, upon the petition of the Minister General of the Friars Minor, issued a Bull "*Exiit qui seminat*" on August 14, 1279, in which he attempted to solve the misunderstandings relative to the interpretations of poverty.[24] In effect the bull provided that, though renunciation of common property is meritorious, it does not include the renunciation of the simple use of things in accordance with the rule, for there can be no profession which could renounce the use of things necessary for sustenance. Everything that had and would be given to the friars was held to be given in ownership to the Holy See unless the donor reserved the ownership to himself. The friars were held entitled

---

[21] Transl. from Ilg, *An Explanation of the Rule of the Friars Minor*, p. 8.

[22] Transl. from Ilg, *op. cit.*, p. 9.

[23] Transl. from Ilg, *op. cit.*, p. 15.

[24] C. 3, *de verborum significatione*, V, 12 in VI°; *BF*, III, n. 127.

to provide even for future necessities, however not too far distant in the future. For the reception of monetary donations it was held not contrary to the rule of the friars to permit them to use *spiritual friends* who would receive such gifts from the benefactors and dispose of them to meet the necessities of the friars. The ownership of this money was to rest always with the benefactors until its conversion for the designated things. The use of things should be in accord with poverty and they should be disposed of by the superiors and *custodes* for the needs of the persons and places as circumstances of persons, time and place required. The reception of legacies was ruled as not permitted if they are centered upon things that are by rule forbidden to the friars, e.g., large estates. However if these were devised to the friars in such a manner that they could be sold by another person and the money received be devoted to the necessities of the friars, they were then to be considered as alms for the friars. The exchange of movable property was permitted to the Ministers by delegation of the Apostolic See. Sales however were to be made through *Procurators* chosen by the Holy See or the Cardinal Protector.

This constitution of Nicholas III did not attain its desired end. Despite the Pope's prohibition of the making of glosses or interpretations to this constitution, controversies continued, causing dissensions in the ranks of the Order. This was brought to the attention of the Council of Vienne. On May 6, 1312, Pope Clement V issued the constitution "*Exivi de paradiso*" [25] which was not intended as a declaration for the discipline of the Order as had been the Bull of Pope Nicholas III, "*Exiit qui seminat.*" It was rather a reassertion of the provisions of its predecessors, with an attempt at the explanation of the doubtful points that had been raised or might be raised in the future.

Total renunciation of property was retained. Inheritance, because it implied ownership of property and by nature extended to money and movable and immovable things, was forbidden. The same prohibition applied to annual revenues, which by law are considered immovable. The Churches and the other buildings of the Friars were not to be excessively large and costly for such

[25] C. 1, *de verborum significatione,* V, 11 in Clem.; *BF,* V, n. 195.

partake of the nature of treasure and abundance and are manifestly inconsistent with the rule and profession of the Friars Minor. The Friars should be especially detached from money and completely cut off from the use of it and while for reasons expressed in the rule (e.g., the care of the sick, the purchase of clothing, etc.) they might make appeals for money to meet their urgent needs, they should conduct themselves as possessing nothing. Granaries and cellars (*cellaria*) were forbidden them. However, it was held lawful for them to have suitable gardens and fields for recollection, recreation and the cultivation of vegetables necessary for themselves, but it was indicated to be contrary to their rule to dispose of such products for monetary considerations. The Friars were forbidden in any way, by any method, to seek to obtain for themselves the goods of those entering the Order, or to act as advisers in regard to their distribution, but it was regarded as permissible for the brethren, considering their necessities, to receive it by way of alms. Finally, a strict *usus pauper* of things was ordered wherever it was thus required by the rule and a *moderatus usus* in other things.

On October 7, 1317, Pope John XXII, by the constitution "*Quorundam exigit,*"[26] ordained that only superiors and the *custodes* with the counsel and consent of the guardians and two discreet priests of the convent, can decide as to the necessity of granaries and cellars for the Friars.

In the year 1317 a controversy arose between the Franciscans and the Dominicans on the question of poverty. The controversy was concerned with the question of whether Christ and the Apostles possessed anything either in common or privately. To permit a more liberal discussion, Pope John XXII, by the constitution "*Quia nonnunquam*" of March 26, 1322,[27] removed the penalties imposed by the Bull "*Exiit qui seminat*" upon those who would attempt to make glosses to the rule of the Friars Minor. The Friars Minor, in defense of their position of using temporal goods without their ownership either in common or privately,

[26] C. 1, *de verborum significatione,* 14, in Extravag. Joan. XXII; *BF,* V, n. 289.

[27] C. 2, *de verborum significatione,* 14, in Extravag. Joan. XXII; *BF,* V, n. 464.

at the General Chapter held in 1322, declared it to be sound and Catholic doctrine to believe that Christ and the Apostles possessed nothing. They substantiated this declaration by the decree "*Exiit qui seminat*" of Pope Nicholas III and appealed to the Supreme Pontiff for a decision. A decision was given on December 8, 1322, by the constitution "*Ad conditorem*,"[28] in which Pope John XXII completely reversed ecclesiastical legislation and policy on the obligations of the vow of poverty in the Order of Friars Minor. Ownership of property was no longer vested in the Holy See but in the individual order. This however, in the opinion of the glossator, seemed to have reference only to the possessions which came to the Friars after this constitution.[29]

Not content, the Friars in another appeal to the Pope in 1323, trying to establish juridically their position, insisted that the Pope accept their views and not be deluded by the enemies of the Order. In response, the constitution "*Cum inter nonnullos*" of November 12, 1323,[30] declared as erroneous and heretical the opinion that Christ and the Apostles had no possessions either privately or in common or that they had the simple use of things with no ownership.[31]

A hundred years later, Pope Martin V, in his constitution "*Amabiles fructus*" published on November 1, 1428,[32] revoked the constitution "*Ad conditorem*" by permitting the Friars Minor *de observantia* absolute renunciation of common ownership of temporal possessions.

Following the foundation of the mendicant orders the right of ownership of property by religious was upheld by Pope Gregory IX (1227–1241) in a letter to all the Prelates of the Church, providing for the eradication of some fifteen abuses in the Church. Among other things all are warned not to be se-

[28] C. 3, *de verborum significatione*, 14 in Extravag. Joan. XXII; *BF*, V, n. 486.

[29] Cf. glossa ad v. *posterum*.

[30] C. 4, *de verborum significatione*, 14 in Extravag. Joan. XXII; *BF*, V, p. 256.

[31] For further discussion of the controversy cf. notes in *BF*, V, pp. 224–225; 233–246; 256–258; 271–280; Holzapfel, *Manuale Historiae Ordinis Fratrum Minorum*, pp. 60–64.

[32] *BF*, VII, n. 1838.

duced by blind avarice for the things that the faithful piously give to the religious. They should in particular avoid taxing things according to their own will and cease forcing the religious to give them what they pretend to call offerings.[33] Then taking into consideration the mendicants [34] who serve Christ in the strictest poverty, he enumerates some twelve abuses to be avoided. Regarding temporal goods prelates are forbidden to require from the religious a share of the fruits of their gardens and dwelling places on the plea that if they did not live there others would give provisions, pay tithes, etc.

In like manner Pope Clement V, at the General Council of Vienne, provided against some thirty abuses which had been used by prelates against the religious. In regard to the property under the care of the religious, he declaimed against their illicit occupation, interdiction and destruction; against the sending of relatives and descendants with their shepherds and domestic animals demanding free maintenance of them from the goods of the monasteries; against compelling abbots and priors to give the prelate's relatives and descendants pensions from monastic goods; and against permitting and tacitly consenting to the violent occupation of monastic possessions by their vassals and other temporal officials. All prelates are ordered to cease all their and their subjects' unjust aspirations and observe inviolably the rights and privileges of the religious, exempt and non-exempt, mendicant and non-mendicant.[35]

The Tridentine Fathers, deeply concerned with the reform of regulars, desired common possession of immovable goods by all religious with the sole exception of two branches of the Franciscan Order, the Capuchins and Friars Minor.

> The Holy Council grants that all monasteries and houses, of men as well as of women, and of mendicants, even those that were forbidden by their constitutions or that had not received permission to this effect by Apostolic privilege, with the exception of the houses of the

[33] C. 16, X, *de excessibus praelatorum,* V, 31; Potthast, n. 8786 a.

[34] C. 17, X, *de excessibus praelatorum,* V, 31.

[35] C. 1, *de excessibus praelatorum,* V, 6 in Clem.; Schroeder, *Disciplinary Decrees,* pp. 431–434.

> brethren of St. Francis, the Capuchins and those called Minor Observants, may in the future possess immovable property.[36]

The legislation of the Council of Trent, though upheld in later ecclesiastical law, suffered at the hands of the civil law. Efforts to strip the Church and religious institutes of every right and privilege to ownership and possession of temporal goods initiated by the laws of Parma, Piacenza and Portugal met with the vigorous resistance of Pope Clement XIII in his constitution "*Alias ad Apostolatus*" of January 30, 1768.[37] In the nineteenth century Pope Pius IX strongly protested the suppression of religious institutes in Sardinia [38] and South America [39] in order that the government might seize their property.[40]

ARTICLE 2. THE CODE AND THE RIGHT OF POSSESSION BY RELIGIOUS

The right of acquisition and possession of temporal goods by religious houses is asserted in canon 531. The canon declares that not only the religious institute but also the province and house are capable of acquiring and possessing property with fixed or founded incomes. It also recognizes the possibility of total exclusion or limitation of this right by the particular rules and constitutions of the institute.[41]

This declaration, pertinent to religious institutes, is an application of the principles laid down in canon 1495 vindicating in paragraph 1 the natural, innate right of the Catholic Church and

---

[36] Conc. Trident., sess. XXV, *de regularibus*, c. 3; transl. from Schroeder, *Canons and Decrees of the Council of Trent*, p. 219.

[37] *Fontes*, n. 464.

[38] Cf. *Alloc.* "*Probe memineritis,*" 22 ian. 1855—*Fontes*, n. 519; alloc. "*Cum saepe,*" 26 iul. 1855—*Fontes*, n. 520.

[39] Cf. Encycl. "*Incredibile,*" 17 sept. 1863—*Fontes*, n. 537; alloc. "*Acerbissimum,*" 22, sept. 1852—*Fontes*, n. 515. Cf. also encycl. "*Quanta cura,*" 8 dec. 1864—*Fontes*, n. 542 and *Syllabus Errorum*—*Fontes*, n. 543.

[40] Cf. McManus, *Administration in Religious Institutes*, pp. 29–33.

[41] Canon 531.—Non modo religio, sed etiam provincia et domus sunt capaces acquirendi et possidendi bona temporalia cum redditibus stabilibus seu fundatis, nisi earum capacitas in regulis et constitutionibus excludatur aut coarctetur.

the Apostolic See to a free and independent ownership of temporal goods, and in paragraph 2, the right of ecclesiastical authority to bestow possession and administration of property upon its churches and moral entities which it had vested with moral juridic personality.[42] The right of acquisition and possession, it must be noted, is an attribute of moral juridic personality. Though it is one of the important rights of a moral person, it is not its prime determinant.[43] Thus the principal factor that contributes the right of acquisition and possession of property to a religious institute, province or house, is their moral personality.[44] This comes to the religious either by prescript of law or by special grant of a competent ecclesiastical superior given in a formal decree.[45] For houses of regulars, with which this study is concerned, moral personality is a consequence of their canonical erection at which moment they become entitled to ownership and acquisition of

[42] Canon 90. Cf. also Goodwine, *The Right of the Church to Acquire Temporal Goods,* pp. 1–5; Beste, *Introductio in Codicem,* p. 350; McManus, *The Administration of Temporal Goods in Religious Institutes,* p. 35; Papi, *The Government of Religious Communities* (New York: P. J. Kenedy and Sons, 1919), p. 160.

[43] Hence Coronata (*Institutiones,* I, n. 558) asserts that they draw a false conclusion, who on the basis of canon 531 deny moral personality to those religious institutes which do not have the right to the acquisition and possession of property.

[44] Moral juridic personality granted to religious houses in ecclesiastical law does not in itself possess the same status in civil law. In the United States religious houses as such are not recognized as ecclesiastical corporations, though they are acknoweldged as private civil corporations subject to the laws of the particular States. Zollman (*American Church Law,* [St. Paul: West Publishing Co., 1933], p. 132) writes that as corporations they "have no higher status than other societies organized by our citizens. They are created for the purpose of managing church property, and are endowed with substantially the same liabilities, and governed by substantially the same rules, as are other private corporations. They are on an equality with natural persons so far as real estate and trusts are concerned." Therefore "it is important," continues Augustine (*Religious and Laymen,* p. 174), "that religious communities, at least those which, according to ecclesiastical law, are capable of holding property, should be *chartered,* because the charter grants them legal existence, fixes their right of making by-laws, and, in a word, endows them with an official character, which the courts must acknowledge." Cf. Beste, *Introductio in Codicem,* p. 351.

[45] Canon 100, §1.

property. The religious house of regulars becomes a moral person by prescript of law. Once the "*beneplacitum*" of the Holy See to establish a religious house is obtained no formal decree of erection is required. The acknowledgment on the part of the competent religious superior that the house is a part of the religious institute is sufficient.[46]

Such is the legislation of common ecclesiastical law relative to property, apart from any particular law of the institute. The Code in canon 531 takes cognizance of the possibility of some religious institutes excluding or limiting ownership, for it adds "unless their capacity [to acquire and possess] is forbidden or restricted by their rules and constitutions."[47] Total exclusion of the right is proper to the Friars Minor and the Capuchins.[48] Property coming to them in any way whatsoever is held by the Holy See as the immediate proprietor, while the Friars, the actual occupants, have its usufruct.[49] Limitations and restrictions of the right may also be found, for example, in the Society of Jesus and the Discalced Carmelites.[50]

For the acquisition and possession of property by religious houses, there is no restriction placed as to the *kind* of property that a moral person may acquire. Precluding any particular law of the institute, the Code indicates it by the general term temporal goods (*bona temporalia*). This term in the Code signifies "all those things which constitute the wealth and possessions of religious institutes."[51] It is not limited only to material objects but extends also to benefits and rights that are not material but

---

[46] Cf. *supra,* pp. 8–9; Larraona, "Commentarium Codicis"—*CpR,* XII (1931), 249.

[47] Canon 531.— . . . nisi earum capacitas in regulis et constitutionibus excludatur aut coarctetur.

[48] Cf. Conc. Trident., sess. XXV, *de regularibus,* c. 3; cf. also *supra* pp. 107–108.

[49] Cf. canon 582, 2o. Cf. also Augustine, *Religious and Laymen,* pp. 177, 178; Coronata, *Institutiones,* I, n. 558, note 3; Fanfani, *De Iure Religiosorum,* n. 153; Wernz-Vidal, *De Religiosis,* n. 215.

[50] Cf. *supra,* p. 45.

[51] McManus, *The Administration of Temporal Goods in Religious Institutes,* p. 1.

which possess an economic value, for example, land, houses, furniture, clothing, securities, stocks and bonds.[52]

Property may be acquired by the house in every way that is allowed it by natural or positive law. All legitimate methods of acquisition permitted by the norms of the sacred canons and particular rules and constitutions may be utilized. Common law sanctions for all moral persons, consequently for religious houses also, all the just modes of acquisition that may be employed by other physical persons.[53] The ordinary means of acquiring temporal goods, comprehended by the Code and generally employed by religious, are the contributions by those entering religious life, income from the industry of the members of the community, pious foundations, free-will offerings by the faithful, testamentary provisions, alms and prescription.[54] This right is not limited only to original but extends also to derivative acquisition and includes income that may be derived from property already in their possession, if it is capable of producing fixed or founded revenues.[55] It is of no consequence whether the conjunction "*or*" (*seu*) be considered here in a conjunctive or disjunctive sense. The nature of the income whether it be fixed or founded remains the same, i.e., comprehending permanent, steady and certain revenues from property already in the possession of the religious, in opposition to income of an unsteady or uncertain character.[56] Thus the right to acquire and possess temporal goods is not restricted to a daily acquisition of what is necessary for immediate support and sustenance. They may acquire and own property, if the particular

---

[52] Creusen, Garesché, Ellis, *Religious Men and Women in the Code,* p. 115.

[53] Canon 1499, §1. Excepted by law is almsgathering. It is proper to only the mendicants in the strict sense. Other regulars need special approbation of at least the local ordinary to gather alms. Cf. *supra,* pp. 69–72.

[54] Cf. *supra,* Part II, pp. 38-99.

[55] The term *fixed* (*stabilibus*) is used in opposition to *occasional.* The former results as if from necessity, as a right to the income from immovable goods, pious foundations or another's juridic obligation. The latter does not result from a right, nor is it certain, but comes as a free-will donation or uncertain alms.—Larraona, "Commentarium Codicis"—*CpR,* XII (1931) 250.

[56] McManus, *The Administration of Temporal Goods in Religious Institutes,* pp. 51, 52; Larraona, *ibid.,* p. 250.

laws of the institute permit it, in a permanent manner with right to draw the regular income that may accrue from it.[57]

The maximum *amount* of property that a religious house may acquire and possess is not determined in the common law of the Church. The determination of such amount may well be left to the particular laws of the institute. A minimum amount is intended and proposed in canon 496 which declares that no religious house should be established unless it can be prudently estimated that a proper livelihood and sustenance will be assured its members either from its fixed income or from the usual alms or from other sources.[58]

---

[57] Papi, *The Government of Religious Communities,* p. 161.
[58] McManus, *op. cit.,* p. 49.

CHAPTER VII

Administration and Investment of Temporal Goods

Article 1. Concept of Administration

The right to acquire and possess temporal goods necessarily includes the right to their administration, that is, to the performance of all acts necessary to the attainment of the purpose toward which these goods are being held. Here, it means the exercise of control over the possessions of religious by competent officials and comprehends the execution of administrative acts involving "the control and care of the temporal goods of the religious institute in order that they may serve the purpose for which they were acquired."[1] These acts, required by necessity or utility include: (1) The maintenance of property in good condition; (2) The obligation of making it productive; (3) The derivation of benefit from it; (4) Its application, payment, and use for legitimate purposes.[2] Thus, as can readily be seen, the care of temporal goods comprehends many acts which can be considered under diverse aspects. Excluding the possibility of various distinction of administrative acts, it is important to note those of *ordinary* and *extraordinary* administration.[3]

[1] McManus, *The Administration of Temporal Goods in Religious Institutes,* p. 79; Larraona, "Commentarium Codicis"—*CpR,* XII (1931), 355, 356; O'Brien, *The Exemption of Religious in Church Law,* p. 252; Vermeersch-Creusen, *Epitome,* I, n. 601; Vromant, *De Bonis Ecclesiae Temporalibus,* n. 172; Wernz, *Ius Decretalium,* III, n. 147; Wernz-Vidal, *De Religiosis,* n. 218.

[2] In its wide sense administration includes also the acquisition of property. Thus it could be reduced to three classes of acts: (1) acquisition; (2) conservation; (3) alienation. Cf. authors referred to in preceding note (n. 1) also Rodericus, *Quaestiones,* I, q. 26, art. 2; Suarez, *De Religione,* tract 8, lib. 2, c. 26, n. 1.

[3] The distinction of administrative acts into *juridical* (contracts, vindication of rights in courts of justice, alienations) and *non-juridical or physical* (cultivation of fields, disposition of means for sustenance, etc.) is of no

Ordinary administrative acts are those which do not exceed the normal exercise of the office of administrator, whether the superior or the person specially appointed for the task.[4] They are acts which are considered regularly necessary for the proper preservation and maintenance of property and the provision for normal, current, and eventual needs. Examples of these acts are: the purchase and sale of goods necessary to meet daily requirements; transactions necessary for the reception of revenues from investments and securities; short-time bank deposits for the purpose of security or convenience; the collection of payments on debts and rentals of houses or lands; the reception of manual gifts; provision for expenses necessary for normal conservation of property and other similiar acts.[5] The extent of the ordinary acts of administration must be determined from the actual rights that are granted to the competent administrators either by the Code or by particular law in the rules and constitutions of the institute.

Extraordinary administrative acts are those which are beyond the power of the administrator. The distinctive feature of these acts is that permission for their performance is not included in the office of the administrator. They can be performed only after the fulfillment of the necessary formalities consisting in obtaining the faculty or consent from the competent superior. This concept of extraordinary administration is precisely juridical. Its determination depends upon the requisites of Canon Law and the particular laws of the institute. In particular law, the im-

---

particular importance in Canon Law except to stress the need for the observance of civil laws in regard to the legal formalities of administration. Cf. McManus, *The Administration of Temperal Goods in Religious Institutes,* p. 80; Larraona, "Commentarium Codicis"—*CpR,* XII (1931), 356.

[4] The Code in canon 516, §2 requires that a special person be designated as procurator for the institute, province or house, to supervise the administration of temporal goods under the direction of the superior. In paragraph 3 of the same canon it recognizes the compatibility of the offices of the local superior and that of the procurator if necessity would urge it.—Cf. Clancy, *The Local Religious Superior,* p. 70.

[5] Larraona, "Commentarium Codicis"—*CpR,* XII (1931), 356; McManus, *The Administration of Temporal Goods in Religious Institutes,* p. 80; O'Brien, *The Exemption of Religious in Church Law,* p. 252.

portance of the act determines whether it is to be considered as being pertinent to ordinary or extraordinary administration. This law may be specific in its determination of the powers of the administrator or it may state general norms, leaving details to the superiors. Of the latter type is the provision of the Code referring the details of administration to particular constitutions of the orders. But specific details may be, and usually are, mentioned in the Code when there is a necessity of intervention of an authority external to the institute.[6] In its chapter on temporal goods and their administration by religious, the Code mentions two instances of extraordinary administration: the placing of investments (canon 533) and alienation of religious property (canon 534).[7]

ARTICLE 2. INVESTMENTS

Canon 533, adverting to the necessity of making investments[8] as prescribed by the constitutions, defines the right and duty of the local ordinary in regard to the investments of money or ecclesiastical property[9] of the religious. It must be noted, how-

---

[6] Cf. canon 532; McManus, *op. cit.*, pp. 81–83; Larraona, "Commentarium Codicis"—*CpR,* XII (1931), 245.

[7] The alienation of religious property is of sufficient importance and scope to be treated in special chapter. Cf. *infra*, pp. 125–150.

[8] Investment in the *strict sense* is the relatively permanent conversion of money or property into other goods which are retained as a source for the perception of revenues. The conversion may be made into immovable or movable property. In a *broad sense* it may mean the mere temporary deposit of money in a bank, for example, for the purpose of security and at the same time the realization of a small profit through the medium of interest. The more probable opinion among authors excludes investments in the broad sense from the requirements of canon 533.—Cf. Augustine, *Religious and Laymen,* p. 181; Larraona, "Commentarium Codicis"—*CpR,* XII (1931), 435; O'Brien, *The Exemption of Religious in Church Law,* p. 254; McManus, *The Administration of Temporal Goods in Religious Institutes,* p. 94; Roth, "Kilka Zagadnień z Zakonnego Prawa Majątkowego"—*Ateneum Kaplanski,* XLIII (1938), 162 note 4.

[9] The terms money (*pecuniae*) and *funds* (*fundi*) as used in this canon mean one and the same thing: property, an object representing a money value.—Larraona, "Commentarium Codicis"—*CpR,* XIII (1932), 92; Roth, *ibid.*, pp. 161, 162.

ever, that the requirements of this canon do not affect in any way religious orders of men. Regulars, on the basis of their exemption from the jurisdiction of the local ordinary, do not need any special permission external to the institute to invest their own funds, even though the money or property to be invested had been given them to promote locally divine worship or works of charity (canon 533, §1, 3°).[10]

The privilege of exemption of regulars is not to be extended to the investment of money that belongs to a parish or mission. Canon 533, §1, 4°, prescribes that all religious, even members of regular orders, must obtain the consent of the local ordinary in order to invest money which had been given to a parish or mission, or which has been given them in behalf of a parish or mission.[11] For a clearer understanding of the provision of this number, a distinction must be made in regard to the object of the donation or gift. From the wording of the text it is twofold: either the parish or mission, or the religious on behalf of the parish or mission.

1. *Donations to a parish or mission.* There is no special need for the determination as to what is meant by a parish. By the term *mission,* on the other hand, is understood a mission parish (*quasi paroecia*) in the vicariates and prefectures apostolic (canon 216, 3).[12] The extension of the term *mission* as used in this

---

[10] Larraona, "Commentarium Codicis"—*CpR,* XIII (1932), 25; McManus, *The Administration of Temporal Goods in Religious Institutes,* p. 109; O'Brien, *The Exemption of Religious in Church Law,* p. 254; Roth, *l.c.,* p. 164; Vermeersch-Creusen, *Epitome,* I, 606; Wernz-Vidal, *De Religiosis,* n. 225.

[11] Canon 533.—§1. 4°. Religiosus quilibet, etsi Ordinis regularis alumnus, si pecunia data sit paroeciae vel missioni, aut religiosis intuitu paroeciae vel missionis.—This includes all donations and offerings as can be deduced from canon 535, §3, 2° which states that it is the right of the local ordinary to demand an account of the funds and bequests referred to in canon 533, §1, 3° and 4°.

[12] Farrell, *The Rights and Duties of the Local Ordinary Regarding Congregations of Women Religious of Pontifical Approval,* p. 149; Beste, *Introductio in Codicem,* p. 352; Ruth, "Kilka Zagadnień z Zakonnego Prawa Majątkowego"—*Ateneum Kaplanskie,* XLIII (1938), 166, Vermeersch-Creusen, *Epitome,* I, 606; Wernz-Vidal, *De Religiosis,* n. 226.

canon, and as proposed by McManus,[13] to include the whole of a territory of a vicariate or prefecture apostolic is alien to the sense of this canon. The position of the words *parish* and *mission* implies that the relationship of a mission to the vicariate or prefecture apostolic is to be understood as analogous to the relationship of a parish to a diocese. That is the suggested sense in the constitution "*Romanos Pontifices*" of May 8, 1881, which is the source of this canon. The constitution would seem to imply a part of the territory under a bishop rather than the whole territory.[14] Thus money given to a religious and intended for a parish or mission becomes, according to the will of the donor, parish or mission property. As such, it comes under the supervision of the local ordinary in its administration.[15]

In addition it is important here to note the various types of parish property or goods that may fall under the administration of religious according to the Code of Canon Law. Four types may be distinguished: [16]

(a) *Property constituting the endowment of the benefice* (*bona beneficilia*). Such is property belonging to the parochial benefice as a juridic moral person and already acquired by the same.[17] The income of the benefice in turn belongs to the person in possession of it.[18] Thus, if the parish is joined to a moral person, in our case a religious house, the income is proper to that moral person. The administration of the property of a benefice

---

[13] *The Administration of Temporal Goods in Religious Institutes,* p. 114.

[14] 14. " . . . Excellit inter haec munus curationis animarum, quod saepe, ut innuimus, religiosis viris demandatur intra fines ab Episcopis praestitutos; *locus autem iis finibus comprehensus missionis nomine designatur."—Fontes,* n. 582. Italics inserted.

[15] Roth, *ibid.,* p. 167. The necessity of supervision by the local ordinary is pertinent only to investments in the strict sense, involving a relatively permanent investment.—Cf. Prümmer, *Manuale Iuris Canonici,* q. 194, d; Nebreda, "De Loci Ordinariorum Iuribus"—*CpR,* VII (1926), 265; Cocchi, *De Religiosis,* ad can. 533, n. 54.

[16] Anonymous, "De Administratione Bonorum in Paroeciis Religiosis"—*Acta Ordinis Fratrum Minorum* (Ad Claras Aquas, Quaracchi, 1882—), LVII (1938), 186–192.

[17] Canon 1410.

[18] Canon 1473.

joined to a religious house, either *pleno iure* or *non-pleno iure*, belongs to him who exercises the office of administrator in the religious house.[19] Regarding parishes that have been only entrusted to religious (*simpliciter concredita*), and not incorporated with the community, the administration of such property must be determined from the particular agreements made between the religious and the local ordinary.

(b) *Property of the parish as such, distinct from the endowment of the benefice and the property of the church.* Under this classification belongs the property that was acquired on behalf of the parish and for the parish. It is property which is destined directly for the good of the members of the parish. The ownership of these goods is not vested in the parochial church, nor in the parochial benefice as a moral person, nor in the territorial district of the parish as a moral person. It is vested in the parish itself, conceived as a moral person constituted by the bulk of property (*massa bonorum*) serving the good and convenience of the parishioners.[20] The administration of these goods is left to the religious pastor who in turn must render an account of this administration to the local ordinary and in the question of investment of this property he is subject to the bishop's consent. The religious superior can only exercise his right of vigilance over the activity of the religious pastor in regard to the administration of these goods.[21]

(c) *Property of the church.* All property that is given over for the construction, conservation, restoration, decoration and the celebration of the divine cult in the church is considered property of the church. Included are also all the immovable and movable goods, furniture, etc. In a word, it comprises all the property that is acquired under any legitimate title by the parish church as a moral person. In determining the lawful superior for the administration one must distinguish whether the church is properly a religious or secular church. A religious church is one which is united with the religious community or house in some

---

[19] Can. 516–532.

[20] Vromant, *De Bonis Ecclesiae Temporalibus*, nn. 61, 64.

[21] Coronata, *Institutiones*, I, n. 635; Fanfani, *De Iure Religiosorum*, n. 452, a; Vromant, *op. cit.*, nn. 174, 197bis.

permanent or stable manner, either by incorporation with the religious community or by perpetual usage. It is not the actual ownership of the church building, but the permanency or stability of its union and use by a religious community that is necessary to the concept of a religious church.[22] Thus in all churches which are united to a religious community in some permanent manner, that is, religious churches, the property of the church is to be administered by the religious superior (can. 630, §4; 609, §1; 415, §3, n. 3) according to the norms of the constitutions of the religious institute (can. 532). The reason for this lies in the fact that since the religious undertake the tasks of construction, conservation, decoration and payment of expenses toward the proper celebration of the divine cult in the church, the administration of the property necessary to the fulfillment of these tasks is left to them.[23] On the other hand in a secular parish, that is one which is cared for by religious for some definite period of time, even though a religious exercises the office of pastor, the legitimate superior for the administration of the property of the church is the local ordinary.[24] However, in both instances, that of the religious church and that of the secular church, an account of the administration of church property must be rendered to the local ordinary[25] unless the religious church is held in ownership by the religious community. This follows from a response of the Pontifical Commission for the Authentic Interpretation of the Code. The Pontifical Commission was asked: Whether in virtue of cc. 631, §3; 535, §3, 2°; 533, §1, 3° and 4°, the ordinary of the

---

[22] Cf. can. 609, §1; Anonymous, "De Administratione Bonorum in Paroeciis Religiosis"—*Acta Ordinis Fratrum Minorum,* LVII (1938), 189; Coady, *The Appointment of Pastors,* The Catholic University of America Canon Law Studies, n. 52 (Washington, D. C.: The Catholic University of America, 1929), pp. 77, 78; Vromant, *De Bonis Ecclesiae Temporalibus,* n. 197bis, note 3.

[23] Anonymous, "De Administratione Bonorum in Paroeciis Religiosis"—*Acta Ordinis Fratrum Minorum,* LVII (1938), 189.

[24] Canon 630, §4; 1519; Anonymous, "De Administratione Bonorum in Paroeciis Religiosis"—*Acta Ordinis Fratrum Minorum,* LVII (1938), 189; Anonymous, "Disquisitio Circa Ius Ordinarii Dioecesani Visitandi Ecclesias Regularium"—*Acta Ordinis Fratrum Minorum,* LV (1936), 98.

[25] Vromant, *De Bonis Ecclesiae Temporalibus,* n. 197bis.

place has the right to demand an account of the administration of foundations and legacies to a religious parish such as is mentioned in can. 1425, §2. The reply was in the affirmative, without prejudice to the prescriptions of canon 630, §4 and canon 1550.[26]

(d) *Property of the religious community.* This comprises the goods that are acquired as emoluments for the work of the pastor by reason of his office and which is given him on behalf of the institute. Included are mass stipends, stole fees, income from the benefice, etc. These goods are acquired by the institute or the Holy See if the institute is incapable of ownership even in common.[27] Their administration is regulated by the norms set for other goods of the religious house, dependent upon the authority of the legitimate superior.[28]

The provision of canon 533, §1, 4° applies only to the investments of money that had been given for a *definite* parish or mission. Money received by a religious for missions in general or for missions of the institute, is to be administered and invested by the religious with due supervision of their competent superiors. If the mission for which the money is intended is specified by the donor, the administration and investment of the donation is subject to the permission of the vicar or prefect apostolic of the mission designated.[29]

2. *Donations to a religious on behalf of the parish or mission.* It is important to note that in this case the religious receives the donation not as a religious but as a pastor. As such it must be administered as parish property under the supervision

---

[26] *AAS*, XVIII (1926), 393 ad IV; transl. from Bouscaren, *The Canon Law Digest*, I, ad can. 1429, p. 699. Cf. also Anonymous, "Disquisitio circa Ius Ordinarii Dioecesani Visitandi Ecclesias Regularium"—*Acta Ordinis Fratrum Minorum,* LV (1936), 98; Beste, *Introductio in Codicem,* pp. 352, 353; McManus, *The Administration of Temporal Goods in Religious Institutes,* p. 113.

[27] Cf. canon 630 with canon 580, 2 and 582.

[28] Cf. canon 532; 516.

[29] Beste, *op. cit.,* p. 353; Larraona, "Commentarium Codicis"—*CpR,* XIII (1932), 94; McManus, *op. cit.,* p. 114; Nebreda, "De Loci Ordinariorum Iuribus"—*CpR,* VII (1926), 266, 267; O'Brien, *The Exemption of Religious in Church Law,* p. 255; Schäfer, *De Religiosis,* n. 197.

of the local ordinary and also under the vigilance of the competent religious superior. These donations cannot be converted toward the needs of the institute of which the pastor is a member, but they must be used for the benefit of the parish or mission.

When the will of the donor is clear, it decides the purpose of the offering.[30] At times, however, it may be difficult to determine whether a donation has been given to the religious as a religious, or for the benefit of the parish or mission. In such a doubt, the presumption in law is that money that is given to rectors of churches is given to the church unless the contrary is proven.[31] The burden of proof thus rests on the pastor or vicar if he claims the donation to be personal rather than to the parish or mission. Circumstances of time, place and manner and person and the like are elements necessarily to be considered in order to clarify the unexpressed will of the donor. Thus, for example, the following offerings could be judged as being made to the religious personally: those of parents, relatives, special friends and benefactors of the religious or the institute; those given on some special occasion such as a feast day of the religious, or for some personal task performed by the religious such as confessor, moderator or teacher.[32] The following examples of offerings are to be judged as given to the religious on behalf of the parish or mission: the sum of money collected on the occasion of special gatherings of the people for the purpose of supporting the parish or mission, such as card parties, carnivals, picnics, and the like; the land and house offered for the support of a missionary; vestments and church equipment sent to the pastor or vicar by a group of individuals, such as a Benefit Society.[33]

[30] McManus (*The Administration of Temporal Goods in Religious Institutes,* p. 114) adds that "it is of prime importance, therefore, in regard to formal donations and gifts, that as far as possible and as soon as possible, the intention of the donor in regard to the purpose of the gift and the reception of the gift should be made manifest by a document capable of supplying proof." Cf. also Leo XIII const. "*Romanos Pontifices,*" 8 maii, 1881, §23—*Fontes,* n. 582.

[31] Canon 1536, §1; cf. *supra,* p. 162.

[32] Larraona, "Commentarium Codicis"—*CpR,* XIII (1932), 96, 97; O'Brien, *The Exemption of Religious in Church Law,* p. 255; Vromant, *De Bonis Ecclesiae Temporalibus,* n. 65.

[33] McManus, *Administration in Religious Institutes,* pp. 115, 116; Roth,

In the question of administration it is of utmost importance to note that the religious superiors and the administrators are not the owners of the temporal goods owned by the community or given for the use of the community. It is their duty to administer temporalities with special care for their preservation so that the purpose of their possession by the community may be fulfilled. They should strive with diligence to preserve the goods intact rather than look forward to increasing the revenues that may be possible through the manipulation of investments. Speculation with community goods and business undertakings of a commercial nature are reprobated in ecclesiastical law. That is the discipline of canon 142 to which the religious are subject in virtue of canon 592.[34] The legislation of canon 142[35] may be summarily stated as follows in the word of Brunini:[36] "Clerics, religious . . . cannot lawfully exercise lucrative commercial trading[37] or artificial trading,[38] if the goods be changed through hired labor, whether the enterprise be conducted through themselves or through others, whether for their own utility or for the utility of others, unless they have been granted permission by proper ecclesiastical authority or unless they are faced with grave necessity affecting their own sustenance or that of those to whom they are obligated."[39]

"Kilka Zagadnień z Zakonnego Prawa Majątkowego"—*Ateneum Kaplanskie,* XLIII (1938), 167.

[34] Canon 592.—Obligationibus communibus clericorum, de quibus in can. 124–142, etiam religiosi omnes tenentur, nisi ex contextu sermonis vel ex rei natura aliud constet.

[35] Canon 142.—Prohibentur clerici per se vel per alios negotiationem, aut mercaturam exercere sive in propriam sive in aliorum utilitatem.

[36] *The Clerical Obligations,* p. 76.

[37] "Strictly commercial trading, *negotiatio lucrativa seu quaestuatio,* is defined as the buying of things with the intention of selling them unchanged at a higher price."—Brunini, *op. cit.,* p. 77.

[38] "Strict artificial trading—*negotiatio artificialis seu industrialis*—may be defined as the buying of material with the intention of changing it by means of *hired* labor and of selling the article at a profit."—Brunini, *op. cit.,* pp. 77, 78.

[39] Cf. *supra,* pp. 33–35. For a list of activities that are not forbidden to clerics and applicable to religious cf. Brunini, *op. cit.,* pp. 82–88.

CHAPTER VIII

ALIENATION OF TEMPORAL GOODS BY REGULARS

ARTICLE 1. PRE-CODE LEGISLATION

A. Historical

FROM the earliest times it had been the practice of the Church to regulate strictly all possible transactions which would affect its property and goods. Subject to these regulations were also the possessions of the religious, as is evidenced in the rulings of the Church given chiefly in the General Councils. The legislation permitting possessions to religious in no way implied complete freedom in their use and administration. It has been the common opinion among authors that the property and goods of religious monasteries, erected by ecclesiastical authority, were to be considered and administered as ecclesiastical goods. Consequently, the laws governing the administràtion of ecclesiastical goods were held to be applicable to the possessions of religious also.[1]

In the twelfth canon of the II Council of Nicaea (787), to counteract the possible ambitions of certain bishops and abbots, it was ordained that "if a bishop or abbot alienate or surrender any part of the farm land belonging to the bishopric or to the monastery in the hands of princes or any other person, his act is invalid according to the canon (Apost. canon 39). Neither is it lawful for him to appropriate any part of it for himself, or to give to his relatives the things that belong to God . . . Nor is property to be surrendered on the plea that it yields no profits;

[1] Bouix, *Tractatus de Jure Regularium,* II, pp. 270, 271, 278; De Luca, *Theatrum Veritatis et Justitiae* (15 vols. in 8, Coloniae Agrippinae, 1706) tom. 12, pars 3, *de alienatione,* disc. 1, nn. 12, 13; Petra, *Commentaria in Constitutiones Apostolicas* V, const. Pauli II, sec. 3, nn. 21-23; Rodericus, *Quaestiones,* I, q. 27, art. 2; Suarez, *De Religione,* tract. 8, lib. 2, c. 26, nn. 5-7.

for in that case it is not to be given to secular rulers who are in the neighborhood, but to clerics or husbandmen. But if resort be had to intrigue so that the ruler buys the land from the husbandmen or cleric, such transaction is likewise invalid and the land shall be restored to the bishopric or the monastery. The bishop or abbot acting thus shall be expelled, the former from his bishopric and the latter from his monastery as those who squander what they did not gather." [2]

Pope Clement V in a decree, considered at the Council of Vienne and specifically directed to the monasteries,[3] in general terms forbade alienation without due reason and authority from the superiors. The decree ordered suspension from office of any religious to whom administration of income and the possessions of a monastery was given, if he transferred the rights or the income or the possessions of the monastery to another whether for the latter's lifetime or only for a certain time. Only in two instances would he be free of this suspension, namely if necessity or utility to the monastery urged such procedure. Even here he needed the consent of the convent or if he was attached to no convent, of his superior.

Pope Paul II, in his constitution "*Ambitiosae*" of March 1, 1468, set down a general law on alienation that served as the norm for regulating alienations in later centuries.[4] He imposed the sentence of excommunication upon those who alienated in a manner contrary to the provisions of ecclesiastical law, as well as upon those who were the recipients of such transactions. Such transfers were also to be considered invalid. In this constitution pontifical approval was required in alienations which consisted of any act of purchase, donation, exchange, sale, mortgage or lease of immovable goods and movable objects of a precious character. This was reaffirmed on July 14, 1555, by Pope Paul IV in his constitution "*Injunctum nobis.*" [5]

The Council of Trent treated alienation in general terms and

[2] C. 19, C. XII, q. 2; transl. from Schroeder, *Disciplinary Decrees*, pp. 149, 150; Mansi, XII 752.

[3] C. 1, *de rebus ecclesiae non alienandis*, III, 4 in Clem.

[4] C. un., *de rebus ecclesiae non alienandis*, III, 4 in Extravag. com.

[5] *Fontes*, n. 88.

spoke only of the prohibition of long-term leases of ecclesiastical goods and the prevention of conversion to, and the usurpation of ecclesiastical goods and rights by the laity.[6] The Sacred Congregation of the Council under the order and authority of Pope Urban VIII, on September 7, 1624, in a general decree, restored the force of the previous constitutions, particularly that of Pope Paul II, "*Ambitiosae.*"[7] Revoking all the privileges of all orders, mendicant and non-mendicant, in whatsoever way they might have been acquired, it ordered the strict observance of the solemnities required by the previous constitutions.[8] Pope Pius IX, in his constitution "*Apostolicae Sedis*" of October 12, 1869, referring to the constitution "*Ambitiosae,*" declared an excommunication *nemini reservata* upon all those who alienated or received ecclesiastical goods without the *beneplacitum* of the Holy See.[9]

Exempt from the solemnities required for alienation, and particularly from obtaining the permission of the Holy See, were the Friars Minor *de Observantia* and the Capuchins, and by a special concession the houses of the professed members of the Society of Jesus. In prescribing the solemnities required for alienation, the Holy See had for its purpose the conservation of immovable goods of the monasteries or convents. Consequently, those regulars who had no possessions, not even in common, did not possess a stable fund and therefore did not come under the laws of alienation. However the incapability of possessing a stable fund did not entirely deny to these regulars the reception of immovable goods. They could accept such goods, not that they were to retain them, but that they, with the permission of the donor, were to have the goods sold and convert the revenues

---

[6] Conc. Trident. sess. XXV, *de ref.*, c. 11; sess. XXII, *de ref.*, c. 11.

[7] *Fontes*, n. 2453.

[8] These solemnities were: 1. Existence of a cause, such as the necessity of the monastery or the utility derived by the monastery by the transaction (Cf. c. 16, C. XII, q. 2); 2. The counsel and consent of the chapter or superior of the monastery (c. 52, C. XII, q. 2; c. 8, X, *de his quae fiunt a praelato sine consensu capituli*, III, 10; c. 1, *de rebus ecclesiae non alienandis*, III, 4 in Clem.); 3. The permission, *beneplacitum*, of the Holy See. Cf. also Ferraris, *Bibliotheca*, ad v. "alienatio" art. 2; Rodericus, *Quaestiones*, I, q. 27, art. 2; Suarez, *De Religione*, tract. 8, lib. 2, c. 27, nn. 2–9.

[9] *Fontes*, n. 552, §4, n. 3.

therefrom toward the satisfaction of their current or imminent needs.[10] Such, too, was the common opinion of the authors.[11]

As to precious movable goods [12] in the possession of the religious, the solemnities of alienation had to be fulfilled, when and if they desired to transfer their ownership in any way. All religious could incorporate such goods into the fund of their churches. Without doubt these possessions came under the requirements of alienation as confirmed by the Sacred Congregation of the Council in a decree to the Friars Minor on March 18, 1719.[13]

B. Types of Alienation

1. Alienations not requiring the "beneplacitum" of the Holy See.

1. *Immovable goods of small value.* That the "*beneplacitum*" of the Holy See was not required for the alienation of property of this kind had been deduced from the 45th chapter of the Council of Agde (506),[14] wherein permission was given to the bishops to dispose of small fields and small vineyards which were of little use to the Church. Neither the Constitution of Pope Paul II "*Ambitiosae*" nor the Council of Trent abrogated this canon, as can be deduced from responses of the Sacred Congregation of

---

[10] Cf. c. 1, *de verborum significatione,* V, 11 in Clem.; Julii III, const., "*Exposcit,*" 21, iul. 1550—*Bull. Rom. Taur.*, VI, 424, 425, §9; *Fontes,* nn. 1868, 1999; also Rodericus, *Quaestiones,* I, q. 26, art. 2.

[11] Cf. Bouix, *Tractatus de Jure Regularium,* II, 286, 287; Ferraris, *Bibliotheca,* ad v. "alienatio" art. 3, nn. 5, 6; Petra, *Commentaria in Constitutiones Apostolicas,* V, const. Pauli IV, sec. 3, n. 24; Rodericus, *Quaestiones,* I, q. 27, art. 3, n. 5.

[12] That is, all those goods which are from the treasury of the Church or which because of their price, artistic merit, rarity, or antiquity confer a special splendor to the Church, such as gold and silver vessels, precious vestments, jewels, ornaments, libraries, important relics, possessions conferring annual revenues and the like.—Ferraris, *Bibliotheca,* ad v. "alienatio" art. 4, nn. 7-11; Schmalzgrueber, *Ius Ecclesiasticum Universum,* III, tit. 13, n. 27.

[13] S. Concilium sic censuit: Quoad mobilia pretiosa Ecclesiae incorporata, esse necessarium beneplacitum Apostolicum.—*Fontes,* n. 3185.

[14] C. 53, C. XII, q. 12; Mansi, VIII, 332.

the Council on January 11, 1596, and December 14, 1613.[15] The only difficulty here was the determination of what was meant by *small value*. Ferraris,[16] arguing from responses of the Sacred Congregation of Bishops and Regulars,[17] set a definite norm of 20 *solidi*. Cardinal de Luca [18] stated that the determination is arbitrary and the circumstances of the church and place must be considered. Fagnanus [19] declared that, because it had not been determined by law, the decision should rest upon the discretion of the judge. Bouix,[20] recounting these opinions, inclined toward that of Ferraris, however, not as an absolute norm but as a directive rule. He stated that at his time the sum considered as *small* should not exceed 500 francs. Wernz [21] writes in effect that this should be determined by circumstances of place and time. On July 30, 1909, the Sacred Congregation of Religious ordered in an instruction that

> In contracting debts or assuming financial liabilities a notable amount is one ranging from 500 to 1000 francs ($100 to $200) in the case of individual monasteries or houses; from 1000 to 5000 francs ($200 to $1000), for provinces or quasi-provinces; from 5000 francs upwards, there the matter belongs to a general order or congregation. If a house, province or general order wishes to take upon itself debts or pecuniary responsibilities in excess of 10,000 francs ($2000), the permission of the Holy See, in addition to the consent of the respective Council, as above, is likewise necessary.[22]

On October 11, 1910, the Apostolic Delegate to the United

---

[15] These decrees are referred to by Fagnanus, *Commentaria*, lib. 3, tit. *de rebus ecclesiae non alienandis*, c. *nulli*, nn. 25, 26.

[16] *Bibliotheca*, ad v. "alienatio" art. 3, nn. 3, 4.

[17] *Faventina*, 22 maii, 1611; *Messanensi*, 29 nov. 1613; *Barensi*, 12 apr. 1689; *Papiensi*, 15 maii, 1710; *Amalphitana*, 8 aug. 1665—as referred to by Ferraris, *l.c.*

[18] *Theatrum Veritatis et Justitiae*, XII, pars 3, *de alienationibus*, disc. 1, n. 117.

[19] *Commentaria*, lib. III, tit. *de rebus ecclesiae non alienandis*, c. *nulli*, n. 26.

[20] *Tractatus de Jure Regularium*, II, pp. 290, 291.

[21] *Ius Decretalium*, III, n. 165.

[22] *AAS*, I (1909), 696. Transl. from *AER*, LIII (1915), 671.

States, by virtue of a rescript of the Sacred Congregation for Religious, authorized for a period of ten years the ordinaries of the dioceses in the United States to permit the religious communities of their dioceses to contract debts to the sum of 50,000 francs ($10,000) without having recourse to the Holy See.[23]

2. *Immovable goods left to the monasteries and churches incapable of retaining them.* This exception has been referred to previously.[24] Here, it may be noted that these orders in matters of alienation were required to use a *syndicus,* that is one who was to protect the donations and the bequests given to the monasteries. Though it was more in accordance with the mind of the Church to have a person other than a religious of the monastery or convent to act in this capacity, a religious could be appointed as *syndicus,* if necessity or utility required it. The use of the *syndicus* was particularly urged for the Friars Minor.[25]

3. *The renting and hiring of property for a three-year period.* This exception was expressly made in the constitution "*Ambitiosae.*"[26] The three years were to be determined not necessarily as three calendar years but as three years during which income was received from property. If, therefore, certain property bore income only every other year, or every three years, the period of the calendar year would be extended for six or nine years. This was the common opinion of authors and was in harmony with ecclesiastical decisions to which they referred.[27]

---

[23] Cf. *AER,* LIII (1915), 676, 677.

[24] Cf. *supra,* pp. 127–128.

[25] Cf. Nicholas III, const. "*Exiit qui seminat,*" 14 aug. 1279—c. 3, *de verborum significatione,* V, in VIo; also Ferraris, *Bibliotheca,* ad v. "Syndicus."

[26] It prohibited "*locationem et conductionem ultra triennium*"—cit. const. "*Ambitiosae*" in c. un. *de rebus ecclesiae non alienandis,* III, 4, in Extravag. com.

[27] Barbosa, *Pastoralis Solicitudo,* pars 3, alleg. 95, n. 4; Ferraris, *Bibliotheca,* ad v. "alienatio" art. 3, nn. 8–10 and additiones ex aliena manu, n. 19; De Luca, *Theatrum Veritatis et Justitiae,* IX, *De locatione et conductione,* disc. 21, nn. 9, 10; Leurenius, *Forum Ecclesiasticum,* lib. III, tit. 13, q. 145, n. 1; Pignatelli, *Consultationes Canonicae,* IV, consultatio 223, nn. 1–6; Schmalzgrueber, *Ius Ecclesiasticum Universum,* III, tit. 18, nn. 29, 34, 35.

4. *The leasing of property which already had been leased.*[28] Where property was already leased each new act of re-leasing was not to be considered as a new alienation but rather as a further execution of what had been determined by previous law. If, however, goods leased in such a manner were reincorporated in the fund of the monastery or church, they could not be leased again without the required solemnities.[29]

5. *Perishable goods.*[30] Such goods are to be understood as movable, non-productive, which do not endure for more than three years or are consumed by use.[31]

6. Alienation of even immovable goods and movable objects of a precious character was allowed without the "*beneplacitum*" when necessity urged and the Pope could not be easily reached, and if there was danger in delay.[32]

2. Alienations requiring the "beneplacitum" of the Holy See.

On the other hand, permission of the Holy See was required in the case of the alienation of the following kinds of property:

1. *Immovable goods and movable goods of a precious character.* Because of the express prohibition in the decrees of the Popes and the Sacred Congregations, there was never any doubt as to the necessity of the permission of the Holy See for the alienation of these goods.

---

[28] "Praeterquam de rebus et bonis in emphyteusi ab antiquo concedi solitis."—Const. "*Ambitiosae*" in c. un. *de rebus ecclesiae non alienandis,* III, 4 in Extravag. com.

[29] Barbosa, *Pastoralis Solicitudo,* pars 3, alleg. 95, nn. 22–36; Fagnanus, *Commentaria,* lib. III, tit. *de rebus ecclesiae non alienandis,* c. *nulli,* nn. 20, 21; Ferraris, *Bibliotheca,* ad v. "alienatio" art. 3, nn. 11–13; Schmalzgrueber, *Ius Ecclesiasticum Universum,* III, tit. 18, nn. 104–106.

[30] "*Praeterquam . . . de fructibus et bonis quae servando servari non possunt.*"—Const. "*Ambitiosae*" in c. un. *de rebus ecclesiae non alienandis,* III, 4, in Extravag. com.

[31] Barbosa, *Pastoralis Solicitudo,* pars 3, alleg. 95, n. 37; Fagnanus, *Commentaria,* in lib. III, tit. *de rebus ecclesiae non alienandis,* c. *nulli,* n. 22; Ferraris, *Biblotheca,* ad v. "alienatio" art. 3, nn. 14, 15.

[32] Barbosa, *Pastoralis Solicitudo,* pars 3, alleg. 95, n. 58; Bouix, *Tractatus de Jure Regularium,* II, p. 293; Ferraris, *Bibliotheca,* ad v. "alienatio" art. 3, n. 16.

2. *Bequests to monasteries.* Sanchez [33] and Suarez [34] held that if a superior refused to accept a bequest, he did not contract the sentence of excommunication because here there is no question of alienation but only simple non-acquisition. Ferraris [35] contended, however, that the repudiation of a legacy is alienation in law. Not only, he claims with Barbosa,[36] is alienation prohibited in regard to the goods acquired but also as to the goods to be acquired. Such goods pass into the ownership of the church or monastery *ipso iure* without the necessity of a formal transfer. Then again a superior could not refuse such bequests unless he first knew that they would come to him and this is already considered rather as something acquired than as something to be acquired. Finally, the superiors must always accept that what is obviously for the utility of the monastery and non-acquisition, in general, is contrary to good administration.

3. *The cutting and selling of trees which exceed what had been determined as a small amount.* In cases where a real necessity demanded it, for example, the need for rooting out old trees less useful and harmful to the garden or orchard, alienation could be made without the *beneplacitum* of the Holy See.[37]

4. *The renting and hiring of property for a long period.* This period was determined by the constitution "*Ambitiosae*" as any term over three years.[38]

5. *Annuities.* Because they were connected with immovable goods which produced income annually, annuities were numbered among immovable goods as it had been determined by the constitution of Clement V, "*Exivi de paradiso*" of May 6, 1312.[39]

---

[33] *Disputationum de Sancto Matrimonio Libri Tres,* Tomus I (Antuerpiae, 1626), lib. VI, disp. 4.

[34] *De Religione,* tract. 8, lib. 2, c. 27, n. 17.

[35] *Bibliotheca* ad v. "alienatio" art. 4, nn. 5–10.

[36] *Pastoralis Solicitudo,* pars 3, alleg. 95, n. 54.

[37] Ferraris, *Bibliotheca* ad v. "alienatio" art. 4, nn. 15–17; Rodericus, *Quaestiones,* I, q. 27, art. 4; Schmalzgrueber, *Ius Ecclesiasticum Universum,* III, tit. 13, n. 36.

[38] Cf. *supra,* p. 130.

[39] C. 1, *de verborum significatione,* V, 11 in Clem.: Cf. also Barbosa, *Pastoralis Solicitudo,* pars 3, alleg. 95, n. 46; Ferraris, *Bibliotheca* ad v. "alienatio" art. 4, nn. 21–24; Reiffenstuel, *Jus Canonicum Universum,* III,

6. *Goods left to a monastery on the condition that they be disposed of freely by the religious.* Despite this condition the *beneplacitum* of the Holy See was deemed necessary. The reason was that once the goods were acquired by a monastery after the death of a testator they became ecclesiastical goods. The disposition of one individual cannot change canonical legislation. If such goods were left for a determined purpose, e.g., for chalices, then such alienations could take place without the solemnities required.[40]

7. *Transfer of goods from one monastery to another even of the same order and province.* Such monasteries, although of the same order, were regarded as distinct from each other especially in regard to the administration of temporal goods. Hence, transfers of this type implied the passage of ownership from one house to another, and therefore were considered as alienation prohibited by the constitutions referred to.[41] In religious orders whose monasteries constitute one social body, under a general superior, it is customary to create a common fund from the superfluous goods of the individual houses as provided by the constitutions of these orders. There seems to be no doubt that in such cases the more needy convents could be provided for without the necessity of going through the solemnities of alienation.[42]

8. *Special Mortgages,* that is, contracts offering a certain and determined piece or pieces of immovable property as security for a debt. There has been no doubt that special mortgages came under the requirements of the constitution "*Ambitiosae.*" Controversies centered only on the extension of the prohibition to general mortgages, which obligated all the goods of the monastery. Reiffenstuel[43] included general mortgages on the ground that

tit. 13, n. 11; Schmalzgrueber, *Ius Ecclesiasticum Universum,* III, tit. 13, n. 11; Heston, *Alienation of Church Property,* pp. 167, 168.

[40] Ferraris, *Bibliotheca,* ad v. "alienatio" art. 4, nn. 26, 27.

[41] Petra, *Commentaria ad Constitutiones Apostolicas,* IV, in constit. 6 Benedicti XII, nn. 34–40; Ferraris, *Bibliotheca,* ad v. "alienatio" art. 4, nn. 31, 32.

[42] Bouix, *Tractatus de Jure Regularium,* II, p. 296.

[43] *Jus Canonicum Universum,* III, tit. 21, n. 34.

they transferred a right and therefore needed the solemnities required. Barbosa[44] and Fagnanus[45] seem to have excluded both the special and general mortgages from the contracts for which the solemnities were required, since in the strict sense they did not come under the terms of alienation, nevertheless, since they were equivalent to alienation, they were prohibited. The preponderance of opinion was for the exclusion of general mortgages.[46] Ferraris, upholding the latter opinion, argued that otherwise regulars would not be able to enter into any contract, since in every contract it is customary to attach a clause obligating possession. This would therefore be too severe a restriction and not according to the mind of the legislators.[47]

9. *Money.* Generally speaking, money should not fall under the concept of property for the alienation of which the solemnities are required. In itself, money was considered a *res mobilis* and, therefore, was not included in the constitutions on the question of alienation, which were concerned only with immovable property and movable objects of a precious character.[48] However, under certain conditions money could be and was considered as falling within the concept of immovable goods and as such could not be alienated without the *beneplacitum* of the Holy See. This would be verified, (1) If the Holy See had granted permission for the alienation of certain immovable goods with the condition that from the money thus received other immovable goods be bought. This money could not be used for any other purpose without

[44] *Pastoralis Solicitudo,* pars 2, alleg. 19, nn. 45, 48.

[45] *Commentaria,* III, tit. *de rebus ecclesiae non alienandis,* c. *nulli,* nn. 29–32.

[46] Pirhing, *Jus Canonicum Nova Methodo Explicatum* (5 vols. in 4, Dilingae, 1674–1678) III, tit. 13, nn. 1–5; tit. 21, nn. 6, 16; Bouix, *Tractatus de Jure Regularium,* II, p. 295; Petra, *Çommentaria ad Constitutione Apostolicas, V, constit.* 6 *Benedicti* XII, nn. 25–30; Wernz, *Ius Decretalium,* III, n. 269.

[47] *Bibliotheca,* ad v. "alienatio" art. 4, nn. 35, 36.—For a more complete study of these opinions cf. Stenger, *The Mortgaging of Church Property,* The Catholic University of America Canon Law Studies, n. 169 (Washington, D. C.: The Catholic University of America Press, 1942) pp. 40–49.

[48] Reiffenstuel, *Jus Canonicum Universum,* III, tit. 13, n. 15.

first obtaining the *beneplacitum;*[49] (2) If the money had been left to the monastery for the purpose of buying immovable or precious goods;[50] (3) If the money was received in the form of annuities and established as a source of annual income;[51] (4) If the money was given as a pious foundation for perpetual Masses.[52]

10. *Donations.* A donation, in a strict sense, is the giving of a lawful object for no other reason than the desire to show liberality or generosity.[53] Pope Alexander III (1159–1181), answering the Bishop of Worcester on the question whether a donation by a religious superior is valid or not, decided that the quantity of the thing given and the customs of the place must be taken into consideration.[54] In another letter to the Bishop of Paris, donations made by a prelate without consulting the Canons were adjudged to be invalid. The prelates were considered only as procurators of ecclesiastical things and not the owners.[55] Pope Clement VIII, in his constitution "*Religiosae Congregationes*" of June 19, 1594,[56] prohibited all religious of whatever congregation, society or institute, from making any type of donation except in

---

[49] De Luca, *Theatrum Veritatis et Justitiae,* XII, pars. 3, *de alienationibus,* disc. 1, n. 19; Bouix, *Tractatus de Jure Regularium,* II, p. 293.

[50] Ferraris, *Bibliotheca,* ad v. "alienatio," art. 4, n. 41; Petra, *Commentaria ad Constitutiones Apostolicas,* V, ad const. 5 Pauli II, sect. 2, n. 31; Pignatelli, *Consultationes-Canonicae,* VI, consult. 65, n. 21.

[51] Ferraris, *Bibliotheca* ad v. "alienatio" art. 4, nn. 42, 43; Bouix, *op. cit.,* II, pp. 293, 294; Schmalzgrueber, *Ius Ecclesiasticum Universum,* III, tit. 13, n. 50.

[52] Bouix, *Tractatus de Jure Regularium,* II, p. 293.

[53] Reiffenstuel, *Jus Canonicum Universum,* III, tit. 24, nn. 2, 3; Schmalzgrueber, *Ius Ecclesiasticum Universum,* III, tit. 24, nn. 13–15; Fernz, *Ius Decretalium,* III, n. 255.

[54] C. 3, X, *de donationibus,* III, 24; JL, n. 13152 (8).

[55] C. 2, X, *de donationibus,* III, 24; cf. glossa ad v. *procurator;* the glossa ad v. *non debet,* attributed to Alanus, states that the procurator could not donate by positive acts (*faciendo*) but could by omitting (*omittendo*). Also in performing such acts, they were permitted to make donations if the amount was small, for a little can be given if it is customary, and in this they (prelates) differ from procurators, for a procurator cannot give anything even though he has a most general administration.

[56] *Fontes,* n. 178.

the general chapter or other general congregation, after mature discussion, with the unanimous consent of all and the permission of the superior approving the adequacy of the cause. To solve the difficulties that had arisen in regard to the interpretation of this constitution, Pope Urban VIII, in his constitution "*Nuper*" of October 16, 1640, permitted donations by religious superiors for reasons of gratitude or the winning and the conservation of the good will of a benefactor toward the order or the convent.[57] This, however, was to be done with discretion and necessarily in accordance with the constitutions and special customs of the particular religious institute. The Sacred Congregation of Religious, in its instruction of July 30, 1909[58] ordered that donations be made only in accordance with the requirements of the constitutions or as determined by the chapter or, lacking the chapter, by the General Superior with his counsellors.

C. *Movable Goods*

An inspection of the decrees concerning alienation of ecclesiastical goods reveals that in the law previous to the present Code of Canon Law, movable goods were not included in the goods requiring solemnities for alienation. As a general norm, in every religious community there existed the right of free administration of the temporalities unless positive law restricted that right. Nowhere in the constitutions prohibiting alienations was the alienation of non-precious goods restricted. Thereby full liberty of administration was left to the wisdom and prudence of the superiors in accordance with the regulations and customs of the individual monasteries and communities.

The reason for this exception of movable goods lay chiefly, as Schmalzgrueber implies, in the silence of the law.[59]

---

[57] *Fontes*, n. 220; cf. also Reiffenstuel, *Jus Canonicum Universum*, III, tit. 24, nn. 32–35.

[58] *Fontes*, n. 4393, n. XIII.

[59] ". . . quod non reperitur prohibitum regulariter intelligitur concessum." —*Ius Ecclesiasticum Universum*, III, tit. 13, n. 38. Cf. also Bouix, *Tractatus de Jure Regularium*, II, 309; Reiffenstuel, *Jus Canonicum Universum*, III, tit. 13, n. 15.

ARTICLE 2. LEGISLATION OF THE CODE

A. Meaning and Object of Alienation

Almost synonymous with the term extraordinary administration, alienation of ecclesiastical property was always of grave concern to the Church. The stringent regulation of alienation is justified when one considers that the goods involved are not owned by the person or persons authorized to administer them but are in possession of a moral ecclesiastical person or the Holy See. To insure the security of ecclesiastical interests in the hands of ecclesiastical or religious superiors, a restraining hand, rigorous and exacting, is necessary. Guided by experience, the Church is fully cognizant of the dangers that accompany unregulated administration of ecclesiastical or religious property. Thus the rules and regulations on alienation are given for the purpose of safeguarding the temporal goods of the Church and assisting the administrators in their task of alienating and obligating, in this case, the property of houses of regulars.[60]

Alienation in its strict juridical meaning implies every act by which ownership of an object is transferred from one person to another either gratuitously (as donations, legacies, etc.) or onerously (by sale, exchange, loan, etc.). It also admits a wider sense, as used in Canon Law, where it includes not only the transactions by which ownership is transferred but also comprises all acts by which ownership is limited, diminished or made less secure without being given up entirely. This latter sense includes any act or contract by which certain ecclesiastical goods are burdened, as for example, by mortgages, loans, leases, contracts of debt, etc.[61] A letter from the Apostolic Delegation at Washington, D. C., to all religious superiors in the United States, on November 13, 1936, in express terms comprehends under the term alienations

---

60 Heston, *The Alienation of Church Property,* p. 71; McManus, *The Administration of Temporal Goods in Religious Institutes,* pp. 118, 119.

61 Doheny, *Practical Problems in Church Finance* (Milwaukee: The Bruce Publishing Co., 1941), p. 22 (hereafter this work is referred to as *Church Finance*); Heston, *The Alienation of Church Property,* p. 69; Larraona, "Commentarium Codicis"—*CpR,* XIII (1932), 188; McManus, *The Administration of Temporal Goods in Religious Institutes,* p. 119; Schäfer, *De Religiosis,* n. 199; Vromant, *De Bonis Ecclesiae Temporalibus,* n. 279.

in the wider sense. "The term *alienation* includes not only purchases or transfers of property, but includes as well any contract, debt or obligation. The Canon Law regards all transactions, which may render the financial condition of the Institute, Province, or religious house less secure, as alienations."[62]

From the viewpoint of the object of alienation, it must be remembered that not every transaction involving the exchange of money or property comes under the law requiring the formalities of alienation. The rules on alienation are limited to the expenditures made from what constitutes the *fixed* or *stable capital* of the religious moral person. Fixed or stable capital is defined as including "all those assets which are not in ordinary circulation, as mediums of barter or exchange, but which constitute the permanent basis of a church body's financial security. It is the sum which has been legitimately set aside to remain intact and be a source of regular income."[63] This stable capital comprises the investments in property or holdings which are of a permanent and morally safe nature. It may consist in securities, such as bonds, stocks, mortgages and the like, which bring in interest or dividends; or in real estate which is owned, rented or leased for the purpose of providing a steady income.[64] If it is designated as fixed or stable capital by competent ecclesiastical authority and permanently invested or duly aggregated to the stable capital of the moral person, it may also consist in an actual deposit of money at interest in a bank.[65]

---

[62] Bouscaren, *The Canon Law Digest, Supplement,* 1941, p. 79. Stenger (*The Mortgaging of Church Property,* pp. 76, 77) adds that "by ordering the solemnities both for the restricted meaning and for any contract wherein the condition of the Church can be made worse, canon 1533 extends the meaning of alienation to its broad sense."

[63] Heston, *The Alienation of Church Property,* pp. 72, 73.

[64] Doheny, *Church Finance,* p. 43; McManus, *The Administration of Temporal Goods in Religious Institutes,* p. 121.

[65] Money as such is usually considered as a medium of exchange and perishable. Thus it is primarily unstable, free or fluctuating capital. However, if it is invested in the sense above, it becomes fixed or stable capital. In a question of doubt concerning the stability or instability of the money received, the presumption in the opinion of authorities appears to be that the money should not be considered as aggregated to the stable capital of the

B. Obligation of Canon 534

Although regulars, on the strength of their privilege of exemption, are independent of the local ordinary in the performance of the acts of administration, they are bound by the various canonical restrictions on alienations. Such is the provision of canon 534 which determines the conditions under which ecclesiastical property belonging to or under the care of religious may be alienated or obligated. Besides the particular rules of this canon which extend to all religious including regulars and other exempt religious,[66] the Code prescribes general norms on alienations in canon 1530–1534. Notwithstanding the express mention only of canon 1531 in canon 534, §1, these general norms are applicable to and obligatory upon religious insofar as their particular prescriptions have not been superseded by canon 534. The reason lies in the fact that property of religious institutes, provinces and houses canonically erected is considered ecclesiastical property. Hence, it must be administered according to the norms regulating the administration of ecclesiastical property given in canons 1530–1534. Canon 534 is only supplementary to the general norms for alienation of ecclesiastical property.[67]

The special legislation of canon 534, §1 provides for (1) The observance of the requirements of canon 1531; (2) An apostolic indult, under the pain of nullity of the contract, for certain types of alienations, and (3) The permission and consent of competent superiors and Council or Chapter.

1. *The Observance of Canon 1531.* This canon provides that *first,* no property may be alienated for less than its appraisal (paragraph 1). This is to safeguard the requirements of canon 1530, §1, 1° which requires a written appraisal by experts of the property to be alienated. This appraisal means the estimate of

---

moral person.—Cf. *supra,* pp. 134–135; Doheny, *op. cit.,* p. 43; Heston, *op. cit.,* pp. 73–75; Larraona, " Commentarium Codicis "—*CpR,* XIII (1932), 191; McManus, *op. cit.,* p. 121.

[66] Letter of the Most Reverend Apostolic Delegate to the United States, 13 nov. 1936—Bouscaren, *The Canon Law Digest* II, 162.

[67] Larraona, "Commentarium Codicis,"—*CpR,* XIII (1932), 185, 186; McManus, *The Administration of Temporal Goods in Religious Institutes,* p. 119.

the objects concerned in view of their alienation and not the price that is actually offered. Where two sums are established in the appraisal, a minimum and a maximum value of the property, the minimum could be used in the petition for alienation and a higher price could be accepted without the necessity of obtaining a new indult. *Secondly,* unless circumstances advise otherwise, alienation must be made by public auction or at least by advertisement, and to the highest bidder (paragraph 2). Public auction or advertisement lends the assurance that all possible profit will be derived since competition among interested parties may well tend to be more advantageous than an individual offer from one party. The provision is for the purpose of preventing the squandering of ecclesiastical property and personal favoritism. It should be noted here also that, from the canonical viewpoint, the highest bid does not confer on the bidder a strict right to demand from the church or religious house the fulfillment of the contract thus initiated, but confers only a preferential right before others entitling him to first consideration when the final decision to sell is made. *Thirdly,* the money received by alienation must be invested in a manner which is safe, permanent, useful and for the benefit of the Church, religious institute, province or house (paragraph 3). It must be remembered that through alienation part of the stable capital is depleted. This depletion can only occur because of a just cause and with the permission of the Holy See. In practice, whenever the Holy See authorizes alienation of ecclesiastical goods it usually authorizes the disbursement of the funds thus received only according to the intention and purpose for which the alienation had been petitioned.[68]

2. *The Necessity of an Apostolic Indult.* Canon 534, §1 prescribes an apostolic indult as necessary, under the pain of nullity of the contract, when there is a question of the disposal of (a) precious objects; (b) alienation and obligation of goods in excess of 30,000 francs ($6000).

---

[68] Augustine, *Religious and Laymen,* pp. 184, 185; Heston, *The Alienation of Church Property,* pp. 92–98; Doheny, *Church Finance,* pp. 28–33; Larraona, "Commentarium Codicis"—*CpR,* XIII (1932), 357–362; McManus, *The Administration of Temporal Goods in Religious Institutes,* pp. 135–140; Vromant, *De Bonis Ecclesiae Temporalibus,* nn. 284, 285.

(a) *Alienation of Precious Objects.* A precious object in the meaning of the Code must be understood in the light of canon 1497, §2, as one which possesses a notable value by reason of art, historical interest, or materials from which it is made.[69] Of particular importance in the alienation of precious objects is the determination of what is meant by a *notable value.* Not every precious object is comprehended under the regulations on alienation, but only those that possess a notable value. The Code is silent as to what actually constitutes this notable value. Neither is there any official declaration of the Holy See on the matter. The Sacred Congregation of the Council, in solving a question of alienation, after recounting the conflicting opinions of authors, notes that the determination of a notable value depends largely upon the circumstance of the changing purchasing power of money. It further concludes that in practice no object is to be considered precious in the meaning of canon 1532, §1, 1° and consequently of canon 534, §1 also, unless it has reached the value of 1000 libellae ($200 gold).[70] In pursuance of this decision (July 12, 1919), the same Sacred Congregation was asked: Whether for the alienation of objects which are in any way precious, the *beneplacitum* of the Holy See is always required or whether the ordinary can permit such an alienation under certain limits of value. The reply was: This question pertains to the Code Commission.[71] The Pontifical Commission issued no reply. Since the only clue to the determination of what constitutes a *notable value* in the mind of the Holy See rests in the previous decision of the Sacred Congregation of the Council (July 12, 1919), it must be considered the practice of the Holy See to require per-

---

[69] Canon 1497, §2. Dicuntur . . . *pretiosa,* quibus notabilis valor sit, artis vel historiae vel materiae causa. Cf. *supra,* p. 128, note 12.

[70] S. C. Conc., Dioecesis *N. Donariorum Votivorum,* 12 iul. 1919—*AAS,* XI (1919), 417, 418; Bouscaren, *The Canon Law Digest,* I, 728, 729; Doheny, *Church Finance,* p. 31; Heston, *The Alienation of Church Property,* p. 106; Larraona, "Commentarium Codicis"—*CpR,* XIV (1933), 40; McManus, *The Administration of Temporal Goods in Religious Institutes,* p. 141; Creuse, Garesché, Ellis, *Religious Men and Women in the Code,* n. 163, p. 122.

[71] S. C. Conc., 14 ian. 1922—*AAS,* XIV (1922), 160; transl. from Bouscaren, *The Canon Law Digest,* I, p. 730.

mission of the Holy See for the alienation of precious objects when they exceed the value of $200 in gold.[72]

(b) *Alienation or Obligation of Property in Excess of 30,000 Francs ($6000).*[73] The sum $6000 must be understood as the limit which cannot be exceeded by ecclesiastical superiors inferior to the Holy See in regard to alienation of goods that are not of a precious character. Such is the principle enunciated for religious institutes in canon 534, §1,[74] and the general ecclesiastical law in canon 1532, §1, 2°.[75] There is no doubt either, that the true standard of value in computing the sum of $6000 is the gold

---

[72] The Code does not specify the standard of money value to be used. It is commonly accepted that "gold coin is the true and recognized unit of value, in contradistinction to paper or other currencies."—Doheny, *Church Finance,* p. 40. This is also clearly enunciated in the letter of the Apostolic Delegate to the United States, November 13, 1936: "The aforesaid sum . . . should be understood . . . in reference to the value of currency based upon gold in distinction to other currencies, gold coin being the true unit of value."—Bouscaren, *The Canon Law Digest,* II, 163.

[73] The Code uses the term 30,000 francs. Authors generally agree and it has been accepted in the letter of the Most Reverend Apostolic Delegate to the United States to all the Religious Superiors, that this sum is equivalent to $6,000 in United States currency. "This ratio continued until January 31, 1934, when President Roosevelt, by a Presidential Proclamation, reduced the gold weight of the dollar, making the gold value only 59.06 percent of the par established in 1900. In view of this substantial and factitious devaluation, one dollar and sixty-nine cents of the devaluated dollar is the present equivalent of the former gold dollar. From this it logically follows that the six thousand gold dollars of 1900–1934 are now equivalent, approximately, to ten thousand one hundred and fifty-nine devaluated dollars. Consequently the thirty thousand francs or lire of canons 534 and 1532 can safely be considered as approximately equivalent to ten thousand devaluated dollars."—Doheny, *Church Finance,* pp. 41–42; cf. also Ellis, "Triginta Millia Libellarum seu Francorum"—*Periodica,* XXVII (1938), 348, 349; Heston, *The Alienation of Church Property,* pp. 111, 112; McManus, *The Administration of Temporal Goods in Religious Institutes,* p. 145.

[74] Canon 534, §1. . . . si agatur de alienandis . . . bonis quorum valor superet summam triginta millia francorum seu libellarum, vel de contrahendis debitis et obligationibus ultra indicatam summam, contractus vi caret nisi beneplacitum apostolicum antecesserit.

[75] Canon 1532.—§1. Legitimus Superior de quo in can. 1530, 1, n. 3, est Sedes Apostolica, si agatur: 2° De rebus quae valorem excedunt triginta millium libellarum seu francorum.

content of money.[76] It is further important to note that this provision applies to alienation or obligations as affecting all types of goods, immovable and movable, providing the latter are stable property and not perishable. The silence of pre-Code law on alienation of movable goods [77] has been remedied in present-day legislation which made the value of the property the primary concern of the Holy See in the question of its alienability. A further reason may be deduced from the fact that movable property which is not perishable, such as livestock, machinery, books, furniture, etc., can be incorporated into the fixed or stable fund of the moral person as a source of permanent or fixed income.[78]

Of grave importance to religious superiors in the United States are the special norms on alienation of temporalities by religious as given in a letter of the Most Reverend Apostolic Delegate to the United States on November 13, 1936, issued under the authority of the Sacred Congregation for Religious.[79] Recalling the necessity of observing the requirements of Canon Law at all times, the Sacred Congregation for Religious, in this letter, adverts to the obligation of a proper and exact observance of canon 534, §1 by all religious including regulars and other exempt religious. Special attention is called to two systems of collecting funds or money. These two systems are: " (1) The issuance of bonds or debentures upon ecclesiastical property and the sale of such bonds or debentures in the public market or to private investors, and (2) The system of soliciting or accepting funds under the so-called annuity agreement providing for payments of an annuity to the donor for life. Both of these systems of obtaining money fall within the provisions of canon 534 " [80] when they involve a sum

[76] Cf. *supra*, p. 142, note 72.

[77] Cf. *supra*, p. 136.

[78] Heston, *The Alienation of Church Property*, p. 82; Larraona, " Commentarium Codicis "—*CpR*, XIV (1933), 40, 41; McManus, *The Administration of Temporal Goods in Religious Institutes*, p. 144; Vromant, *De Bonis Ecclesiae Temporalibus*, n. 280 bis.

[79] For a reprint of the letter cf. Doheny, *op. cit.*, Appendix II, pp. 93–98; Bouscaren, *The Canon Law Digest*, II, 161–166.

[80] Bouscaren, *The Canon Law Digest*, II, 162.

exceeding six thousand dollars and would be both unlawful and invalid if made without a papal indult.[81]

"An apostolic indult[82] is required not only in the event of a single transaction exceeding the sum of six thousand dollars, but an apostolic indult is necessary in every case in which a coalescence of the debts or obligations of every kind and nature exceeds the said sum of six thousand dollars."[83]

3. *Permission of Competent Superiors and Consent of Council or Chapter.* Canon 534, §1 provides that in cases where the temporal goods to be alienated are not in excess of the sum of 30,000 francs ($6000) the written permission of the superior is necessary and sufficient if given according to the norms of the respective constitutions and with the consent and favorable vote of his Chapter or Council expressed by secret ballot.[84] These provisions, except as to sufficiency of the consent of subordinate superiors, apply to all alienations, debts and obligations, including those in excess of $6000 as well as precious goods valued at $200 or more.

---

[81] Doheny, *Church Finance,* p. 69.

[82] NOTE: The papal indult does not imply the acceptance by the Holy See of responsibility for the transaction, but merely removes the obstacles of law in order to complete the transaction. Neither does it oblige the religious to complete the alienation or take upon themselves its obligations.—Larraona, "Commentarium Codicis"—*CpR,* XIV (1933), 29, 30, 44; McManus, *op. cit.,* p. 147.

[83] The letter of the Apostolic Delegate here continues to illustrate by examples the coalescence of distinct operations of alienation or of one transaction involving distinct objects belonging to the same juridical person when the value of the articles taken together is in excess of $6,000. This is done to illustrate the law of the Code and a reply of the Pontifical Code Commission of July 20, 1929: "An vi canonis 1532, §1, 2º requiratur licentia S. Sedis ad alienandas per modum unius plures res ecclesiasticas eiusdem personae, quae simul sumptae valorem excedunt triginta millium libellarum seu francorum. Resp. Affirmative.—*AAS,* XXI (1929), 574. Cf. also, Bouscaren, *op. cit.,* I, p. 731; Doheny, *Church Finance,* p. 72, note 10; Heston, *The Alienation of Church Property,* p. 113.

[84] Canon 534, §1. . . . secus requiritur et sufficit licentia, in scriptis data, Superioris ad normam constitutionum cum consensu sui Capituli seu Consilii per secreta suffragia manifestato; cf. also letter of the Most Reverend Apostolic Delegate, 13 nov. 1936—Bouscaren, *The Canon Law Digest,* II, 162.

Alienation of the latter however requires an added solemnity, the apostolic indult.[85]

The sum under $6000 for which the consent of the Chapter or Council is required is not stated in the Code. Larraona,[86] taking up the question, insists that a literal interpretation of this precept, making it applicable to each and every sum under $6000, is not consonant with practice and particular legislation. Toward the determination of a norm to guide administrators of the temporalities of religious he proposes a twofold argument. The first, he asserts, according to the norm of canon 6, 3°, is given in the criterion proposed in pre-Code law by the constitution "*Inter ea*" (July 30, 1909) of the Sacred Congregation for Religious.[87] The second, he deduces in view of canon 20 by the application of juridic analogy considering parallel canons treating on alienations, debts and obligations undertaken by local ordinaries (canons 1532, 1541). In either case, Larraona concludes, the formalities of canon 534, §1 are not required for small sums. He further proposes that this canon does not oblige when there is a question of transactions involving sums of less than 1000 *libellae* ($200). In practice particular constitutions, which are referred to in this canon, may determine the competency of the superior and the extent of the obligation of these formalities of written permission and consent of the Chapter or Council.[88] If the constitutions simply restate the canon, the obligation of the formalities must be determined in the manner proposed by Larraona. Larraona

[85] Larraona, "Commentarium Codicis,"—*CpR,* XIV (1933), 169; McManus, *The Administration of Temporal Goods in Religious Institutes,* p. 149.

[86] "Commentarium Codicis,"—*CpR,* XIV (1933), 169–177.

[87] Cf. *supra,* pp. 129–130.

[88] For example, the Constitutions of the Friars Minor (n. 289) read: Pro alienandis bonis quorum valor continetur intra decem millia et triginta millia libellarum seu francorum, requiritur et sufficit licentia Ministri generalis, data in scriptis et cum consensu Definitori generalis per secreta suffragia manifestato. Si valor non excedit summam decem millium francorum seu libellarum, sufficit scripta licentia Ministri provincialis, praevio consensu sui Definitorii etiam per secreta suffragia manifestato. Definitorium vero cuiuslibet provinciae determinet valorem pro diversitate regionum, infra quem praeter licentiam Ministri provincialis, consensus Dicretorii localis sufficere possit.

further notes that minor superiors must observe the formalities of canon 534, §1 at all times, except in very small things.[89]

A safeguard against arbitrary transactions on the part of the superiors is provided by their obligation of eliciting the consent of the chapter or council and not only its advice. This consent is necessary for the validity of the transaction according to the law of the Code as stated in canon 105, 1°.[90] Authors are divided as to whether the formalities of obtaining written permission and secret ballot are necessary for the validity of the act. McManus[91] contends that lacking proof of the law itself, "the prescript of canon 1680, §1 is particularly applicable, viz., that 'only then should an act be considered null when it lacks essentially constitutive elements, or when solemnities or conditions have been omitted which are prescribed by the sacred canons under pain of nullity.' Writing and secrecy are solemnities, but it is not evident that canon 534 prescribes them under pain of nullity, and therefore it would seem that the omission of these solemnities would not nullify the act as far as canon 534 is concerned. However, if the constitutions prescribe them for validity, the constitutions are law in this regard."

C. *Kinds of Transaction as Affected by Canon 534*

1. *Transactions Governed by Canon 534.*

Transactions governed by canon 534 include:

1. All acts or contracts by which ecclesiastical property is exposed to danger or loss. Such is the law of the Code as expressed in canon 1533.[92] According to this canon all the solemni-

[89] Cf. Clancy, *The Local Religious Superior,* p. 75.

[90] Augustine, *Religious and Laymen,* p. 188; Larraona, "Commentarium Codicis"—*CpR,* XIV (1933), 179; McManus, *The Administration of Temporal Goods in Religious Institutes,* p. 130.

[91] *The Administration of Temporal Goods in Religious Institutes,* p. 130. For authors holding opposite view cf. McManus, *op. cit.,* p. 130, note 39; Larraona, "Commentarium Codicis"—*CpR,* XIV (1933), 178–180.

[92] The application of this canon to religious property is particularly stressed in the letter of the Most Reverend Apostolic Delegate to the United States (November 13, 1936): "A proper and exact observance of canon 534, §1 and canon 1533 requires compliance with the formalities prescribed for so-called alienations."—Bouscaren, *The Canon Law Digest,* II, 162.

ties required for alienation are to be transferred also to all contracts whereby the condition of the Church could be made less secure.[93] It is concerned primarily with the juridical financial condition of the Church by which its juridic right of ownership would be jeopardized in the eyes of a court of law.[94]

2. All acts and contracts which involve the transfer of ownership of temporal goods pertinent to the fixed or stable capital of the religious moral person, such as sales, donations, payments on debts from stable capital.[95]

3. Contracts by which temporalities of religious moral persons are offered as security for their fulfillment, including: (a) Pledge (*pignus*). When the possession of the property is given over to another as security while the ownership is retained. (b) Mortgage.[96] Previous to the Code common opinion held that only special mortgages came under the law establishing the requirements of alienation. This has been sustained in the Code in virtue of canon 1538, §1. General mortgages would not seem to be primarily intended under the concept of alienation.[97] However it is more logical to conclude with Stenger, who writes that "the textual examination of canon 1533 must extend the concept of alienation to the transfer of a *ius ad rem* and hence to a general mortgage when the stable capital may be subjected to satisfy the debt. Even if the term *hypotheca* mentioned in canon 1538 did not include a general mortgage, the phrase *aere alieno contrahendo* in the same canon would include it." [98] (c) Long term rentals of property belonging to the stable capital.[99] The

---

[93] Canon 1533.—Sollemnitates ad normam can. 1530–1532 requiruntur non solum in alienatione proprie dicta, sed etiam in quolibet contractu quo conditio Ecclesiae peior fieri possit.

[94] Heston, *The Alienation of Church Property*, pp. 118–133; Larraona, "Commentarium Codicis"—*CpR*, XIII (1932), 189; Stenger, *The Mortgaging of Church Property*, pp. 83–89; Wernz, *Ius Decretalium*, III, n. 154.

[95] Cf. *supra*, p. 138; McManus, *The Administration of Temporal Goods in Religious Institutes*, p. 123; Stenger, *op. cit.*, pp. 89, 90.

[96] Cf. *supra*, pp. 133–134.

[97] McManus, *Administration in Religious Institutes*, pp. 123, 124, note 16; Vromant, *De Bonis Ecclesiae Temporalibus*, n. 329.

[98] *The Mortgaging of Church Property*, p. 160, Conclusions nn. 7, 8, also pp. 101–103.

[99] Canon 1541.

prescripts of canon 1531 must also be observed in this case.[100] Rentals of property for periods longer than nine years and concerned with an annual rental sum in excess of $6000 necessitate permission of the Holy See for validity. These two elements must exist concomitantly. For rentals not in excess of nine years even though in excess of $6000, or rentals in excess of nine years but below $6000, the permission of the legitimate superiors is needed according to the norms of canon 1541, §2 and the prescripts of particular law.[101] (d) Long term leases of property pertaining to stable capital.[102] Leases differ from rentals insofar that only immovable property can be leased while both immovable and movable property can be rented. Rental implies only the right to use the property, while in a lease the practical equivalent of property rights is conferred upon the lessee without any actual transfer of ownership. Likewise leases generally extend for a much longer period of time than rentals. As far as it may concern religious, the laws governing renting and leasing of property are the same. If the so-called act of "*redemption of the canon*" takes place, by which, instead of a yearly sum or rental (the canon), the lessor accepts a lump sum and hence implies acquisition of title to property by the former lessee, the act becomes equivalent to alienation and consequently the requirements of canon 534 must be fulfilled.[103]

2. *Transactions Not Governed by Canon 534.*[104]

In general, all purchases or payments made with money that is

[100] Cf. *supra*, pp. 139–140.

[101] The Code in keeping with canon 1529 leaves the determination of details of contracts to prevailing civil law. Hence the consideration of Canon Law must be supplemented by a study of the civil law in force in the given locality.—Heston, *The Alienation of Church Property*, pp. 181–184; Doheny, *Church Finance*, p. 58; McManus, *The Administration of Temporal Goods in Religious Institutes*, pp. 150, 151; Vromant, *De Donis Ecclesiae Temporalibus*, n. 340.

[102] Cf. canon 1542.

[103] Heston, *op. cit.*, pp. 185, 186; McManus, *op. cit.*, pp. 151, 152; Vromant, *op. cit.*, nn. 341, 342. Leasing of property in the Code (emphyteusis) has no counterpart in English or American law, but is very closely akin to what we know as a 99-year lease.—Bouscaren, *The Canon Law Digest*, I, p. 733, note.

[104] Herewith the reader is referred to lists of acts as drawn up by Doheny,

not of the stable or fixed capital of the religious moral person do not come under the requirements of canon 534. In particular the following acts, though they are similar to alienation, do not fall within the scope of alienation in the sense of the Code of Canon Law:

1. Expenditures needed in meeting current expenses.
2. Mutual acceptance of money or securities without explicit contractual obligations even though a moderate rate of interest be paid.
3. By custom, the sale of old furnishings for the purpose of purchasing new equipment.
4. Money used for the purchase and construction of buildings for religious which they would otherwise have to rent. Necessary repairs are also excluded. However, improvements and enlargements of church edifices and extinction of other debts of the religious moral persons need specific authorization.
5. Money used for the construction of buildings when it is already available.
6. Money and securities even those pertaining to stable capital, withdrawn for the purpose of purchasing or constructing buildings which will yield income (schools, hospitals, etc.). Authors consider this and the following transaction as conversion rather than alienation.
7. Transfer of parts of stable capital to safer investments and at least equally lucrative. The withdrawal of securities to change them into simple bank deposits at interest is not acknowledged by all authors as being free from the requirements of this canon.
8. Money that is given with the express intention that it be used for specific purposes providing these purposes are legitimate and with no intention of prejudicing the ecclesiastical character of religious goods.
9. Return of property to the original seller if the original sale included the plan for repurchase at his option.
10. Money that is obtained through the so-called *construction*

Church Finance, pp. 58, 59; Heston, *The Alienation of Church Property,* pp. 76–78; Larraona, "Commentarium Codicis"—*CpR,* XIII (1932), 194, 195; McManus, *The Administration of Temporal Goods in Religious Institutes,* pp. 124–126.

mortgage and *money purchase* mortgage. The former is one given to a creditor to secure a loan used in building an edifice. It must be noted that the only property mortgaged is the building under construction and the land on which it stands. The mortgage here does not affect the existing stable fund of the institute but only the property in the process of its acquisition. The latter is one contracted in the sale wherein the vendor is the mortgagee and the purchasing religious agency is the mortgagor. These "can be allowed without the solemnities of alienation when in the former the plot of ground on which the building is to be erected has been acquired for that purpose, the initial payment comes from non-stable capital and the amortization and interest are paid from current revenue and when in the latter the initial payment for the property comes from non-stable capital and the amortization and interest payments come from current revenues." [105]

11. Money or property that has been bequeathed to an institute incapable of common possessions.[106]

12. The refusal of legacies or donations. Although such refusals are not permitted (canons 580, §2; 1536) they do not come under the requirements of canon 534. Non-acquisition is not to be confused with alienation.

---

[105] Stenger, *The Mortgaging of Church Property,* pp. 160, 161, conclusion n. 9, also pp. 107–113.

[106] Cf. *supra,* pp. 217, 218, 221.

CONCLUSIONS

1. THE pre-Code conditions for the erection of a religious house requiring the consent of the persons concerned and the suitable sustenance of at least twelve religious who would reside in a religious house, are no longer necessary. However, they may be used as a norm for determining the necessity of having a new religious house in the locality.

2. Before granting permission for the establishment of a religious house, the local ordinary must make a prudent estimate as to whether proper livelihood and sustenance will be assured not only to the new house but also to the already existing religious houses in the locality. This prudent judgment should be made concerning: (1) The needs and opportunities of the religious house; (2) The amount of temporal aid and the guarantee of required aid; (3) The purpose and special work of the institute.

3. All private possessions held by religious are contrary not only to the particular law of the institute but also to general ecclesiastical law. However, a probable opinion, based on pre-Code law, permits the use of the dependent *peculium* if custom, privilege or indult sanction it.

4. Almsgathering in its canonical sense must be accepted as a personal appeal to the charity of the faithful by seeking offerings from door to door. Hence it does not embrace all forms of appeal for temporal aid. Regulars who are not mendicants strictly so-called must obtain only the permission of their superiors and of the local ordinary, unless special privileges exclude all need of permission of the local ordinary.

5. Pious foundations given to exempt religious institutes, but for the purpose of promoting an enterprise which is proper to the diocese, do not come within the concept of exemption from the jurisdiction of the local ordinary.—Founded mass stipends are distinct from manual mass stipends and the administration regarding them must be determined by the canonical requirements for the administration of pious foundations.

6. Material remuneration for the exercise of the sacred ministerial functions by religious is dependent upon the regulations of Provincial Councils, Diocesan Synods and custom. Lacking these, recourse may be had to a form of "gentleman's agreement" referred to as natural or canonical equity.

7. Religious orders, provinces and houses, considered as moral persons may acquire temporal goods and may seek all the safeguards provided by the laws of prescription. As to the limit of time for prescription the special privileges enjoyed by religious before the Code are not revoked.

8. Common law sanctions to all moral persons, consequently to religious houses also, all the just modes of acquisition of property that may be employed by other physical persons, subject to the additional requirements of their particular laws.

9. Regulars, on the strength of their privilege of exemption, need no permission from the local ordinary to invest their own funds, even though the money or the property be given to them to promote locally the aim of divine worship or the works of charity. The privilege of exemption does not extend to the investment of money that was acquired on behalf of a parish or mission.

BIBLIOGRAPHY

SOURCES

Acta Apostolicae Sedis, Commentarium Officiale, Romae, 1909–

Acta Sanctae Sedis, 41 vols., Romae, 1865–1908.

Bullarii Romani Continuatio Summorum Pontificum, 19 vols., Prati, 1756–1883.

Bullarium Franciscanum, 7 vols., Romae, 1759–1904, Supplementum, Romae, 1908.

Bullarum Diplomatum et Privilegiorum Sanctorum Romanorum Pontificum Taurinensis Editio, 24 vols. et Appendix, Augustae Taurinorum, 1857–1872.

Canones et Decreta Sacrosancti Oecumenici Concilii Tridentini, Romae, 1904.

Codex Iuris Canonici Pii X Pontificis Maximi iussu digestus Benedicti Papae XV auctoritate promulgatus praefatione Fontium Annotatione et Indice Analytico–Alphabetico ab Emo Petro Card. Gasparri auctus, Romae: Typis Polyglottis Vaticanis, 1917. Reimpressio, 1934.

Codicis Iuris Canonici Fontes cura Emi Petri Card. Gasparri editi, 9 vols., Romae (postea Civitate Vaticana): Typis Polyglottis Vaticanis, 1923–1939. (Vols. VII–IX ed. cura et studio Emi Iustiniani Card. Serédi.)

Collectanea in Usum Secretariae Sacrae Congregationis Episcoporum et Regularium, Ed. A. Bizzarri, Romae, 1863.

Corpus Iuris Canonici, editio Lipsiensis II (Richter-Friedberg), 2 vols., Lipsiae: Tauchnitz, 1879–1881, editio anastatice repetita, Lipsiae, 1928.

Decretales D. Gregorii Papae IX, una cum Glossis Restitutae, Romae, 1582.

Decretum Gratiani emendatum et notationibus illustratum una cum Glossis, 2 vols., Romae, 1582.

Jaffé, Philippus, *Regesta Pontificum Romanorum ab Condita Ecclesia ad annum post Christum natum, 1198,* Editionem secundam correctam et auctam auspiciis Gulielmi Wattenbach curaverunt S. Loewenfeld, F. Kaltenbrunner, P. Ewald, 2 vols. in 1, Lipsiae, 1885–1888.

Liber Sextus Decretalium D. Bonifatii Papae VIII, suae integritati cum Clementinis et Extravagantibus, earumque Glossis Restitutis, Romae, 1582.

Mansi, J. D., *Sacrorum Conciliorum Nova et Amplissima Collectio,* 53 vols., Vols. 1–31, Florentiae, Venetiis, Parisiis, 1759–1798; Vols. 31b–53, Parisiis, Leipzig, Arnhem, 1901–1927.

Potthast, A., *Regesta Pontificum Romanorum inde ab anno post Christum natum 1198 ad annum 1304,* 2 vols., Berolini, 1874, 1875.

Regula et Constitutiones Fratrum Minorum, Ad Claras Aquas (Quaracchi) prope Florentiam: Typographia Collegii S. Bonaventurae, 1922.

Schroeder, Henry J., *Canons and Decrees of the Council of Trent,* St. Louis, Mo.: B. Herder Book Co., 1941.

REFERENCE WORKS

Aertnys, J. — Damen, C. A., *Theologia Moralis secundum doctrinam S. Alphonsi de Ligorio,* 9. ed., 2 vols., Galopiae: Typis M. Alberts Filii, 1918.

Alphonsus Maria de Ligorio, S., *Theologia Moralis,* cura et studio Leonardi Gaudé, 4 vols. Romae, 1905-1912; Vol. II, Romae, 1907.

Appeltern, Victorius ab, *Compendium Praelectionum Juris Regularis Adm. R. P. Piati Montani,* ed. altera, Parisiis, 1913.

[Bachofen], Charles Augustine, *A Commentary on the New Code of Canon Law,* 8 vols., Vol. III, *Religious and Laymen,* 3. ed., St. Louis, Mo.: B. Herder Book Co., 1922.

Barbosa, Augustinus, *Iuris Ecclesiastici Libri Tres,* Lugduni, 1650.

———, *Pastoralis Sollicitudo seu de Officio et Potestate Episcopi,* 3 parts in 2 vols., Lugduni, 1656.

Barraclough, Geoffrey, *Papal Provisions,* Oxford: Basil Blackwell, 1935.

Benedicti XIV Opera Omnia in XVII tomos distributa, Vol. XI, *De Synodo Dioecesana,* Prati, 1844.

Beste, Udalricus, *Introductio in Codicem,* Collegeville, Minn.: St. John's Abbey Press, 1938.

Blat, Albertus, *Commentarium Textus Codicis Iuris Canonici,* 6 vols., Vol. II, *De Personis,* ed. altera, Romae: Libreria del Collegio "Angelico," 1921.

Bouix, D., *Tractatus de Jure Regularium,* 2 vols., Parisiis, 1857.

Bouscaren, T. Lincoln, *The Canon Law Digest,* 2 vols., Milwaukee: The Bruce Publishing Co., 1934–1943.

Brunini, Joseph Bernard, *The Clerical Obligations of Canons 139 and 142,* The Catholic University of America Canon Law Studies, n. 103, Washington, D. C.: The Catholic University of America, 1937.

Chelodi, Ioannes, *Ius de Personis iuxta Codicem Iuris Canonici,* ed. altera a Sac. Ernesto Bertagnolli recognita et aucta, Tridenti: Libr. Edit. Tridentum, 1927.

Clancy, Patrick M. J., *The Local Religious Superior,* The Catholic University of America Canon Law Studies, n. 175, Washington, D. C.: The Catholic University of America Press, 1943.

Coady, John Joseph, *The Appointment of Pastors,* The Catholic University of America Canon Law Studies, n. 52, Washington, D. C.: The Catholic University of America, 1929.

Cocchi, Guidus, *Commentarium in Codicem Iuris Canonici ad Usum Scholarum,* 5 vols. in 8, Liber II, *De Personis,* Pars II, *De Religiosis,* 2. ed., Taurinorum Augustae: Officina Libraria Marietti, 1926.

Connolly, Nicholas, *The Canonical Erection of Parishes,* The Catholic University of America Canon Law Studies, n. 114, Washington, D. C.: The Catholic University of America, 1938.

Coronata, Matthaeus Conte a, *Institutiones Iuris Canonici ad Usum Utriusque Cleri et Scholarum,* 5 vols., Vol. I, Taurini: Ex Officina Libraria Marietti, 1928.

Creusen, Joseph—Ellis, Adam C.—Garesché, Edward F., *Religious Men and Women in the Code,* 4. English ed., Milwaukee: The Bruce Publishing Co., 1940.

Delgado, Conradus, *De Relationibus inter Parochum Religiosum et eius Superiores Regulares cum Respectu Particulari ad Ius Speciale O.F.M.,* Romae: Catholic Book Agency, 1940.

De Luca, Joannes Baptista Cardinalis, *Theatrum Veritatis et Justitiae,* 15 vols. in 8, Coloniae Agrippinae, 1706.

Doheny, William J., *Practical Problems in Church Finance,* Milwaukee: The Bruce Publishing Co., 1941.

Fagnanus, Prosper, *Commentaria in Quinque Libros Decretalium,* Venetiis, 1696.

Fanfani, Ludovicus, *De Iure Religiosorum ad Normam Codicis Iuris Canonici, 2 ed.,* Taurini-Romae: Ex Officina Librari Marietti, 1925.

Farrell, Benjamin, *The Rights and Duties of the Local Ordinary Regarding Congregations of Women Religious of Pontifical Approval,* The Catholic University of America Canon Law Studies, n. 128, Washington, D. C.: The Catholic University of America Press, 1941.

Ferraris, F. Lucius, *Prompta Bibliotheca Canonica, Iuridica, Moralis, Theologica necnon Ascetica, Polemica, Rubricistica, Historica,* 8 vols., Romae, 1885–1892; *Supplementum,* ed. Januarius Bucceroni, Romae, 1899.

Flanagan, Bernard Joseph, *The Canonical Erection of Religious Houses,* The Catholic University of America Canon Law Studies, n. 179, Washington, D. C.: The Catholic University of America Press, 1943.

Gerster a Zeil, Thomas Villanova, *Ius Religiosorum in Compendium Redactum pro Iuvenibus Religiosis,* Taurini: Officina Libraria Marietti, 1935.

Geser, Fintan, *The Canon Law Governing Communities of Sisters,* St. Louis, Mo.: B. Herder Book Co., 1938.

Goodwine, John, *The Right of the Church to Acquire Temporal Goods,* The Catholic University of America Canon Law Studies, n. 131, Washington, D. C.: The Catholic University of America Press, 1941.

Garcias, Nicholaus, *Tractatus de Beneficiis,* 2 vols., Genevae, 1658.

Hannan, Jerome Daniel, *The Canon Law of Wills,* Philadelphia: The Dolphin Press, 1935.

Harrigan, Robert J., *The Radical Sanation of Invalid Marriages,* The Catholic University of America Canon Law Studies, n. 116, Washington, D. C.: The Catholic University of America, 1938.

Hesten, Edward Louis, *The Alienation of Church Property in the United States,* The Catholic University of America Canon Law Studies, n. 132, Washington, D. C.: The Catholic University of America Press, 1941.

Hinschius, Paulus, *Decretales Pseudo-Isidorianae et Capitula Angilramni,* Lipsiae, 1863.

Holzapfel, Heribert, *Manuale Historiae Ordinis Fratrum Minorum* latine redditum a G. Hazelbeck, Friburgi Brisgoviae: B. Herder Book Co., 1909.

Hostiensis, Cardinalis (Henricus de Segusio), *Commentaria in Quinque Libros Decretalium,* 5 vols. in 3, Venetiis, 1581.

———, *Summa Aurea,* Lugduni, 1568.

Ilg, John, *An Explanation of the Rule of the Friars Minor,* 2. ed., n.p., 1940.

Kazenberger, Kilian, *The Book of Life or a Brief Literal Exposition of the Holy Rule of the Seraphic Father St. Francis, Founder of the Order of Friars Minor,* transl. by a Father of the Province of the Most Holy Name, n.p., 1905.

Lauretus de Franchis, *Controversiae inter Episcopos et Regulares atque Observationes Zacharii Pasqualigii,* Romae, 1656.

Leurenius Petrus, *Forum Ecclesiasticum,* 5 vols., Venetiis, 1729.

McManus, James Edward, *The Administration of Temporal Goods in Religious Institutes,* The Catholic University of America Canon Law Studies, n. 109, Washington, D. C.: The Catholic University of America, 1937.

McVann, James, *The Canon Law on Sermon Preaching,* New York: The Paulist Press, 1940.

Mattheuci, Augustinus, *Officialis Curiae Ecclesiasticae,* Venetiis, 1734.

Melo, Antonius, *De Exemptione Regularium,* The Catholic University of American Canon Law Studies, n. 12, Washington, D. C.: The Catholic University of America, 1921.

Meyer, L. G., *Alms-gathering by Religious,* an historical synopsis, Licentiate Dissertation in Canon Law, Washington, D. C.: The Catholic University of America, 1940.

Miller, Newton Thomas, *Founded Masses according to the Code of Canon Law,* The Catholic University of America Canon Law Studies, n. 34, Washington, D. C.: The Catholic University of America, 1926.

Mocchegiani, Petrus, *Iurisprudentia Ecclesiastica,* 3 vols., Ad Claras Aquas (Quaracchi), 1904–1905.

Monacelli, Franciscus, *Formularium Legale Practicum Fori Ecclesiastici,* 4 vols., ed. 3 romana, Romae, 1844.

Navarrus (Martinus Aspilcueta), *Opera Omnia,* 6 vols., Romae, Vols. 1–4, 1618; Vols. 5, 6, 1621.

O'Brien, Joseph D., *The Exemption of Religious in Church Law,* Milwaukee: The Bruce Publishing Co., 1943.

Ojetti, Benedictus, *Synopsis Rerum Moralium et Iuris Pontificii,* 3. ed., 4 vols., Romae, 1909–1914.

Papi, Hector, *The Government of Religious Communities,* New York: P. J. Kenedy and Sons, 1919.

———, *Religious in Church Law,* New York: P. J. Kenedy and Sons, 1924.

Pejška, Joseph, *Ius Canonicum Religiosorum,* 3. ed., Friburgi Brisgoviae: B. Herder Book Co., 1927.

Petra Vincentius, *Commentaria ad Constitutiones Apostolicas,* 5 vols. in 2, Venetiis, 1729.

Pignatelli, Jacobus, *Consultationes Canonicae,* 11 vols., Coloniae Allobrogorum, 1700.

Pirhing, Ernricus, *Jus Canonicum Nova Methodo Explicatum,* 5 vols. in 4, Dilingae, 1674–1678.

Pourrat, P., *Christian Spirituality from the Time of Our Lord till the Dawn of the Middle Ages,* 3 vols., London: Burns, Oates and Washbourne Ltd., Vol. 1, transl. by W. H. Mitchell and S. P. Jacques, 1922; Vol. II, transl. by S. P. Jacques, 1924; Vol. III, transl. by W. H. Mitchell, 1927.

Prümmer, Dominicus, *Manuale Iuris Canonici in Usum Scholarum,* ed. 4 et 5 aucta, Friburgi Brisgoviae: B. Herder and Co., 1927.

Raymundus a Peñafort, S., *Summa Iuris Canonici,* Veronae, 1744.

Reiffenstuel, Anacletus, *Jus Canonicum Universum editio novissima cui accessit Tractatus de Regulis Iuris,* 6 vols., Romae, 1831–1834.

Robinson, Paschal, *The Writings of St. Francis of Assisi,* Philadelphia, 1906.

Rodericus, Emanuel, *Quaestiones Regulares et Canonicae,* 3 vols., Antuerpiae, 1528.

Sanchez, Thomas, *Disputationum de Sancto Matrimonio Libri Tres,* Tomus I, Antuerpiae, 1626.

Schäfer, Timotheus, *Compendium de Religiosis ad Normam Codicis Iuris Canonici,* Münster, I. W.: Ex Officina Libraria Aschendorff, 1927.

Schmalzgrueber, Franciscus, *Ius Ecclesiasticum Universum,* 5 vols. in 12, Romae, 1843–1845.

Schroeder, Henry J., *Disciplinary Decrees of the General Councils,* St. Louis, Mo.: B. Herder Book Co., 1937.

Sipos, Stephanus, *Enchiridion Iuris Canonici,* 3. ed., Pécs: Typographia "Haladás R. T.," 1936.

Stenger, Joseph Bernard, *The Mortgaging of Church Property,* The Catholic University of America Canon Law Studies, n. 169, Washington, D. C.: The Catholic University of America Press, 1942.

Suarez, Franciscus, *Opera Omnia,* ed. nova a Carolo Berton, Parisiis: Apud Ludovicum Vives, 1856–1861, 28 vols., Vols. XIII–XVI, *De Religione.*

Taunton, Ethelred, *The Law of the Church,* St. Louis, Mo., 1906.

Tellenbach, Gerd, *The Church, State and Christian Society at the Time of the Investiture Contest,* transl. by R. F. Bennet, Studies in Mediaeval History, n. 3, Oxford: Basil Blackwell, 1940.

Thomae Aquinatis, *Opera Omnia,* Venetiis, 1587, Tomus XVII, Opusculum XVII, *Contra pestiferam doctrinam retrahentium homines a religionis ingressu.*

———, *Summa Theologica,* emendata a De Rubeis, Billuart et aliorum Notis Selectis Ornata, 6 vols., Taurini (Italia): Marietti, 1937.

Turner, Sidney Joseph, *The Vow of Poverty,* The Catholic University of America Canon Law Studies, n. 54, Washington, D. C.: The Catholic University of America, 1929.

Vermeersch, A.—Creusen, J., *Epitome Iuris Canonici cum Commentariis ad Scholas et ad Usum Privatum,* 3 vols., Vol. I, 2. ed., 1924; Vol. II, 2. ed., 1925; Vol. III, 1923, Mechlinae-Romae: H. Dessain.

Vromant, G., *De Bonis Ecclesiae Temporalibus ad Usum Utriusque Cleri, praesertim Missionariorum,* 2. ed., Louvain: Museum Lessianum, 1934.

Wernz, Franciscus X., *Ius Decretalium ad Usum Praelectionum in Scholis Textus Canonici sive Iuris Decretalium,* 2. ed., 6 vols., Romae: Prati, 1906–1913. Vol. III, *Ius Administrationis Ecclesiae Catholicae,* Romae, 1908.

Wernz, F.—Vidal, Petrus, *Ius Canonicum ad Codicis Normam Exactum,* 7 vols. in 8, Tomus III, *De Religiosis,* Romae: Apud Aedes Universitatis Gregorianae, 1933.

Zollman, Carl, American Church Law, St. Paul: West Publishing Co., 1933.

ARTICLES

Anonymous, "Annotationes"—*Periodica,* XI (1923), 34–38.

Anonymous, "De Administratione Bonorum in Paroeciis Religiosis"—*Acta Ordinis Fratrum Minorum,* LVII (1938), 186–192.

Anonymous, "Disquisitio circa Ius Ordinarii Diocesani visitandi Ecclesias Regularium"—*Acta Ordinis Fratrum Minorum,* LV (1936), 96–98.

Capello, F., "De Praescriptione"—*Jus Pontificium,* IV (1924), 21–25.

Ellis, Adam, "Triginta Millia Libellarum seu Francorum"—*Periodica,* XXVII (1938), 348–353.

Gearin, M. C., "The Confessor and the Vow of Religious Poverty"—*AER,* LXI (1919), 136–153.

Goyeneche, S., "Annotationes"—*CpR,* IV (1923), 34–39.

———, "Consultationes"—*CpR,* XI (1930), 261–263; I (1920), 340–343.

———, "De Transitu ad Aliam Religionem"—*CpR,* I (1920), 22–29; 73–77; 107–112; 217–226; 295–300; 359–365; II (1921), 116–124; 141–148; 173–176.

Larraona, A., "Commentarium Codicis"—*CpR,* I (1920), 134–139; 171–177; II (1921), 201–210; 275–287; III (1922), 45–53; IV (1923), 39–46; V (1924), 324-334; 417-436; XII (1931), 244-252; 353-359; 435-442; XIII (1932), 24–35; 92–99; 184–195; XIV (1933), 38–44; 169–182; 252–256.

Larraona, A., "Consultationes"—*CpR,* I (1920), 112–114.

——, "De Paupertate Simplici"—*CpR,* I (1920), 333–340; II (1921), 9–13; 40–45; 71–76; 104–107.

Maroto, Philippus, "Annotationes"—*CpR,* I (1920), 166–169; 169–171; V (1924), 122–134.

Nebreda, Eulogius, "De Loci Ordinariorum Iuribus circa Pia Legata Donationesve tum Religiosis tum Eorum Ecclesiis etiam Paroecialibus facta"—*CpR,* VII (1926), 107–118; 191–198; 261–271; 317–333.

Piontek, Cyril, "A Gentleman's Agreement"—*The Jurist,* III (1943), 284–305.

——, "Pennies Collections and Other Free-will Offerings in the Code of Canon Law"—*AER,* CIX (1943), 190–199; 272–279; 358–365.

Roth, Jan, "Kilka Zagadnień z Zakonnego Prawa Majątkowego"—*Ateneum Kapłanskie,* XLII (1938), 161–170.

——, "Zbieranie Jałmużn przez Osoby Zakonne"—*Ateneum Kapłanskie,* XXXVIII (1936), 279-287.

Salsmans, I., "Annotationes"—*Periodica,* VII (1914), 165–168.

Steiger, Josephus, "De Propagatione et Diffusione Vitae Religiosae, Synopsis Historica"—*Periodica,* XIII (1924), (29)-(60); (73)-(100); (153)-(180).

Voltas, P., "Consultationes"—*CpR,* I (1920), 275–279.

Vromant, G., "De Licentiis Requisitis ad Erigendam Domum Religiosam"—*Jus Pontificium,* VIII (1928), 212–215.

——, "Obligatio Vitae Communis apud Missionarium Religiosum"—*Periodica,* XVIII (1929), 25*–35*.

PERIODICALS

Ateneum Kapłanskie, Włocławek, Seminarjum Duchowne, 1909–

Ateneum Kapłanskie, Włtocławek, Seminarjum Duchowne, 1909–

American Ecclesiastical Review, The, Philadelphia, 1889–1943, Baltimore, 1944—

Commentarium Pro Religiosis, Romae, 1920; ab anno 1935: *Commentarium pro Religiosis et Missionariis.*

Jurist, The, Washington, D. C., 1941—

Jus Pontificium, Romae, 1921—

Periodica de Re Canonica et Morali utili praesertim Religiosis et Missionariis, 1905—; ab anno 1927: *Periodica de Re Canonica, Morali, Liturgica.*

ABBREVIATIONS

AAS—*Acta Apostolicae Sedis.*

AER—*The American Ecclesiastical Review* (Later *The Ecclesiastical Review*).

ASS—*Acta Sanctae Sedis.*

BF—*Bullarium Franciscanum.*

Bull. Rom. Taur.—*Bullarum Diplomatum et Privilegiorum Sanctorum Romanorum Pontificum Taurinensis editio.*

Bull. Rom. Cont.—*Bullarii Romani Continuatio.*

CpR—*Commentarium pro Religiosis.*

Fontes—*Codicis Iuris Canonici Fontes cura . . . Gasparri editi.*

J (K-E-L) Jaffé (Kaltenbrunner, Ewald, Loewenfeld).

Mansi—*Sacrorum Conciliorum Nova et Amplissima Collectio.*

CPI—*Pontificia Commissio ad Codicis Canones authentice interpretandos,*

Periodica—*Periodica de Re Canonica et Morali utili praesertim Religiosis et Missionariis.*

S.C.C.—Sacra Congregatio Concilii.

S.C. de Prop. Fide—Sacra Congregatio de Propaganda Fide.

S.C. Ep. et Reg.—Sacra Congregatio Episcoporum et Regularium.

S.C. Rel.—Sacra Congregatio de Religiosis.

INDEX

BIOGRAPHICAL NOTE

ROMUALD EUGENE KOWALSKI was born at Milwaukee, Wisconsin, on August 10, 1914. After completing his elementary studies at St. Adalbert and Sts. Cyril and Methodius Schools, Milwaukee, Wisconsin, he attended St. Bonaventure's High School, Sturtevant, Wisconsin. In August, 1931, he entered the Novitiate of the Franciscan Order at Pulaski, Wisconsin, and in the following year, August 15, 1932, made his profession as a member of the Order of Friars Minor of the Province of the Assumption of the Blessed Virgin Mary. He received the B.A. degree in 1936 from St. Francis College, Burlington, Wisconsin, where he completed his philosophical studies. His theological studies were taken up at St. Mary of the Angels' Seminary, Green Bay, Wisconsin, where he was ordained to the priesthood on June 22, 1939. In September, 1941, he entered the School of Canon Law at the Catholic University of America, where he received the Baccalaureate Degree in Canon Law in May, 1942, and the Licentiate Degree in Canon Law in May, 1943.

CANON LAW STUDIES*

1. Freriks, Rev. Celestine A., C.PP.S., J.C.D., Religious Congregations in Their External Relations, 121 pp., 1916.
2. Galliher, Rev. Daniel M., O.P., J.C.D., Canonical Elections, 117 pp., 1917.
3. Borkowski, Rev. Aurelius L., O.F.M., J.C.D., De Confraternitatibus Ecclesiasticis, 136 pp., 1918.
4. Castillo, Rev. Cayo, J.C.D., Disertacion Historico-Canonica sobre la Potestad del Cabildo en Sede Vacante o Impedida del Vicario Capitular, 99 pp., 1919 (1918).
5. Kubelbeck, Rev. William J., S.T.B., J.C.D., The Sacred Penitentiaria and Its Relation to Faculties of Ordinaries and Priests, 129 pp., 1918.
6. Petrovits, Rev. Joseph, J. C., S.T.D., J.C.D., The New Church Law on Matrimony, X-461 pp., 1919.
7. Hickey, Rev. John J., S.T.B., J.C.D., Irregularities and Simple Impediments in the New Code of Canon Law, 100 pp., 1920.
8. Klekotka, Rev. Peter J., S.T.B., J.C.D., Diocesan Consultors, 179 pp., 1920.
9. Wanenmacher, Rev. Francis, J.C.D., The Evidence in Ecclesiastical Procedure Affecting the Marriage Bond, 1920 (Printed 1935).
10. Golden, Rev. Henry Francis, J.C.D., Parochial Benefices in the New Code, IV-119 pp., 1921 (Printed 1925).
11. Koudelka, Rev. Charles J., J.C.D., Pastors, Their Rights and Duties According to the New Code of Canon Law, 211 pp., 1921.
12. Melo, Rev. Antonius, O.F.M., J.C.D., De Exemptione Regularium, X-188 pp., 1921.
13. Schaaf, Rev. Valentine Theodore, O.F.M., S.T.B., J.C.D., The Cloister, X-180 pp., 1921.
14. Burke, Rev. Thomas Joseph, S.T.D., J.C.D., Competence in Ecclesiastical Tribunals, IV-117 pp., 1922.
15. Leech, Rev. George Leo, J.C.D., A Comparative Study of the Constitution "Apostolicae Sedis" and the "Codex Juris Canonici," 179 pp., 1922.
16. Motry, Rev. Hubert Louis, S.T.D., J.C.D., Diocesan Faculties According to the Code of Canon Law, II-167 pp., 1922.
17. Murphy, Rev. George Lawrence, J.C.D., Delinquencies and Penalties in the Administration and the Reception of the Sacraments, IV-121 pp., 1923.

* Below n. 100 only the following numbers are still available: Nn. 3, 4, 9, 25, 34, 57 and 75. Beginning with n. 100 only the following are unavailable: Nn. 100-111 inclusive, and n. 113.

18. O'Reilly, Rev. John Anthony, S.T.B., J.C.D., Ecclesiastical Sepulture in the New Code of Canon Law, II-129 pp., 1923.
19. Michalicka, Rev. Wenceslas Cyril, O.S.B., J.C.D., Judicial Procedure in Dismissal of Clerical Exempt Religious, 107 pp., 1923.
20. Dargin, Rev. Edward Vincent, S.T.B., J.C.D., Reserved Cases According to the Code of Canon Law, IV-103 pp., 1924.
21. Godfrey, Rev. John A., S.T.B., J.C.D., The Right of Patronage According to the Code of Canon Law, 153 pp., 1924.
22. Hagedorn, Rev. Francis Edward, J.C.D., General Legislation on Indulgences, II-154 pp., 1924.
23. King, Rev. James Ignatius, J.C.D., The Administration of the Sacraments to Dying Non-Catholics, V-141 pp., 1924.
24. Winslow, Rev. Francis Joseph, O.F.M., J.C.D., Vicars and Prefects Apostolic, IV-149 pp., 1924.
25. Correa, Rev. Jose Servelion, S.T.L., J.C.D., La Potestad Legislativa de la Iglesia Catolica, IV-127 pp., 1925.
26. Dugan, Rev. Henry Francis, A.M., J.C.D., The Judiciary Department of the Diocesan Curia, 87 pp., 1925.
27. Keller, Rev. Charles Frederick, S.T.B., J.C.D., Mass Stipends, 167 pp., 1925.
28. Paschang, Rev. John Linus, J.C.D., The Sacramentals According to the Code of Canon Law, 129 pp., 1925.
29. Piontek, Rev. Cyrillus, O.F.M., S.T.B., J.C.D., De Indulto Exclaustrationis necnon Saecularizationis, XIII-289 pp., 1925.
30. Kearney, Rev. Richard Joseph, S.T.B., J.C.D., Sponsors at Baptism According to the Code of Canon Law, IV-127 pp., 1925.
31. Bartlett, Rev. Chester Joseph, A.M., LL.B., J.C.D., The Tenure of Parochial Property in the United States of America, V-108 pp., 1926.
32. Kilker, Rev. Adrian Jerome, J.C.D., Extreme Unction, V-425 pp., 1926.
33. McCormick, Rev. Robert Emmett, J.C.D., Confessors of Religious, VIII-266 pp., 1926.
34. Miller, Rev. Newton Thomas, J.C.D., Founded Masses According to the Code of Canon Law, VII-93 pp., 1926.
35. Roelker, Rev. Edward G., S.T.D., J.C.D., Principles of Privilege According to the Code of Canon Law, XI-166 pp., 1926.
36. Bakalarczyk, Rev. Richardus, M.I.C., J.U.D., De Novitiatu, VIII-208 pp., 1927.
37. Pizzuti, Rev. Lawrence, O.F.M., J.U.L., De Parochis Religiosis, 1927. (Not Printed.)
38. Bliley, Rev. Nicholas Martin, O.S.B., J.C.D., Altars According to the Code of Canon Law, XIX-132 pp., 1927.
39. Brown, Mr. Brendan Francis, A.B., LL.M., J.U.D., The Canonical Juristic Personality with Special Reference to its Status in the United States of America, V-212 pp., 1927.

40. CAVANAUGH, REV. WILLIAM THOMAS, C.P., J.U.D., The Reservation of the Blessed Sacrament, VIII-101 pp., 1927.
41. DOHENY, REV. WILLIAM J., C.S.C., A.B., J.U.D., Church Property: Modes of Acquisition, X-118 pp., 1927.
42. FELDHAUS, REV. ALOYSIUS H., C.PP.S., J.C.D., Oratories, IX-141 pp., 1927.
43. KELLY, REV. JAMES PATRICK, A.B., J.C.D., The Jurisdiction of the Simple Confessor, X-208 pp., 1927.
44. NEUBERGER, REV. NICHOLAS J., J.C.D., Canon 6 or the Relation of the Codex Juris Canonici to the Preceding Legislation, V-95 pp., 1927.
45. O'KEEFE, REV. GERALD MICHAEL, J.C.D., Matrimonial Dispensations, Powers of Bishops, Priests, and Confessors, VIII-232 pp., 1927.
46. QUIGLEY, REV. JOSEPH A. M., A.B., J.C.D., Condemned Societies, 139 pp., 1927.
47. ZAPLOTNIK, REV. JOHANNES LEO, J.C.D., De Vicariis Foraneis, X-142 pp., 1927.
48. DUSKIE, REV. JOHN ALOYSIUS, A.B., J.C.D., The Canonical Status of the Orientals in the United States, VIII-196 pp., 1928.
49. HYLAND, REV. FRANCIS EDWARD, J.C.D., Excommunication, Its Nature, Historical Development and Effects, VIII-181 pp., 1928.
50. REINMANN, REV. GERALD JOSEPH, O.M.C., J.C.D., The Third Order Secular of Saint Francis, 201 pp., 1928.
51. SCHENK, REV. FRANCIS J., J.C.D., The Matrimonial Impediments of Mixed Religion and Disparity of Cult, XVI-318 pp., 1929.
52. COADY, REV. JOHN JOSEPH, S.T.D., J.U.D., A.M., The Appointment of Pastors, VIII-150 pp., 1929.
53. KAY, REV. THOMAS HENRY, J.C.D., Competence in Matrimonial Procedure, VIII-164 pp., 1929.
54. TURNER, REV. SIDNEY JOSEPH, C.P., J.U.D., The Vow of Poverty, XLIX-217 pp., 1929.
55. KEARNEY, REV. RAYMOND A., A.B., S.T.D., J.C.D., The Principles of Delegation, VII-149 pp., 1929.
56. CONRAN, REV. EDWARD JAMES, A.B., J.C.D., The Interdict, V-163 pp., 1930.
57. O'NEILL, REV. WILLIAM H., J.C.D., Papal Rescripts of Favor, VII-218 pp., 1930.
58. BASTNAGEL, REV. CLEMENT VINCENT, J.U.D., The Appointment of Parochial Adjutants and Assistants, XV-257 pp., 1930.
59. FERRY, REV. WILLIAM A., A.B., J.C.D., Stole Fees, V-136 pp., 1930.
60. COSTELLO, REV. JOHN MICHAEL, A.B., J.C.D., Domicile and Quasi-Domicile, VII-201 pp., 1930.
61. KREMER, REV. MICHAEL NICHOLAS, A.B., S.T.B., J.C.D., Church Support in the United States, VI-136 pp., 1930.
62. ANGULO, REV. LUIS, C.M., J.C.D., Legislation de la Iglesia sobre la intencion en la application de la Santa Misa, VII-104 pp., 1931.

63. Frey, Rev. Wolfgang Norbert, O.S.B., A.B., J.C.D., The Act of Religious Profession, VIII-174 pp., 1931.
64. Roberts, Rev. James Brendan, A.B., J.C.D., The Banns of Marriage, XIV-140 pp., 1931.
65. Ryder, Rev. Raymond Aloysius, A.B., J.C.D., Simony, IX-151 pp., 1931.
66. Campagna, Rev. Angelo, Ph.D., J.U.D., Il Vicario Generale del Vescovo, VII-205 pp., 1931.
67. Cox, Rev. Joseph Godfrey, A.B., J.C.D., The Administration of Seminaries, VI-124 pp., 1931.
68. Gregory, Rev. Donald J., J.U.D., The Pauline Privilege, XV-165 pp., 1931.
69. Donohue, Rev. John F., J.C.D., The Impediment of Crime, VII-110 pp., 1931.
70. Dooley, Rev. Eugene A., O.M.I., J.C.D., Church Law on Sacred Relics, IX-143 pp., 1931.
71. Orth, Rev. Clement Raymond, O.M.C., J.C.D., The Approbation of Religious Institutes, 171 pp., 1931.
72. Pernicone, Rev. Joseph M., A.B., J.C.D., The Ecclesiastical Prohibition of Books, XII-267 pp., 1932.
73. Clinton, Rev. Connell, A.B., J.C.D., The Paschal Precept, IX-108 pp., 1932.
74. Donnelly, Rev. Francis B., A.M., S.T.L., J.C.D., The Diocesan Synod, VIII-125 pp., 1932.
75. Torrente, Rev. Camilo, C.M.F., J.C.D., Las Procesiones Sagradas, V-145 pp., 1932.
76. Murphy, Rev. Edwin J., C.PP.S., J.C.D., Suspension Ex Informata Conscientia, XI-122 pp., 1932.
77. MacKenzie, Rev. Eric F., A.M., S.T.L., J.C.D., The Delict of Heresy in its Commission, Penalization, Absolution, VII-124 pp., 1932.
78. Lyons, Rev. Avitus E., S.T.B., J.C.D., The Collegiate Tribunal of First Instance, XI-147 pp., 1932.
79. Connolly, Rev. Thomas A., J.C.D., Appeals, XI-195 pp., 1932.
80. Sangmeister, Rev. Joseph V., A.B., J.C.D., Force and Fear as Precluding Matrimonial Consent, V-211 pp., 1932.
81. Jaeger, Rev. Leo A., A.B., J.C.D., The Administration of Vacant and Quasi-Vacant Episcopal Sees in the United States, IX-229 pp., 1932.
82. Rimlinger, Rev. Herbert T., J.C.D., Error Invalidating Matrimonial Consent, VII-79 pp., 1932.
83. Barrett, Rev. John D. M., S.S., J.C.D., A Comparative Study of the Third Plenary Council of Baltimore and the Code, IX-221 pp., 1932.
84. Carberry, Rev. John J., Ph.D., S.T.D., J.C.D., The Juridical Form of Marriage, X-177 pp., 1934.
85. Dolan, Rev. John L., A.B., J.C.D., The Defensor Vinculi, XII-157 pp., 1934.

86. HANNAN, REV. JEROME D., A.M., S.T.D., LL.B., J.C.D., The Canon Law of Wills, IX-517 pp., 1934.
87. LEMIEUX, REV. DELISE A., A.M., J.C.D., The Sentence in Ecclesiastical Procedure, IX-131 pp., 1934.
88. O'ROURKE, REV. JAMES J., A.B., J.C.D., Parish Registers, VII-109 pp., 1934.
89. TIMLIN, REV. BARTHOLOMEW, O.F.M., A.M., J.C.D., Conditional Matrimonial Consent, X-381 pp., 1934.
90. WAHL, REV. FRANCIS X., A.B., J.C.D., The Matrimonial Impediments of Consanguinity and Affinity, VI-125 pp., 1934.
91. WHITE, REV. ROBERT J., A.B., LL.B., S.T.B., J.C.D., Canonical Ante-Nuptial Promises and the Civil Law, VI-152 pp., 1934.
92. HERRERA, REV. ANTONIO PARRA, O.C.D., J.C.D., Legislacion Ecclesiastica sobra el Ayuno y la Abstinencia, XI-191 pp., 1935.
93. KENNEDY, REV. EDWIN J., J.C.D., The Special Matrimonial Process in Cases of Evident Nullity, X-165 pp., 1935.
94. MANNING, REV. JOHN J., A.B., J.C.D., Presumption of Law in Matrimonial Procedure, XI-111 pp., 1935.
95. MOEDER, REV. JOHN M., J.C.D., The Proper Bishop for Ordination and Dimissorial Letters, VII-135 pp., 1935.
96. O'MARA, REV. WILLIAM A., A.B., J.C.D., Canonical Causes for Matrimonial Dispensations, IX-155 pp., 1935.
97. REILLY, REV. PETER, J.C.D., Residence of Pastors, IX-81 pp., 1935.
98. SMITH, REV. MARINER T., O.P., S.T.Lr., J.C.D., The Penal Law for Religious, VII-169 pp., 1935.
99. WHALEN, REV. DONALD W., A.M., J.C.D., The Value of Testimonial Evidence in Matrimonial Procedure, XIII-297 pp., 1935.
100. CLEARY, REV. JOSEPH F., J.C.D., Canonical Limitations on the Alienation of Church Property, VIII-141 pp., 1936.
101. GLYNN, REV. JOHN C., J.C.D., The Promoter of Justice, XX-337 pp., 1936.
102. BRENNAN, REV. JAMES H., S.S., M.A., S.T.B., J.C.D., The Simple Convalidation of Marriage, VI-135 pp., 1937.
103. BRUNINI, REV. JOSEPH BERNARD, J.C.D., The Clerical Obligations of Canons 139 and 142, X-121 pp., 1937.
104. CONNOR, REV. MAURICE, A.B., J.C.D., The Administrative Removal of Pastors, VIII-159 pp., 1937.
105. GUILFOYLE, REV. MERLIN JOSEPH, J.C.D., Custom, XI-144 pp., 1937.
106. HUGHES, REV. JAMES AUSTIN, A.B., A.M., J.C.D., Witnesses in Criminal Trials of Clerics, IX-140 pp., 1937. .
107. JANSEN, REV. RAYMOND J., A.B., S.T.L., J.C.D., Canonical Provisions for Catechetical Instruction, VII-153 pp., 1937.
108. KEALY, REV. JOHN JAMES, A.B., J.C.D., The Introductory Libellus in Church Court Procedure, XI-121 pp., 1937.

109. McManus, Rev. James Edward, C.SS.R., J.C.D., The Administration of Temporal Goods in Religious Institutes, XVI-196 pp., 1937.
110. Moriarty, Rev. Eugene James, J.C.D., Oaths in Ecclesiastical Courts, X-115 pp., 1937.
111. Rainer, Rev. Eligius George, C.SS.R., J.C.D., Suspension of Clerics, XVII-249 pp., 1937.
112. Reilly, Rev. Thomas F., C.SS.R., J.C.D., Visitation of Religious, VI-195 pp., 1938.
113. Moriarity, Rev. Francis E., C.SS.R., J.C.D., The Extraordinary Absolution from Censures, XV-334 pp., 1938.
114. Connolly, Rev. Nicholas P., J.C.D., The Canonical Erection of Parishes, X-132 pp., 1938.
115. Donovan, Rev. James Joseph, J.C.D., The Pastor's Obligation in Prenuptial Investigation, XII-322 pp., 1938.
116. Harrigan, Rev. Robert J., M.A., S.T.B., J.C.D., The Radical Sanation of Invalid Marriages, VIII-208 pp., 1938.
117. Boffa, Rev. Conrad Humbert, J.C.D., Canonical Provisions for Catholic Schools, VII-211 pp., 1939.
118. Parsons, Rev. Anscar John, O.M.Cap., J.C.D., Canonical Elections, XII-236 pp., 1939.
119. Reilly, Rev. Edward Michael, A.B., J.C.D., The General Norms of Dispensation, XII-156 pp., 1939.
120. Ryan, Rev. Gerald Aloysius, A.B., J.C.D., Principles of Episcopal Jurisdiction, XII-172 pp., 1939.
121. Burton, Rev. Francis James, C.S.C., A.B., J.C.D., A Commentary on Canon 1125, X-222 pp., 1940.
122. Miaskiewicz, Rev. Francis Sigismund, J.C.D., Supplied Jurisdiction According to Canon 209, XII-340 pp., 1940.
123. Rice, Rev. Patrick William, A.B., J.C.D., Proof of Death in Prenuptial Investigation, VIII-156 pp., 1940.
124. Anglin, Rev. Thomas Francis, M.S., J.C.D., The Eucharistic Fast, VIII-183 pp., 1941.
125. Coleman, Rev. John Jerome, J.C.D., The Minister of Confirmation, VI-153 pp., 1941.
126. Downs, Rev. Joseph Emmanuel, A.B., J.C.D., The Concept of Clerical Immunity, XI-163 pp., 1941.
127. Esswein, Rev. Anthony Albert, J.C.D., Extrajudicial Penal Powers of Ecclesiastical Superiors, X-144 pp., 1941.
128. Farrell, Rev. Benjamin Francis, M.A., S.T.L., J.C.D., The Rights and Duties of the Local Ordinary Regarding Congregations of Women Religious of Pontifical Approval, V-195 pp., 1941.
129. Feeney, Rev. Thomas John, A.B., S.T.L., J.C.D., Restitutio in Integrum, VI-169 pp., 1941.
130. Findlay, Rev. Stephen William, O.S.B., A.B., J.C.D., Canonical

Norms Governing the Deposition and Degradation of Clerics, XVII-279 pp., 1941.

131. GOODWINE, REV. JOHN, A.B., S.T.L., J.C.D., The Right of the Church to Acquire Property, VIII-119 pp., 1941.

132. HESTON, REV. EDWARD LOUIS, C.S.C., Ph.D., S.T.D., J.C.D., The Alienation of Church Property in the United States, XII-222 pp., 1941.

133. HOGAN, REV. JAMES JOHN, A.B., S.T.L., J.C.D., Judicial Advocates and Procurators, XIII-200 pp., 1941.

134. KEALY, REV. THOMAS M., A.B., Litt.B., J.C.D., Dowry of Women Religious, IX-152 pp., 1941.

135. KEENE, REV. MICHAEL JAMES, O.S.B., J.C.D., Religious Ordinaries and Canon 198, V-164 pp., 1942.

136. KERIN, REV. CHARLES A., S.S., M.A., S.T.B., J.C.D., The Privation of Christian Burial, XVI-279 pp., 1941.

137. LOUIS, REV. WILLIAM FRANCIS, M.A., J.C.D., Diocesan Archives, X-101 pp., 1941.

138. MCDEVITT, REV. GILBERT JOSEPH, A.B., J.C.D., Legitimacy and Legitimation, X-247 pp., 1941.

139. MCDONOUGH, REV. THOMAS JOSEPH, A.B., J.C.D., Apostolic Administrators, X-217 pp., 1941.

140. MEIER, REV. CARL ANTHONY, A.B., J.C.D., Penal Administration Procedure Against Negligent Pastors, XI-240 pp., 1941.

141. SCHMIDT, REV. JOHN ROGG, A.B., J.C.D., The Principles of Authentic Interpretation in Canon 17 of the Code of Canon Law, XII-331 pp., 1941.

142. SLAFKOSKY, REV. ANDREW LEONARD, A.B., J.C.D., The Canonical Episcopal Visitation of the Diocese, X-197 pp., 1941.

143. SWOBODA, REV. INNOCENT ROBERT, O.F.M., J.C.D., Ignorance in Relation to the Imputability of Delicts, IX-271 pp., 1941.

144. DUBÉ, REV. ARTHUR JOSEPH, A.B., J.C.D., The General Principles for the Reckoning of Time in Canon Law, VIII-299 pp., 1941.

145. MCBRIDE, REV. JAMES T., A.B., J.C.D., Incardination and Excardination of Seculars, XX-585 pp., 1941.

146 KRÓL, REV. JOHN T., J.C.D., The Defendant in Ecclesiastical Trials, XII-207 pp., 1942.

147. COMYNS, REV. JOSEPH J., C.SS.R., A.B., J.C.D., Papal and Episcopal Administration of Church Property, XIV-155 pp., 1942.

148. BARRY, REV. GARRETT FRANCIS, O.M.I., J.C.D., Violation of the Cloister, XII-260 pp., 1942.

149. BOLDUC, REV. GATIEN, C.S.V., A.B., S.T.L., J.C.D., Les Études dans les Religions Cléricales, VIII-155 pp., 1942.

150. BOYLE, REV. DAVID JOHN, M.A., J.C.D., The Juridic Effects of Moral Certitude on Pre-Nuptial Guarantees, XII-188 pp., 1942.

151. CANAVAN, REV. WALTER JOSEPH, M.A., LITT.D., J.C.D., The Profession of Faith, XII-143 pp., 1942.

152. Desrochers, Rev. Bruno, A.B., Ph.L., S.T.B., J.C.D., Le Premier Concile Plénier de Québec et le Code de Droit Canonique, XIV–186 pp., 1942.
153. Dillon, Rev. Robert Edward, A.B., J.C.D., Common Law Marriage, X-148 pp., 1942.
154. Dodwell, Rev. Edward John, Ph.D., S.T.B., J.C.D., The Time and Place for the Celebration of Marriage, X-156 pp., 1942.
155. Donnellan, Rev. Thomas Andrew, A.B., J.C.D., The Obligation of the Misa pro Populo, VII-131 pp., 1942.
156. Eltz, Rev. Louis Anthony, A.B., J.C.L., Cooperation in Crime.
157. Gass, Rev. Sylvester Francis, M.A., J.C.D., Ecclesiastical Pensions, XI-206 pp., 1942.
158. Guiniven, Rev. John Joseph, C.SS.R., J.C.D., The Precept of Hearing Mass, XIV-188 pp., 1942.
159. Gulczynski, Rev. John Theophilus, J.C.D., The Desecration and Violation of Churches, X-126 pp., 1942.
160. Hammill, Rev. John Leo, M.A., J.C.D., The Obligations of the Traveler According to Canon 14, VIII-204 pp., 1942.
161. Haydt, Rev. John Joseph, A.B., J.C.D., Reserved Benefices, XI-148 pp., 1942.
162. Huser, Rev. Roger John, O.F.M., A.B., J.C.D., The Crime of Abortion in Canon Law, XII-187 pp., 1942.
163. Kearney, Rev. Francis Patrick, A.B., S.T.L., J.C.L., The Principles of Canon 1127.
164. Linahen, Rev. Leo James, S.T.L., J.C.D., De Absolutione Complicis In Peccato Turpi, 114 pp., 1942.
165. McCloskey, Rev. Joseph Aloysius, A.B., J.C.D., The Subject of Ecclesiastical Law According to Canon 12, XVII-246 pp., 1942.
166. O'Neill, Rev. Francis Joseph, C.SS.R., J.C.D., The Dismissal of Religious in Temporary Vows, XIII-220 pp., 1942.
167. Prince, Rev. John Edward, A.B., S.T.D., J.C.D., The Diocesan Chancellor, X-136 pp., 1942.
168. Riesner, Rev. Albert Joseph, C.SS.R., J.C.D., Apostates and Fugitives from Religious Institutes, IX-168 pp., 1942.
169. Stenger, Rev. Joseph Bernard, J.C.D., The Mortgaging of Church Property, 186 pp., 1942.
170. Waldron, Rev. Joseph Francis, A.B., J.C.D., The Minister of Baptism, XII-197 pp., 1942.
171. Willett, Rev. Robert Albert, J.C.D., The Probative Value of Documents in Ecclesiastical Trials, X-124 pp., 1942.
172. Woeber, Rev. Edward Martin, M.A., J.C.D., The Interpellations, XII-161 pp., 1942.
173. Benko, Rev. Matthew Aloysius, O.S.B., M.A., J.C.D., The Abbot *Nullius*.

174. Christ, Rev. Joseph James, M.A., S.T.L., J.C.D., Dispensation from Vindictive Penalties.
175. Clancy, Rev. Patrick M. J., O.P., A.B., S.T.Lr., J.C.D., The Local Religious Superior, X-229 pp., 1943.
176. Clarke, Rev. Thomas James, J.C.D., Parish Societies, XII-147 pp., 1943.
177. Connolly, Rev. John Patrick, S.T.L., J.C.D., Synodal Examiners and Parish Priest Consultors, X-223 pp., 1943.
178. Drumm, Rev. William Martin, A.B., J.C.D., Hospital Chaplains.
179. Flanagan, Rev. Bernard Joseph, A.B., S.T.L., J.C.D., The Canonical Erection of Religious Houses, X-147 pp., 1943.
180. Kelleher, Rev. Stephen Joseph, A.B., S.T.B., J.C.D., Discussions with non-Catholics: Canonical Legislation, X-93 pp., 1943.
181. Lewis, Rev. Gordian, C.P., J.C.D., Chapters in Religious Institutes, XII-169 pp., 1943.
182. Marx, Rev. Adolph, J.C.D., The Declaration of Nullity of Marriages Contracted Outside the Church, X-151 pp., 1943.
183. Matulenas, Rev. Raymond Anthony, O.S.B., A.B., J.C.L., Communication, a Source of Privileges.
184. O'Leary, Rev. Charles Gerard, C.SS.R., J.C.D., Religious Dismissed After Perpetual Profession, X-213 pp., 1943.
185. Power, Rev. Cornelius Michael, J.C.D., The Blessing of Cemeteries.
186. Shuhler, Rev. Ralph Vincent, O.S.A., J.C.D., Privileges of Regulars to Absolve and Dispense, XII-195 pp., 1943.
187. Ziolkowski, Rev. Thaddeus Stanislaus, A.B., J.C.D., The Consecration and Blessing of Churches, XII-151 pp., 1943.
188. Heneghan, Rev. John Joseph, S.T.D., J.C.D., The Marriages of Unworthy Catholics: Canons 1065 and 1066.
189. Carroll, Rev. Coleman Francis, M.A., S.T.L., J.C.L., Charitable Institutions.
190. Ciesluk, Rev. Joseph Edward, Ph.B., S.T.L., J.C.L., National Parishes in the United States.
191. Coburn, Rev. Vincent Paul, A.B., J.C.L., Marriages of Conscience.
192. Connors, Rev. Charles Paul, C.S.Sp., A.B., J.C.L., Extra-Judicial Procurators in the Code of Canon Law.
193. Coyle, Rev. Paul Raymond, A.B., J.C.L., Judicial Exceptions.
194. Fair, Rev. Bartholomew Francis, A.B., S.T.L., J.C.L., The Impediment of Abduction.
195. Gallagher, Rev. Thomas Raphael, O.P., A.B., S.T.Lr., J.C.L., The Examination of the Qualities of the Ordinand.
196. Gannon, Rev. John Mark, S.T.L., J.C.L., The Interstices Required for the Promotion to Orders.
197. Goldsmith, Rev. J. William, B.C.S., S.T.L., J.C.L., The Competence of Church and State over Marriage—Disputed Points.

198. Goodwine, Rev. Joseph Gerard, A.B., S.T.B., J.C.L., The Reception of Converts.
199. Kowalski, Rev. Romuald Eugene, O.F.M., A.B., J.C.L., Sustenance of Religious Houses of Regulars.
200. McCoy, Rev. Alan Edward, O.F.M., J.C.L., Force and Fear in Relation to Delictual Imputability and Penal Responsibility.
201. McDevitt, Rev. Vincent John, Ph.B., S.T.L., J.C.L., Perjury.
202. Martin, Rev. Thomas Owen, Ph.D., S.T.D., J.C.L., Adverse Possession, Prescription and Limitation of Actions: The Canonical "Praescriptio."
203. Miklosovic, Rev. Paul John, A.B., J.C.L., Attempted Marriages and Their Consequent Juridic Effects.
204. Mundy, Rev. Thomas Maurice, A.B., S.T.L., J.C.L., The Union of Parishes.
205. O'Dea, Rev. John Coyle, A.B., J.C.L., The Matrimonial Impediment of Nonage.
206. Olalia, Rev. Alexander Ayson, S.T.L., J.C.L., A Comparative Study of the Christian Constitution of States and the Constitution of the Philippine Commonwealth.
207. Poisson, Rev. Pierre-Marie, C.S.C., A.B., Ph.L., Th.L., J.C.L., Droits Patrimoniaux des Maisons et des Églises Religieuses.
208. Stadalnikas, Rev. Casimir Joseph, M.I.C., J.C.L., Reservation of Censures.
209. Sullivan, Rev. Eugene Henry, S.T.L., J.C.L., Proof of the Reception of the Sacraments.
210. Vaughan, Rev. William Edward, J.C.L., Constitutions for Diocesan Courts.
211. Lyons, Rev. Joseph Henry, J.C.L., The Joinder of Issue in Canonical Trials.

www.ingramcontent.com/pod-product-compliance
Lightning Source LLC
LaVergne TN
LVHW050232080826
844660LV00012B/517

* 9 7 8 0 8 1 3 2 2 3 8 6 5 *